Ethical Consensus and the

MORALITY AND THE MEANING OF LIFE

Edited by:
Professor Albert W. Musschenga (Amsterdam)
Professor Paul J.M. van Tongeren (Nijmegen)

Advisory Board:
Professor Frans De Wachter (Louvain)
Professor Dietmar Mieth (Tübingen)
Professor Kai E. Nielsen (Calgary)
Professor Dewi Z. Phillips (Swansea)

In this series the following titles have been published:

Ethical Consensus and the Truth of Laughter

The Structure of Moral Transformations

Hub Zwart

KOK PHAROS PUBLISHING HOUSE
KAMPEN - THE NETHERLANDS
1996

The translation of this book has been subsidized by the Netherlands Organization for Scientific Research (NWO)

© 1995, Kok Pharos Publishing House
P.O. Box 5016, 8260 GA Kampen, the Netherlands
Cover design by Rob Lucas
ISBN 90 390 0412 9 / CIP
ISSN 0928-2742
NUGI 631/619

Table of Contents

Introduction

The Beginning of Moral Philosophy as a Philosophical Problem

One of moral philosophy's basic questions is the one concerning its beginning. For instance, should it be located in the *discovery*, or in the *justification* of moral truth; in the *object* or in the *subject* of moral evaluation? As discovery precedes justification from a *chronological* point of view, it seems justifiable to argue that the beginning of moral philosophy must be located in the act of discovering moral truth, that is, in the moral truth as it reveals itself to us or forces itself upon us. Yet, one might object that the recognition of moral truth as it presents itself to us, already presupposes a moral subject, someone who is susceptible to it, who already has some knowledge concerning duties, norms or values, or at least an ability to recognize them. It is in the judgement or apprehension by a subject that moral truth will emerge. Moreover, should the moral subject be absent, nothing would be of any value, and the world would be devoid of moral significance. From a *logical* point of view, therefore, the subject seems to precede the object.

Moreover, apart from the issue concerning the subjective or objective nature of moral knowledge, a second question concerning the beginning of moral philosophy is vexing us. Should we start from established morality, that is, from the moral consensus which manages to maintain itself and is guiding contemporary moral life, or from experiences of uneasiness or discontent? Should established morality be contested and criticized, or rather consolidated, reinforced and legitimized by moral philosophy? In subsequent sections I will point out that in contemporary moral discourse something like a *consensus sapientium* seems to have emerged among moral philosophers, which basically consists of the idea that it is the goal of moral philosophy to strengthen, justify and reconstruct established morality, and to secure and immunize it against experiences of chronic discontent. The basic objective of this book, however, will consist of the effort to contest some of these established truths which are mistakenly considered beyond contestation. Instead of reconstructing and consolidating established morality - the 'Aristotelian' option (in terms of ancient Greek morality) - I will opt for a 'Socratic' approach, challenging what is mistakenly taken to be self evident, exposing established consensus to a moral truth it is unable to incorporate.

The basic contention put forward in this book is that both the logical and the chronological beginning, of moral philosophy as well as of morality as such, is to be found in the subversive experience of laughter. It is in the experience of laughter that the vulnerability of established morality finds itself exposed, that moral truth reveals itself to us, and that moral subjectivity is in fact produced. I presume that this remarkable claim demands some preliminary elucidation before being elaborated more fully in the subsequent sections and chapters of this book.

To begin with, moral philosophy is commonly considered a particular branch of philosophical reflection which aims at explaining morality as such. Basically, it confronts us with the question of *why* we consider a certain act or a certain state of affairs justified, problematic or even repulsive from a moral point of view. The basic difference between ethics and morality, between moral philosophy and moral opinion is said to reside in the fact that, in the case of moral philosophy, moral judgements are accompanied by an effort to justify or ground them, that is, by a well-considered, more or less systematic moral account. However, as opinions often happen to be accompanied by some kind of justification or other, while moral philosophies often contain some elements which remain ungrounded or unexplained, I consider the difference between morality and moral philosophy of a relative and gradual rather than a principal nature. Furthermore (but this will be more fully explained elsewhere), I consider moral subjectivity to be the *outcome* or *product* rather than the *origin* of moral experience. And finally, it is my conviction that the question regarding moral philosophy's beginning is too often thwarted by the fact that the notion 'beginning' is interpreted in terms of an absolute origin or ground, whereas morality's (or moral philosophy's) starting point must rather be considered to be of a relative and historical nature, and never an unprecedented event. Moreover, the beginning of morality is something which is permanently recaptured and resumed once a certain moral regime managed to establish itself.

Yet it cannot be denied that the history of morality displays some decisive ruptures or instances of discontinuity in which a certain moral regime suddenly finds itself fundamentally contested and challenged by unprecedented and incompatible moral experiences. Its apparent self-evidence suddenly finds itself exposed to subversive laughter, an experience which, under certain historical conditions, might even announce the commencement of a new moral epoch. This commencement, however, is never a transition from the immoral to the moral, or from primitivism and deficiency to enlightenment - although, once the new regime has finally established and secured its domination, its prehistory often tends to be represented in such a way. It is quite clear that this must be considered a strategy of self-justification rather than an effort to discern the true nature of the change. What is at stake here is a transformation of the basic way moral truth is experienced, articulated and interpreted. Somehow, the basic conditions of moral life have changed and unprecedented forms of moral subjectivity and moral experience are produced. It is not a transition from immorality to morality, however, not an absolute commencement or a creation *ex nihilo*. Rather it is an answer to a question, a solution to a problem. It is the replacement of certain basic forms of moral subjectivity by others which are incompatible with it, and efforts by the old regime to incorporate them or silence them turn out to be of no avail.

But perhaps the most remarkable aspect of my claim, and the one most urgently in need of preliminary clarification, will be the connection between morality and laughter. At first glance, the very association of the two might seem ridiculous in itself. Morality seems to exclude, rather than to imply laughter - it seems a perfectly *serious* philosophical (or theological) genre. Let me therefore provisionally explain why and how I consider them to be connected, although the bulk of the argument will of course be elaborated more carefully (and, I hope, more convincingly) in the remainder of the book. I already indicated that morality's beginning is of a relative nature and that there is no absolute transition from the non-moral to the moral. Morality is not produced by the moral subject. Rather, it is a world we enter. Even a completely transformed morality is a response to something else which was already there. The moral subject is formed or constituted by a moral life already existing in which he inevitably becomes involved. It is, to use an image borrowed from Ricoeur (1975), like a conversation which had already been going on for quite some time before we entered it, and which is bound to be continued should we disappear from the scene. We take the floor when others have already spoken.

But why should morality be something to talk about and to discuss, and even to contest, rather than something which could or should be taken for granted? What incites us to participate in the debate - and in some cases even to become moral philosophers ourselves? The answer is to be found in our *discontent* with the discourse of the others. Had it not been for the unsatisfactory nature of the conversation already existing, we would never have commenced speaking ourselves. For some reason or other, we consider current moral discourse one-sided and defective. We sense that it presents us with a reduced and distorted picture of the moral world. Something is absent or forgotten, something still remains to be said, a basic truth seems to be neglected. We reject, but at the same time remain highly dependent on the discourse which already came into existence before we ourselves became involved in it. Most of the concepts and arguments we rely on in our effort to recover concealed or forgotten aspects of moral truth were already introduced by others. We did not coin them ourselves, but borrow them from the very discourse we come to reject as basically defective. In other words, although established discourse might seem to conceal important aspects of moral life, it at the same time enables and allows us to address the issues at hand more adequately.[1] We would not have

---

[1] Cf. Gadamer (1960/1990): we speak a language already spoken by others; we use words, concepts and arguments borrowed from others, instead of inventing them ourselves. Even the questions we raise in response to its deficiencies are triggered by the discourse we

noticed the importance of these hidden or forgotten issues, nor would we have been able to formulate them, had it not been for the existence *and* the defectiveness of what is already established, had it not been for the efforts at articulation already made by our predecessors or contemporaries. Moral philosophy, therefore, is a secondary mode of speech - a series of critical glosses on the speech of others, its merits and its defects. It is not a *prima philosophia*, but rather a way of reading. Moral philosophy is never *merely* meta-ethical but always proves to be normative in the end. Meta-ethics can serve as a temporary technical device, but eventually our personal commitment to moral truth - our *daimonion*, as Socrates called it - is bound to reveal itself.

Now there are several strategies for exposing the defects of the discourse of the other, one of which is critical argument. However, under certain specific historical circumstances, the apparent self-evidence of established moral discourse has gained such a dominance, such a capacity of resistance or incorporation, such an ability to conceal its basic vulnerability, that its validity simply seems beyond contestation. Notwithstanding the moral subject's basic discontent, he remains unable to challenge the dominant discourse effectively by means of critical argument. Or, to borrow a phrase from Michel Foucault, individuals find themselves faced with a certain rationality, a moral regime that dominates moral discourse to such an extent that they cannot offer any resistance without raising the suspicion of being *unreasonable*. They (that is, we) find ourselves confronted with a discourse quite unable to recognize its own deficiencies. Although we are forced to accept its basic claims, our chronic discontent nevertheless persists. That is, although we are forced to participate in this discourse, we remain basically ambivalent, and our attitude towards established morality contains both a Yes and a No.

Then, all of a sudden, the basic vulnerability of the dominant regime dawns on us or is revealed to us - and this is the experience of laughter. Although given the circumstances established morality cannot be criticized, it can be ridiculed. And this is the (albeit relative) beginning of our effort to articulate the neglected and disregarded moral truth that had been forcing itself upon us and vexing us, although we remained unable to discern its significance for quite some time. Moral criticism, and the subsequent dawning of a new moral discourse or moral regime, is preceded by the experience of laughter. All the crucial ruptures in the history of morality were accompanied by and made possible by laughter. It subdued and undermined the dominant forms of moral subjectivity, constituted by the old regime, and allowed for unprecedented forms of moral subjectivity to emerge and constitute themselves. True laughter is the ground and starting point of moral transformations, and an experience of epochal significance. The basic scenario of laughter can be discerned in the moral transformations such as occurred during the fourth century B.C. (chapter three), the

---

enter.

first half of the sixteenth century A.D. (chapter four), and at the end of the nineteenth century A.D. (chapter five).

The first two chapters of this book will be of an introductory nature. In chapter one, I will present an outline of what in my case can be considered as the unsatisfactory 'discourse of the other': a particular moral logic called liberalism (or, the compartmentalization of moral life). For although this particular logic does not constitute the actual subject matter of my book, it is what made me embark on my effort to retrieve the philosophy of laughter obscured by it. It entails a particular understanding of moral life which, rather than being indisputable or self-evident, must be considered the temporary outcome of a certain historical development, an outcome whose basic 'platitudes' (Rorty) are bound to find themselves exposed to laughter. Furthermore, it presupposes, instrumentalizes and reinforces *certain* forms of moral subjectivity, disqualifying others as primitive, unreasonable or immoral. Yet, this moral regime which managed to become established and now seems unable to recognize its own deficiencies, still finds itself accompanied by a sense of uneasiness which already points to something which is hidden or neglected, a moral truth about to reveal itself in the experience of laughter - an experience which entails a challenge to the established consensus. Furthermore, I will claim that moral philosophy, rather than being a more or less scientific discourse elaborated on the basis of certain stable and secured moral principles or truths, basically and originally is a comic genre, and I will indicate the extent to which an abstract or even misguided understanding of moral subjectivity is bound to hamper our conception of moral experience as such. Notably, I will indicate the way the significance of laughter tends to be misrepresented in contemporary moral discourse. Attention will be drawn to the efforts of the moral regime to contain or incorporate laughter by reducing it to 'irony'. In the subsequent chapter, I will turn to some possible representatives of a rival approach, that is, to philosophers who can be considered as 'philosophers of laughter', namely Mikhail Bakhtin, Friedrich Nietzsche, George Bataille and Michel Foucault, in order to retrieve a basic understanding of laughter as a phenomenon of philosophical significance. Several *forms* of laughter - notably 'true' versus 'subdued' laughter - will be distinguished, and several *genres* of laughter (notably parody and irony) will be discussed. Finally, in the decisive chapters of this book, I will turn to three epochal figures (a philosopher, a theologian and a playwright) whom I consider as prominent protagonists (or even 'heroes') of laughter, representing the moments of transition and transformation already indicated above: Socrates (fourth century B.C., chapter three), Martin Luther (sixteenth century A.D., chapter four) and Henrik Ibsen (nineteenth century A.D., chapter five). Their work (or, in the case of Socrates, his speech acts, his verbal performance as recorded by Plato) will be subjected to what I will refer to as a *re*reading, a careful analysis from the point of view of laughter, a way of reading based on the contention that for strategic reasons, the serious aspects of their achievements have been persistently overemphasized, disregarding the significance of laughter. In other words, *re*reading is a way of reading that recognizes the extent to which certain texts, although generally supposed to be in support of, or at least in tune with established morality, are basically alien to it; a way of reading that focuses attention on those aspects of the text which came to be disregarded as residual.[2]

I already indicated that moral philosophy is not to be regarded as *prima philosophia*, a rational reconstruction of a universal moral truth grounded in certain indisputable principles. Rather, it is an effort to respond to what is said by others, that is, to a moral discourse already established. Moral truth is not something which can be captured in certain formula or propositions. It is something that reveals itself in the very process of reading and writing and therefore cannot be isolated from its 'context of discovery' or secured and justified in a systematic way. In other words, instead of containing a systematic series of arguments, this book is the account, the record of a reading process, as moral philosophy is basically a practice of writing, while writing is basically a way of reading - or rather *re*reading: a way of reading which reveals the extent to which certain discursive unities, regarded as being in support of the established consensus (and whose incompatible and disturbing features are usually pacified by means of strategies of revision, 'explanation' and biased reading), are basically at odds with it.

This book was originally meant to be a revised version in English of my thesis in Dutch - a review of moral theories on ethical consensus formation in both moral philosophy and health care ethics, published in 1993. From what has been said above, however, it will be clear that some changes have occurred. Rather than containing a systematic reconstruction of the Dutch version, it is a book in its own right, belonging to the same 'responsive' and 'explorative' genre, being the outcome of a similar 'responsive' reading/writing process (rather than a reconstruction or justification of what had already been said or explored before). It is a continuation, rather than a recapitulation of previous research. The research is reported 'immediately' as it were, rather than systematically presenting and justifying its 'results'. Furthermore, in the course of the rewriting process, some important shifts occurred. In view of the international and more general character of the new book, all references to (Dutch) health care ethics were dropped. As to moral experiences which can be considered as contesting or at least questioning the established ethical consensus (the basic issue of both books), the emphasis on the tragic that dominated the Dutch version gave way to an emphasis on the comical in this one. And finally, the sections on Socrates, Luther and Ibsen, being rather unsatisfactory and provisional paragraphs in the original book, grew into decisive chapters in this one.

---

[2] Or *ri*sidual: something *merely* comical.

Kierkegaard, in his book on irony (1989), allowed his style to suit his subject. As a contemporary reviewer phrased it, the work not only treated of irony but *was* irony. Kierkegaard conceded that the form of his treatise 'departed somewhat' from conventional scholarly methods, but asked the reader to forgive his jocundity, just as he himself sometimes sang at his work, in order to lighten the burden. The basic objective of my book is not to set off the reader laughing, although I do hope that it will contribute to the effort of making some forms of laughter possible again by retrieving the comic origins of moral criticism as a genre. All the same, I suspect that my way of reading and writing will be considered as somewhat too carefree and unrestricted to pass as academic by some. For instance, I do not profess to have written an exhaustive summary of the philosophical literature on laughter. On the contrary, some remarkable omissions will be noted. I will rely on Nietzsche rather than Kierkegaard, for instance, on Bakhtin rather than Bergson. I agree beforehand that much remains to be said. As to my use of foreign languages, all titles and quotations in the main text are translated (with a few exceptions, but in those cases the translation is usually provided by a footnote). In the footnotes, however, I sometimes prefer to cite the original text in German, French or Latin.

Apart from the philosophers mentioned in the text, I am greatly indebted to the editors of the *Morality and the Meaning of Life* series (Bert Musschenga, Paul van Tongeren and Kristin De Troyer), to Lucy Jansen for correcting and improving my use of the English language, to my fellow-participants in the *7th International Bakhtin Conference* (Moscow, 29 June 1995) who allowed me to present a draft version of some sections of the book and shared their comments with me, and (last but not least) to Martin Drenthen, Jaap Gruppelaar, Rien Janssens, Danforth Johnson, Cyril Lansink, Anton Simons and Donald Wesling who read and commented on draft versions of the manuscript, to my benefit.

Nijmegen
18 February 1996
450th Anniversary of Luther's death / Carnival's Eve

Chapter 1

Established Morality and Discontent

1. DOES MORAL PHILOSOPHY CONSTITUTE A SCIENCE?

The history of moral philosophy is not a tale of scientific progress, one that relates the gradual accumulation and elaboration of expert knowledge, where real progress has been made and some chronic misconceptions are finally dismissed once and for all. Rather, it is a more or less cyclical tale about the recognition, concealment or rejection, retrieval or recurrence of moral truths. The claim that moral philosophy is not *yet* a science, but could (and therefore should) be transformed in such a way that it might *become* a science, prevents us from recognizing the truly 'ethical' in ethics. We will never be able once and for all to define rigid criteria for moral action, and indeed, every epoch has formulated its own criteria. But this does not imply that it is utterly pointless or even ridiculous to reflect on what constitutes moral behaviour, even if we will never be able to produce an exhaustive account of moral life for all eternity.

For several reasons, moral philosophy[1] has been compared to medicine. For instance, although medicine and ethics offer general rules of conduct, both still rely to a significant extent on sensible judgement in concrete problem situations. That is, both contain practical knowledge, lacking the exactitude usually ascribed to (for example) physics and its scientific applications, and therefore remaining dependent on the sensibility and experience of the individual practitioner involved. Practical knowledge has to be applied to the specific circumstances of the case at hand, and this implies uncertainty, ambiguity and interpretation. On the other hand, in the case of medicine, remarkable scientific progress has been made, notably during the last decades. In fact, medicine has succeeded in becoming a science, in accumulating and elaborating extensive bodies of expert knowledge and in abolishing countless misconceptions and delusions once and for all. Medicine had *tried* to become a modern science ever since Descartes, and now it seems as if it has finally succeeded in achieving its goal. Although Descartes himself was somewhat reluctant with regard to moral philosophy's scientific potential, others cherished similar hopes in the case of ethics. And yet, ethics (or moral philosophy) still finds itself in much the same situation as medicine did before it became a science.

Indeed, before the dawn of modern science, the art of medicine found itself in a rather difficult position. It lacked most of the scientific knowledge and technical

---

[1] Or ethics: I consider them as synonyms.

means which today are taken for granted. Hippocratic medicine, for instance, although considered almost sacred by subsequent medical traditions, suffered from a bad reputation in its own time, and the modern reader is struck by the defensive mode of speech in which the bulk of the Hippocratic corpus was actually written. In ancient Greece, medicine was mocked and ridiculed by popular opinion as well as by contemporary philosophers and poets, and this situation continued for many centuries. The seventeenth century French playwright Molière, for instance, gave voice to a popular tradition of long standing when he ridiculed medicine and its practitioners in several of his comedies. In one of them, *L'amour Médecin*, it is claimed that the physician's competence consists in nothing but translating into Latin what one already knows, namely that the patient is ill. And when four physicians are asked for their opinion on a certain case, two of them start a theoretical debate on an ancient dispute which apparently carries more weight for them than the well-being of their patient, while the other two invoke the authority of Hippocrates and suggest that nothing at all should be done, and that one should refrain from all medical interventions in order to prevent any harmful consequences from occurring.

In the case of ethics, a similar risk of ridicule still constitutes a serious threat. Whereas medicine has been transformed into a science, or rather, a scientific practice, ethics has remained 'pre-scientific' and traditional in view of the fact that it still combines its diagnostics of the actual moral condition with a continuous *re*reading, a permanent and critical appropriation of its philosophical inheritance - and this inevitably implies hesitancy and reserve when it comes to making decisions, because the philosophical inheritance is notorious for its lack of consensus, apart from its being untimely and the problems of application which result from this. In short, ethics still remains a practice which consists of and combines two basic skills: the ability to 'read' or judge moral cases, and the ability to appreciate philosophical discourse. While medicine was transformed from a limited and even primitive practice into a modern, scientific one, similar efforts in the field of ethics did not produce the same effect. In the case of ethical discourse, one can still recognize the attachment to ancient writings as well as the chronic lack of consensus, arising in part from the absence of a *consensus sapientium* in the transmitted corpus - in short: the very features that popular wisdom ridiculed and attributed to medicine for centuries. And the same goes for the tendency towards restraint when it comes to real life decisions and applications.

It is against this background that a certain tendency in contemporary ethical discourse has gained prominence, a tendency which basically consists of the effort to secure a common ground, an ethical consensus which would allow moral philosophy to become more like a science, and to escape persistent public ridicule. It is claimed that there are certain basic moral principles or ideas which cannot be contested by anyone without being inconsistent, unreasonable or simply immoral. It should be the ethicist's objective to reconstruct and justify in a more or less systematic way such a set of basic moral claims which count as non-controversial and self-evident, and which actually shape our moral and social life. Once such a set of basic claims or principles has been secured, a more or less systematic application of these principles to a broad range of moral or policy problems becomes possible, and the ponderous burden of reading and rereading the philosophical corpus will become less inevitable, while chronic dissension can be significantly diminished. Now the question is whether this effort to escape public ridicule does not fall subject to a more fatal, philosophical laughter.

The attempt to turn ethics into a more serious genre, and perhaps even into a scientific one (for science is serious by definition), is remarkable if the *history* of moral philosophy as a genre is taken into consideration. For some reason or other, contemporary ethics does not seem very familiar with its own history. Notably the fact that, since time immemorial, moral criticism used to be intimately connected with comedy and laughter, became increasingly obscured. From a historical point of view, my effort to connect (or rather, *re*connect) morality and laughter is not as astonishing as it might seem. But why should ethics care about its history? What is wrong with contemporary ethics trying to become a more serious genre? What objections can be raised against the effort to secure a common ground, a set of non-controversial moral principles and basic ethical techniques if it could be of some assistance in solving matters of public policy in a fair and reasonable way?

In order for such questions to be answered in a convincing way, the contemporary effort to transform ethics into a more serious, more scientific discipline should be discussed at length, as I tried to do in some previous publications (Zwart 1993, 1995). As to the present study, however, such an endeavour, inevitable as it may seem, would put me in a difficult position. For although my uneasiness with certain prominent aspects of the established ethical consensus is what induced me to write the book, the established consensus itself is not the principal target of my research. On the contrary, the greater part of the book will be devoted to the moral significance of laughter as an experience of contestation. Such an exercise, however, would undoubtedly remain incomprehensible without at least some explanation as to the reason why, that is, without at least a hint as to the way it relates to the present situation. Indeed, the basic objective of my 'exercise in retrieval' (Taylor 1989, p. xi) of the time-old connection between ethics and laughter is to understand modernity. Therefore, in this first chapter I will present a picture of the kind of discourse I happen to reject, but hasten to add that it is not intended as a thorough exposition of contemporary moral discourse as such. Those in favour of the contested view will perhaps claim that, instead of producing a fair picture of what is being rejected, I simply laugh it off by means of a mere caricature, lacking sufficient academic *acribeia*. On the other hand, to be more explicit about what one rejects than about what one embraces would be inordinate as well. Therefore, let me emphasize beforehand that, as the picture of the contemporary ethical consensus presented in this chapter intends to summarize an understanding elaborated more carefully elsewhere, it is not in itself an effort to convince those in favour of the established consensus that they are hopelessly mistaken. My purpose simply is to clarify why I consider an effort to retrieve the ancient connection between ethics and laughter worthwhile. My subsequent *re*reading from the point of view of laughter of some remarkable episodes of the history of morality will point out that laughter is bound to reveal the limited and temporal nature of an established discourse that mistakenly considers itself to be extra-temporal and incontestable. As to the present, I basically will contend that the established consensus, though liberating and broad-minded as it may seem, contains some severe restriction and constraints that cannot be brought to light as long as its basic convictions remain unchallenged. In fact, I am convinced that, in order to produce an adequate and convincing judgement regarding the present situation, a retrieval of the truth of laughter will prove indispensable. In chapter five, when the moral significance of laughter has been sufficiently explored, an effort will be made to determine its significance in terms of the present more accurately.

2. THE ETHICS OF COMPARTMENTALIZATION AND THE TWILIGHT OF MORAL TRUTH

The effort to turn ethics into a more serious genre by securing a common ground (or 'ethical consensus') can be identified by means of certain typical terms and phrases. To begin with, it is said to involve a shift from 'content' to 'procedure'. Furthermore, moral life is compartmentalized into a 'public' and a 'private' realm, into public regulation and private emotions or attachments. In the public realm, the individual is expected to behave reasonably, to respect others, and to negotiate rights, interests and claims in order to achieve the best possible solution to a given problem for all of the parties involved, taking into account all the rights and interests at stake. In the private realm, however, one is allowed to commit oneself to any particular world view or moral ideal, undisturbed by the fact that such a view or such an ideal might seem untenable or even ridiculous to others, as long as such a commitment does not result in harm to others, or in impeding the process of consensus formation in the public realm, conducted by ethical experts. In the public sphere, we are to comply to an ethic of peaceful negotiation and regulation. By regulating public behaviour, private eccentricity is said to be secured. I will refer to this view as liberalism but hasten to add that what I have in mind is an articulation of the basic structure of contemporary public discourse (as it is apparently shared by an impressive number of individuals of widely differing political and religious denomination) rather than any political conviction in particular.

What is implied in such a view is basically a 'method of avoidance', an effort to turn all controversial items into private matters, thereby 'de-listing' them from the public agenda.[2] It is an effort to pacify public life by means of effective compartmentalization. The reduced and minimalized agenda for ethics, basically containing a set of procedural solutions to policy problems, is justified by the claim that eventually the only alternative to such a strategy of avoidance is moral warfare (or even civil war). The objective of moral deliberation is not to reveal the ultimate moral truth of human existence, for this has become a personal matter, but to maintain a situation of peaceful co-existence of incompatible world views and basic commitments. As to the ultimate moral truth of human existence, pluralism is inescapable. Ethics (at least the social or policy branch of ethics) should withdraw itself from the realm of incompatible 'comprehensive' doctrines, of substantial understandings of moral life, and transform itself into a fairly neutral or even procedural discourse. It should not aim at solving theoretical problems which it will remain unable to solve and which are bound to remain the object of endless struggle and contestation. Rather, ethics should restrict and limit itself to the non-controversial and the procedural. The compartmentalization of moral life into a public and a private realm implies the exclusion of moral truth from public debate.

This self-restriction is justified by a historical account, a typical narrative or 'standard account' (Toulmin 1990) the plot of which can be summarized as follows. Premodern society was grounded in a shared understanding of moral truth, a common, substantial view of moral life. In the sixteenth century, the self-evidence of this truth gave way to pluralism, a process which before long resulted in massive, violent confrontations between mutually incompatible moral truths. Subsequently, the Enlightenment emerged as an effort to develop a rationalistic ethic acceptable to all moral subjects regardless of their particular world views or their traditional religious attachments. The project of Enlightenment, however, although it succeeded in liberating modern individuals from many pre-modern constraints, still contained an appeal to a certain moral truth, a normative ideal of moral subjectivity, a substantial view of human nature which was supposed to be realized progressively in history. In the present, 'postmodern' condition, even this limited appeal to the progress of reason and to the rational nature of man has become problematic and is considered an untenable, 'metaphysical' remnant. Indeed, the appeal to reason is to give way to the more limited demand to be 'reasonable', that is, to a philosophy of

---

2 The phrase 'method of avoidance' was coined by Rawls (1987), one of its most prominent protagonists. The phrase 'de-listing' was coined by Callahan (1981), in order to criticize such an approach. Cf. Zwart (1993).

moral deliberation and mutual respect which is still reminiscent of the Enlightenment in certain respects but refrains from the effort to ground its ethic in a substantial moral view of man. Ethics should basically restrict itself to formulating the ideal conditions for moral deliberation. Although no one can be forced to accept the claim that human beings are rational or that ethics can be grounded in a 'law of reason' which is beyond contestation, everyone can be expected to behave reasonably in the public realm - whatever picture of human life is cherished in private. In private life, responsibility and human freedom may well be ridiculed, but in our public life an ever-increasing amount of responsibility has to be accepted.

In this chapter I will indicate why I consider this historical account, as well as the effort to reconstruct a non-controversial, reasonable consensus justified by it, basically flawed. To begin with, the basic conditions of public deliberation, to be accepted by all reasonable human beings, are far from neutral or restricted. Rather, their origin must be located in certain specific and historical, indeed, substantial claims regarding the moral truth of human existence. Furthermore, instead of allowing pluralism to flourish, they in fact contain severe constraints on moral life; they are restricting rather than restricted. Finally, they mistakenly take for granted and assume a certain kind of moral subjectivity which is in fact produced and reinforced by them.

In *Cosmopolis* Toulmin (1990) already dismissed some misguided assumptions underlying what he refers to as the 'standard account of modernity'. One of them is the claim that, whereas in the Middle Ages the church had severely impeded science, reason and individual autonomy to flourish, in the seventeenth century ecclesiastical constraints on science (including moral philosophy) and human life (including its moral aspect) were relaxed instead of reinforced, and theological commitments were less rigorous and demanding than before. According to Toulmin, the very reverse was true. While the sixteenth century was indeed a period of remarkable freedom and open-mindedness, during the seventeenth century a rigid ecclesiastical and theological regiment came to be imposed which corresponded to a similar attitude of toughness in the realm of philosophy.[3] Much like the Counter-Reformation on the theological level, seventeenth-century philosophy should be regarded a 'Counter-Renaissance' in which the tolerant, practical and skeptical attitude of Renaissance thinkers like Erasmus and Montaigne was replaced by a theoretical quest for certainty and firm foundations. Although Erasmus in *Praise of Folly* had ridiculed contemporary philosophical and theological discourse, he did not aim at replacing it by an indisputable and incontestable stable ground. Progress and Enlightenment in the

---

3 The Russian philosopher M. Bakhtin, who will be introduced in chapter two, agrees with this. Cf. 'The fifteenth century was an age of considerable freedom in France' - there was, for instance, 'no sharp line between familiar speech and "correct" language' (Bakhtin 1968, p. 320), and many similar remarks.

realm of philosophy, Toulmin claims, meant restriction and constraint rather than free-thinking.

A similar claim could be made for the subsequent transformation from the modern (or 'rationalistic') ethics of Enlightenment to the postmodern (or 'liberalistic') ethics of compartmentalization. Whereas the new, postmodern ethics might seem less demanding and less restrictive at first glance, I will maintain that its basic gesture is one of exclusion and restriction. Indeed, it is my contention that postmodern constraints on public moral discourse are more instead of less severe than the ones preceding it. Postmodern individuals find themselves forced to participate in public deliberation and the process of consensus formation while inclinations among some individuals or sections of the population to remain aloof, to remain hesitant about taking part in it, are increasingly considered problematic. Moreover, although it is suggested that the deliberation process is able to tolerate virtually all possible contributions, certain speech acts are disqualified and excluded beforehand as being 'fundamentalistic' or as disturbing the process of consensus formation, or as representing views which are not considered acceptable to all reasonable individuals. In short, what we are dealing with here is an ethic of deliberation in which a compulsion to take part in a certain kind of public discourse is intrinsically connected with a tendency towards exclusion. Or to put it otherwise, in order to be granted access to public discourse, we have to become a certain kind of moral subject - someone willing to negotiate, willing to refrain from making any public appeals to 'private' moral truths. We postmoderns have to consent to a particular form of moral exchange in order to find ourselves included among its participants, and we are denied the right to commit ourselves publicly to deviant discursive modes. The compartmentalization of moral life implies that we agree to settle for consensus at the expense of truth - although we are of course still granted the right to remain susceptible to deviant moral demands in private. Any effort to present ourselves as *public* guardians of moral truth (as guardians of the inviolable significance of uncurbed nature, for example) is disqualified as being an inadmissible expression of fanaticism and intolerance. By means of these and other similar procedures of exclusion, the established consensus is permanently reproduced, maintained and reinforced at the expense of deviant discursive modes which are dismissed as obsolete relics or rejected as symptoms of fundamentalism. In short, we find ourselves confronted with a moral regime that cannot be questioned without raising the suspicion of being unreasonable, and that successfully immunizes itself against contestation, considering its basic principles self-evident and inevitable, unwilling to admit that its picture of moral life contains a substantial claim to moral truth (and therefore remains contestable by definition). The speech acts of those who remain hesitant to accept these restrictions and who refuse to consider their speech acts as either contributions to the consensus formation process or as articulations of private, highly idiosyncratic truths, are not taken into consideration. Their views are considered to be at odds with a moral regime whose basic objective is the reduction of public tensions by redefining them as conflicts of interests, that is, by compartmentalizing moral language into a public and a private vocabulary.

My discontent with this established moral logic does not evolve out of the idea that it should be our objective to realize or at least approximate what Habermas (1987) referred to as an 'ideal communication', devoid of any strategic constraints, for such an ideal must not only be considered fictitious and utopian, it is grounded in a thoroughly misguided understanding of moral discourse. *Every* effort to articulate moral experience, or to establish an ethical discourse is bound to reveal certain aspects, while others are forgotten or concealed, and even the postmodern (or liberal) regime most certainly has its merits, apart from its defects. Rather, I would like to emphasize that what we are confronted with here is a discursive regime which *presents* itself as highly permissive, while it is in fact severely restrictive. In short, it is a regime which seems unable to recognize its own constraints, its own violence and domination, and therefore runs the risk of becoming a liberal *ideology*, a discursive *coup d'état* which no longer admits its strategic objectives nor recognizes its effects.

Indeed, we must acknowledge that every moral discourse entails constraints. They can be contested, and moral discourse can be transformed, but this implies the replacement of the established constraints by others. We participate in this struggle, this process of contestation and transformation in order to promote a discursive situation which allows the particular life form or moral practice represented and pursued by us to flourish. The idea that some constraints are neutral or at least generally acceptable, and therefore cannot be accused of encouraging or impeding certain ways of life as compared to others, is fictitious and bound to convey an ideological bias in favour of one of the ways of life at stake.

In short, what is advocated here is a picture of moral discourse as a strategic situation, a struggle between incompatible ways of life, where every discursive genre or mode of speech, indeed every single speech act, every single word is both revealing and concealing, encouraging and restrictive. There are no neutral forms of speech. It is a strategic or *agonistic* situation involving several discursive tendencies mutually impeding, contesting or reinforcing each other. What is advocated here is not simply a recognition, but an intensification of this *agon*, rather than its avoidance - for avoidance merely implies the unquestioned domination of one particular discursive tendency at the expense of other possibilities.

It is an understanding of discourse supported by the views of the Russian philosopher and literary scientist Mikhail Bakhtin (1988) who describes social discourse in terms of a temporary ideological equilibrium which for a certain period of time manages to maintain a certain coherence and unity but finds itself faced with and penetrated by a continuing clash of 'voices', that is, finds itself permanently contested and 'dialogized', and remains involved in an agonistic and polemic situation. Every form of life produces its characteristic modes of speech, and modern society is a *heteroglossia* of voices, a plurality of speech genres, a permanent struggle of centripetal and centrifugal discursive forces. The dominant mode of speech of a certain epoch finds itself continuously challenged by the vocabularies, the modes of speech or dialects which are characteristic of more peripheral life forms. There are no neutral words, no neutral vocabularies. Every mode of speech is contested, contestable, contesting. Every speech unit has its own environment, its own history, belongs to a certain life form, a certain occupation for instance, a certain view of life, and will subsequently find itself appropriated, exploited and transformed by those who participate in social discourse.

Bakhtin refers to contemporary society as a 'living novel'. There are languages of generations, of professions, of parties and age groups, of the authorities as well as of various classes and circles. There are languages of officials, labourers and students, while even the languages of the military student, the high school student and the trade school student are all different languages (p. 290).[4] Even languages of the day exist, as well as family jargons. All these languages serve their own specific socio-political purposes, each has its own slogans, its own vocabulary, its own emphases (p. 263). In no way can they live in peace and quiet with each other and therefore social discourse is a perpetual struggle, although the internal stratification and differentiation of every national language tends to be subdued somewhat by forces that serve 'to unify and centralize the verbal-ideological world' (p. 270) and to impose a 'common' view, embodied in a common 'neutral' language, that is, a verbal approach considered as normal for a given sphere of society. Every concrete utterance serves as a point where the centrifugal and centripetal forces of language confront one another. In the next chapter, Bakhtin's views will be explored more carefully, but at this point I merely wish to emphasize that I take them to encourage and confirm the claim that an apparently neutral standard account of contemporary ethics can never be neutral (or non-controversial) from an agonistic, Bakhtin-like view on social discourse. A 'common neutral language' is always a *particular* vocabulary or mode of speech, and as such it is the outcome of a particular history, expressing a substantial view of moral life, and encouraging certain life forms while impeding others. The compartmentalization of moral life into a private realm of truth and a public sphere of restriction and regulation, is far from self-evident or neutral. While apparently confirming the actual decline of moral truth in public life, it basically is an attempt of one particular truth, one particular substantial view of

---

4 Cf. Nietzsche's remark on the peculiar features of student's German - notably its inclination toward irony (*Human, All Too Human II*, 'The Wanderer and his Shadow', § 228).

moral life to gain dominance over its rivals. Being neutral, or rather, seeming neutral, is an effect of domination.

Now what is this 'substantial' view of moral life that is implied in the seemingly neutral strategy of compartmentalization and where do we find the history which produced it? It goes without saying that an adequate reconstruction of the view involved as well as of its history is quite beyond the scope of this book, let alone a mere chapter. Still, a few significant aspects can be marked. In his book *The Flight from Authority*, Jeffrey Stout (1981) describes how, during the modern epoch, the decline of truth in public discourse gave rise to the differentiation of morality as a relatively autonomous domain and the subsequent development of moral philosophy into an autonomous academic discipline, disengaging itself from the constraints of traditional ecclesiastical authorities. Furthermore, his book contains a description of how the 'crisis of authority', brought about by the Reformation, stimulated the quest for a moral consensus, a public compromise between incompatible truths. By tracing the *history* of the established moral account, the assumption that there is an incontestable central core of human experience which has no history is questioned. This central core turns out to be a particular view, the outcome of a particular history. According to Stout, although the Reformation was basically motivated by the quest for an indisputable ground, it in fact produced a multiplication of authorities, with pietism (that is, the appeal to inner certainty as the standard of truth) as its ultimate result. The church as a body gave way to pious atoms. Every single conscience constituted a separate authority, bereft of any means to settle disagreement among truth claims, and unwilling to accept rational justifications. Furthermore, the pietistic turn implied an emphasis on the moral at the expense of the strictly religious and dogmatic aspect of faith, a development which eventually resulted in the separation of public and private morality.

Now pietism is not merely a particular version of protestantism, nor simply a certain doctrine or regional version of a creed. Rather it implies a certain form of moral subjectivity, grounded in the Protestant separation of the worldly and the spiritual realm or regiment (the Two Worlds Theorem). Whereas the public sphere (the worldly regiment) was left to the politics of power and calculation (although perhaps, under certain favourable circumstances, and in spite of corrupted human nature, a more or less just and reasonable policy could be realized), the *essential* part of human life came to be located in the private and inner sphere. As a participant in public life the Christian individual restricted himself to advocating a settlement or compromise that would not constitute a threat to his basic spiritual and moral commitments. That is, he opted for a kind of equilibrium, a restricted, limited and reasonable status quo, in order to secure a pietistic inner world of truth. Whereas public compromise was motivated by prudent self-interest and calculation, religious and moral issues belonged to the sphere of moral sentiment and inner experience, inaccessible to criticism. This implied an active, negotiating attitude as a participant in social discourse, and a passive, receptive attitude in the private sphere. That is, it implied a willingness to subject oneself to 'human law' up to the point where this human law prevented one from acting in accordance with personal conscience ('divine law'). In a perfect world the state would disappear, but in real life it was an evil which had to be accepted. All this implied a permanent tension between personal freedom and public compliance. The government both secured and threatened personal autonomy. It was considered incapable of, or at least unauthorized to pronounce judgement in matters of religious and moral truth, and therefore assigned a more restricted function: to recognize, respect and maintain personal autonomy in order to allow the individual to subject himself to certain (often highly idiosyncratic) religious demands. In his personal life, the individual was sovereign, and answerable only to God. The evolving equilibrium, however, was permanently at risk: the authorities might threaten personal autonomy, while a fanatic individual (expanding the spiritual regiment to the public sphere) might incite moral warfare. Public compromise guaranteed social stability, and allowed for the development of a public policy directed at public welfare. It had nothing to do with moral truth, however, which was considered a personal and not a public experience.

In short, Protestantism, notably pietism, prepared the way for liberalism, that is, for liberal etatism, a moral view presented by J.S. Mill in his essay *On Liberty* (1859/1974). According to Mill, liberalism is a social or political ethics, a reflection on the way power can be legitimately exercised by society over the individual. It emphasizes a rigid demarcation between the public and the private sphere and defines the duties which can be enforced upon individuals in the public sphere, leaving ample room for the right to eccentricity in the private sphere. In the parts which only concern himself, Mill writes, the independence of the individual is absolute. Over himself, his own body and mind, the individual is sovereign. This sovereignty is limited, however, by the moral demand not to inflict harm upon others.

The subject of Mill's essay, therefore, is the nature and limits of the power which can be legitimately exercised by society over the individual. Liberalism is to provide an answer to the question of how and to what extent individuals are to be governed, that is, it deals with the question of how both individual and collective tyranny should be checked. In the nineteenth century, modern society had acquired the technical means to exercise social tyranny on a formidable scale, far beyond comparison with any previous kind of political oppression, leaving fewer means to escape and penetrating much more deeper into the details of life. Thus, individual freedom had to be guaranteed. Still, Mill considered the enforcement of some restraints on human action inevitable: some rules of conduct simply had to be imposed. The question therefore was how to make the fitting adjustment between individual independence and social control. Now according to Mill, the only purpose for which power can be rightfully exercised over any member of a civilized community, against his will, is to prevent harm to others. The individual has the right to frame the plan of his own life so long as he does not harm his fellow creatures. Although at first glance this might seem to allow for only a limited range of interferences by the government, on further reflection it becomes clear that, as many of our acts do have implications for other human beings, liberalism came to encourage and justify a substantial and gradually increasing exercise of public power. That is, although liberalism apparently aims at restricting the impact of governmental action on private life, the 'harm-principle' provides the modern state with a perfect justification for becoming increasingly involved, at least in a regulative manner, in countless aspects of social intercourse - an involvement which is bound to intensify as society grows more an more complex and the mutual dependence of individuals will increase. In order to protect others against the tyranny of the self and, by implication, the self against the tyranny of others, the individual becomes subject to an increasing number of restrictions - and this constitutes the basic *aporia* of liberalism. In ancient Greek or Roman societies, although at first glance their modes of exercising power were often far more despotic and far less democratic, the extent to which public policy penetrated social intercourse, conducting individual life from birth to death, both in sickness and in health, was far less intense. Indeed, Michel Foucault (1989/1995) pointed out that, although contemporary liberalism's basic concern appears to be the fear of governing-too-much, the actual extent of its involvement as a political regime in practically all the details of human life is truly astonishing. In fact, Foucault recognized that liberalism is basically a kind of 'etatism', a set of technologies for governing individuals. It is a political regime that exercises power over individuals in a remarkably efficient way, producing a stable consensus, securing an adapted form of moral subjectivity by inventing and utilizing efficient techniques and instruments of power (Foucault 1980).

Indeed, liberalism presupposes (or rather, produces) a certain form of moral subjectivity. According to Mill, despotism (a more archaic form of etatism, a more primitive mode of exercising power) is legitimate when it comes to dealing with barbarians, and liberalism has no application to any state of things prior to the time when mankind had become capable of improvement by 'free and equal discussion'.[5] In other words, one has to comply with liberalism's basic demands in order to find one's right to eccentricity respected - that is, only certain forms of eccentricity are accepted. Other, truly incompatible forms of life are faced with the prospect of tyranny, and in his *Discipline and Punish* Foucault (1975) has provided us with a

---

[5] 'Until then, there is nothing for them but implicit obedience to an Akbar or a Charlemagne, if they are so fortunate as to find one' (p. 69).

vivid picture of the modern forms of tyranny which eventually allowed the liberal state to emerge and the corresponding forms of moral subjectivity to be constituted. Liberalism is basically a mode of exercising power, a technique for governing individuals, demanding and producing a certain kind of conversion and adaption, a certain level of obedience and consent, a certain (trans)formation of moral subjectivity. Its basic gesture is the compartmentalization of moral life into a private realm of eccentricity and a public realm of constraint. Ethical consensus remains an ideological equilibrium justifying a temporary state of affairs.

Now the logic at work in both pietism and liberalism implies a rather restricted agenda for moral philosophy. It is no longer directed at the discovery of moral truth but rather at establishing a public compromise, allowing the individual to engage in his eccentric quest for truth while preventing harm to others. Basic experiences of moral truth and moral embarrassment are excluded from the ethical agenda since ethics aims at consensus formation and behaviour regulation. At best, two separate agendas for ethics are allowed: one for public and one for private use. Be this as it may, the picture of moral life implied in the ethics of compartmentalization is far from neutral or non-controversial. Rather it contains certain substantial claims with regard to moral life which should be open to contestation. Moreover, it implies a certain form of moral subjectivity (the compartmentalized Self) which is the outcome of certain historical experiences and anything but universal or self-evident.

Notwithstanding the 'genealogical' affinity between the Protestant and the liberalist view on government, some important differences can be discerned as well. Whereas from a Protestant point of view public life is depicted in more or less negative terms, liberalism has a more positive and affirmative understanding of the management of public life. It is not *merely* a compromise, for the individual *is* basically a citizen and public policy can certainly be fair and reasonable. In short, what has occurred is a historical shift from a negative, more or less Protestant, to a somewhat more positive, liberal appreciation of the state. Whereas Protestantism is first and foremost concerned with the individual, with the way the individual is to guide his own life in order to become a certain kind of moral subject, liberalism is not interested in private morality as such, but in the social conditions which have to be realized in order for certain forms of moral subjectivity to flourish and constitute themselves. Liberalism is first and foremost a social ethics, a perspective on the use of social power. It is, in short, a version of what I will refer to as *etatism*. Notwithstanding its explicit concern with individual freedom, its main 'subject' is not the individual but the state.[6]

---

6 It is important to note, however, that although Protestantism originally started as a 'bottom-up' understanding of moral transformation, it gradually became more and more etatistic. This fate already announced itself in the case of Luther. In order to counter the fanaticism of those whom he polemically referred to as *Schwärmer* and who threatened to

The historical shift from a rather negative towards a much more positive appreciation of public policy and the public realm (that is, the shift from a Protestant to a liberal understanding of ethical consensus) is described by John Rawls in *The Idea of an Overlapping Consensus* (1987).[7] According to Rawls, ethics should opt for consolidation rather than contestation. It is the task of a philosopher to articulate a conception of justice acceptable to all 'reasonable' individuals[8] in a pluralistic society, a conception which can be considered a general standard by means of which public institutions are to be permanently scrutinized. In a pluralistic society, such a consensus is absolutely indispensable. In order to understand our contemporary situation, however, one has to realize that the quest for consensus is an *answer* to a specific historical *problem*, a problem which constitutes the basic experience, the beginning and starting-point of modern times and has remained our basic problem - the problem of pluralism and the risk of moral warfare it implies. Modern society's principal objective is to avoid a situation of massive and violent confrontation between incompatible moral or religious truths, to avoid the recurrence of religious wars such as the ones accompanying the dawn of modern times. This quest for ethical consensus is the outcome of a historical experience. The modern individual came to recognize that a willingness to compromise in the public sphere in order to avoid irreconcilable conflicts, and to opt for a *modus vivendi* between incompatible truths, is inevitable and more reasonable than to persist in violent confrontation. At first this willingness to compromise was merely a matter of prudence, best-interest and calculation (the Protestant attitude) and the public consensus was accepted merely for strategic reasons. A corresponding transformation of moral subjectivity itself (the emergence of the compartmentalized Self) was not yet implied. At a later stage, however, the willingness to compromise was transformed into a *moral* issue and became part of moral subjectivity itself: one of the basic convictions that constituted the moral subject. Dissension gave way to the constitution of a particular kind of moral subjectivity, to the establishment of a particular moral regime, liberalism, which is still governing us, and which still provides the moral ground structure for our public arrangements. The modern

---

overthrow the still vulnerable compartmentalization between church and state as it was initially advocated by him, he found himself forced to support the transformation of the Lutheran Church into an instrument of etatism. Faced with a violent confrontation between peasants and state, he decided to side with the state against the peasants, although initially he had supported (some of) their claims, while their revolt had (at least to a considerable extent) been inspired by the spiritual upheaval he himself had inaugurated. But more of this in chapter four.

[7] The fact that many prominent spokesmen of liberal ethics are political rather than moral philosophers, confirms the claim that liberalism is basically a social ethic.

[8] That is, all individuals who have successfully accommodated themselves to the dominant form of moral subjectivity.

28

individual is forced to participate in modern society and to consent to the basic moral convictions it embodies, but is granted the right (albeit within restricted boundaries) to determine his own eccentric (but harmless) life plan.

In certain respects, however, Rawls' account seems rather concealing and ideological. It is suggested that the individuals involved were willing to undergo this transformation on their own accord. Others, like Marx in *The Capital, Part I* and Foucault in *Discipline and Punish*, revealed the violent nature of this change, which resulted in the constitution of the modern subject and the establishment of the liberal regime (i.e. the compartmentalization of moral life). History reveals that reason is always preceded by force. In order for a certain moral regime to become established, a violent *coup d'état* seems inevitable. Henceforth, we no longer seem able to challenge its basic truth without raising the suspicion of being 'unreasonable'. All individuals are forced to comply to a particular standard for moral subjectivity. In fact, by means of punishment and forced labour, a certain form of conscience, a certain sense of accountability or responsibility is produced. By neglecting or obscuring the violent nature of these historical events, philosophy tends to give way to an ideological justification of the established regime. Indeed, according to Rawls, philosophy's basic aim is consolidation and justification, requiring of individuals that they finally accept the restrictive guidelines for moral deliberation, finally renounce their responsiveness to incompatible moral demands, that is: finally be *converted*. For the transformation of the moral subject which occurred during the modern epoch was in a very fundamental way a conversion, rather similar to the conversion which preceded it during the first half of the Middle Ages. Both conversions seemed rather superficial and violent at first, but gradually resulted in the internalization of certain basic demands and in an exclusion of incompatible forms of life - by means of a form of exercising power referred to by Foucault as 'pastoral' power.

Eventually, we become unable to challenge the basic moral convictions of established culture. The only way to reveal their being less self-evident than they seem, is to compare them with the basic moral convictions of a world we know comparatively well, although it is a world quite unlike ours, the moral world of ancient Greece and Rome. According to Nietzsche, this vanished world allows us to formulate certain experiences regarding the present that would otherwise remain incomprehensible.[9] Indeed, as Hans Achterhuis (1984) and others have pointed out, the ancient Greek and Roman world constitutes a comic mirror to the modern one, as both worlds are radically separated from each other by what can be referred to as a complete reversal and transformation of all values - an *Umwertung aller Werte*, as Nietzsche's version of comic reversal is called. The Greek, for instance, greatly preferred idleness to work and considered the latter as utterly degrading. In the

---

9 *Human, All Too Human II*, 'Mixed opinions and aphorisms', § 218.

sixteenth century, however, protestants like Luther (not coincidentally a miner's son) and humanists like Coornhert initiated the abuse of idleness and the praise of labour - a genre, a conviction which soon became one of the omnipresent and quasi self-evident platitudes of the great ethico-political discourse of modernity. All of a sudden, the rural populace was depicted as excessively lazy, backward and prodigal by the spokesmen of official discourse (Achterhuis 1984, p. 40 ff.). While the popular masses of Europe, notwithstanding their fierce and large-scale resistance, were gradually transformed into a massive reservoir of labour, a new genre made its appearance, beginning with Moore's *Utopia*. The one thing all these perfectly organized, utopian societies, invented by Moore and his followers had in common was their persistent emphasis on the significance of labour. From the very start, however, this new genre found itself accompanied by a comic and popular double, a cycle of legends about an counter-utopian land of gluttony and idleness, the *pays de Cocagne* (Achterhuis, p. 84; cf. Bakhtin 1968, p. 297), in which popular resistance against wage work expressed itself in a popular (that is, comical and parodical) manner. In the Land of Cockaigne, the same harsh penalties that were directed against idleness in real life, were used as a punishment for being too eager to work.

The ideological features in Rawls' account apparently result from his unwillingness to recognize the power aspect of the particular moral logic it tries to justify - a logic which aims at establishing itself at the expense of other possibilities. Philosophy is reduced to the effort of supporting the established consensus (involving certain basic ingredients of moral subjectivity such as tolerance, willingness to compromise and negotiate, and fairness) and of producing certain guidelines and procedures for moral deliberation, instead of challenging the established truth regime. Of course, this is abolishing true pluralism rather than accepting it. Once we have adopted this kind of moral subjectivity, the moral logic supported by Rawls does seem inevitable, but this already requires the subjugation of real pluralism. Indeed, Rawls himself points to the fact that the increasing detachment of the modern individual from traditional and religious life forms and commitments, resulting in an unclear and indefinite identity, is bound to facilitate their participation in the democratic institutions of contemporary society (Rawls 1972) - much like the conversion to Christianity was facilitated by the decline of traditional and local attachments and ways of life. The impetus at work here is the effort to secure and reinforce that which has been established (being itself the outcome of a previous transformation) and to reject any rival philosophical understandings, such as the *Socratic* one, which rather considers philosophy a practice of fundamental contestation, challenging what appears to be self-evident, revealing fundamental uncertainty and embarrassment, exposing the vulnerability of basic moral convictions, unwilling to accept compromise at the expense of moral truth or to support established consensus for the sake of securing established forms of moral subjectivity. Notably, in Plato's *Apology*, Socrates emerges as a fanatic of moral truth, appealing to a higher duty, a divine mission to irritate his fellow citizens, arousing them from their ideological slumber and inciting them to question what *seems* firmly established. Someone, furthermore, who displays a basic readiness to ridicule the moral answers generally accepted as true, and to mock the protagonists of the official, standard account. Rawls, when he embarks on his effort to elaborate procedures for ethical decision making, already knows (quite unlike Socrates) what kind of results such a procedure is supposed to yield, already knows the *answer* his philosophy is supposed to support or provide. His effort is fundamentally biased in favour of the established moral regime, the standard moral account. The method of avoidance (the ethics of compartmentalization) is basically a strategy of consolidation, whereas the basic objective of philosophers like Socrates and Foucault is contestation.

In his most recent book *Political Liberalism*, Rawls' version of the standard account of modernity is recapitulated and further clarified (Rawls 1993). The modern world is not taken for granted, but compared with its historic mirror, the ancient world. Ancient religion, Rawls tells us, was public in the sense that all citizens were expected to participate in public celebrations, although the details of what one believed in terms of doctrine were not of great importance. Medieval Christianity, however, was not only public but also doctrinal (with a creed that was to be believed), as well as authoritarian. Now although Luther and Calvin were as dogmatic and intolerant as their Roman foes had been - they never intended to further toleration - the Reformation must be considered the historical origin of political liberalism. Gradually, as we have seen, toleration as a mere *modus vivendi* gave way to the discovery of the possibility of a stable pluralist society. Political liberalism is the answer to a question: how is it possible to maintain over time a stable and just society of free and equal citizens in the absence of a shared comprehensive (religious, philosophical or moral) doctrine? Such a thing is possible, Rawls claims, if one narrows the range of disagreement by avoiding those moral topics on which these comprehensive doctrines divide and by restricting the agenda of ethics to determining fair terms for cooperation and intercourse between free and equal citizens. Moreover, liberalism merely articulates the basic principles and ideas that already are implicitly accepted and recognized by all reasonable individuals. Those principles can (or rather, should) be endorsed by all citizens, whatever their religious view. In order for a just and stable cooperation of free and equal citizens to be maintained, the appeal to comprehensive truths should give way in public life to consensus, that is, to the primacy of the political and the established.

Furthermore, the political sphere is explained by Rawls in what I refer to as an etatistic, top-down manner (p. 136 ff.). Political power is always coercive power, Rawls contends, and the government alone has the authority to use force. Yet, the exercise of political power is proper only when it is exercised in accordance with this basic structure all free and equal citizens will freely agree to.[10] Although the state has the power to punish and to correct by force, the basic political values normally have sufficient weight to override all other values that come in conflict with it. Political values normally outweigh whatever values may seem at odds with them, as they articulate the basic framework of social life, the very groundwork of our existence, the fundamental terms of cooperation.

In the decisive section devoted to 'The political conception of the person' (p. 29 ff.), however, Rawls agrees that a certain form of moral subjectivity is presupposed by liberalism. Ethical consensus as understood by Rawls implies that individuals have a double (that is, compartmentalized) identity: an institutional, political or public one and a noninstitutional, nonpolitical, nonpublic one. Besides their institutional identity, they have affections, devotions and loyalties that resist objective evaluation. Indeed, citizens normally have two views, and their overall view can be divided into two parts (p. 140). Yet, although our moral identity often changes considerably over time (usually slowly but sometimes suddenly) these changes or conversions do not imply a change in our public or institutional identity. Therefore, the dominant form of moral subjectivity (the compartmentalized Self including a stable institutional identity) has to be accepted by all individuals and may even be enforced. The principles of justice that constitute society's basic structure are such as reasonable individuals normally comply with. They constitute a permanent feature of public culture, and normally need not be enforced by means of the oppressive use of state power (as had been the case in the society of the Middle Ages) because they imply a basic moral structure all reasonable individuals will readily assent to. We may, however, force individuals to be 'reasonable'.

Moreover, Rawls admits that the problem of social stability had been on his mind from the very outset (p. 141). Eventually he claims, however, that liberalism will produce a fair amount of political stability, one strong enough to resist the 'normal tendencies to injustice' (p. 142) by encouraging individuals to acquire a normally sufficient sense of justice so that they will generally comply with society's basic institutions (p. 141 ff.). Political liberalism appeals not to force but to public reason, that is, to the sense of justice of free and equal citizens viewed as reasonable and rational. The fact of pluralism, moreover, is not an unfortunate condition of human life, as we might say of pluralism as such, allowing for doctrines that are not only irrational but mad and aggressive. Rather, the fact of reasonable pluralism is the outcome of the free exercise of free human reason under conditions of liberty (p. 144).

---

[10] '[I]n a democratic society public reason is the reason of equal citizens who [exercise] political and coercive power over one another' (p. 214).

Once again, what is neglected in such an account is a basic fact of which history informs us, namely that the 'reasonable' individual, free and equal, and willing to accept 'fair terms of cooperation' had to be produced by force. In *The Capital, Part 1* Marx explains the emergence of the massive reservoir of labour power presupposed by the kind of society that was coming into existence at that time. In Marx' account, the true origin of modern society is revealed. It is a history of violence, plunder and terrorism. Marx relates how, in the sixteenth century, the self-supporting rural population was violently transformed into a massive labour reservoir by means of expropriating and oppression. All of a sudden, they found themselves deprived of their means of existence, were chased away from the lands they had commonly cultivated since time immemorial by means of policies such as 'inclosure of commons' and 'clearing of estates'. Eventually, they became 'free and equal' and were forced to accept the 'fair terms of cooperation' of the emerging labour market. In fact, they were transformed into servile, dependent, poverty-stricken labourers. Those who dared to put up resistance, became the victim of a ruthless policy directed at the extermination of 'idleness', 'laziness' and 'pauperism' by means of what Marx refers to as 'grotesque-terroristic' punishment as well as a series of harsh disciplinary techniques such as the famous 'Houses of Terror'. This transfiguration of the rural population into individuals that would comply with the new ideal of personhood called *homo laborans* was what made modern society possible. Rawls, in his anecdote about the 'original position' and the historical shift from *modus vivendi* to liberalism, totally ignores the history that finally made individuals reasonable and willing to cooperate, taking for granted the idea that paid labour constitutes the basic structure of human existence. Actual history is a comic mirror bound to expose the ideological nature of nineteenth century 'political economy' as well as of twentieth century 'political liberalism'.

Indeed, what is neglected is the fact that, compared to the 'oppressive' and 'authoritarian' Middle Ages, contemporary society's basic feature is its astonishing uniformity in terms of the forms of life it is able to tolerate. Wage work has become a basic condition for admittance to public intercourse. This, the forced unification of forms of life, the demand that, whatever we do, we must remain 'reasonable' and willing to work and, above all, willing to accept compartmentalization, is what constitutes the 'groundwork of our existence'. But let me not be misunderstood. I do not call for a relapse into a medieval world or for a fundamental political transformation of the present, nor do I consider the Land of Cockaigne a serious or even tempting prospect. What is advocated here is a *philosophical* recognition of the power aspect of moral life. Any effort to conceal this aspect, to present the established consensus as non-controversial and incontestable, will find itself exposed the truth of laughter. In the next section, two further examples of consolidation and avoidance will be presented: the moral views of Peter Strawson and Richard Rorty.

Special attention will be given to the latter's understanding of Socrates, his initial appreciation of him as well as his subsequent rejection of him as a philosophical hero (before subjecting some of Plato's Socratic dialogues to a more thorough *re*reading in chapter three).

3. THE METHOD OF AVOIDANCE, OR: THE LOSS OF PROBLEMS

A perfect example of the 'method of avoidance' or the 'ethics of compartmentalization' is provided by Strawson (1970). As has been indicated above, there is a remarkable tendency in established moral discourse to start with a certain rhetoric gesture: a proposal to distinguish, that is, to separate. In the case of Strawson, it is the distinction between *the region of the ethical* (to be abandoned by moral philosophy) and *the sphere of morality* (to which moral philosophy should exclusively devote her attention). According to Strawson, all individuals will be fascinated by some personal moral ideal or other, seizing them, impressing them. These ideals are 'true' in a very fundamental way. But moral philosophy will never succeed in integrating them into a coherent, comprehensive unity. He writes:

> The region of the ethical is a region in which there are truths which are incompatible with each other. There exist, that is to say, many profound general statements which are capable of capturing the ethical imagination... They can be incorporated into a metaphysical system, or dramatized in a religious or historical myth. Or they can exist - their most persuasive form for many - as isolated statements such as, in France, there is a whole literature of, the literature of the maxim. I will not give examples, but I will mention names. One cannot read Pascal or Flaubert, Nietzsche or Goethe, Shakespeare of Tolstoy, without encountering these profound truths... In most of us the ethical imagination succumbs again and again to *these* pictures of man, and it is precisely as truths that we wish to characterize them while they hold us captive (p. 101).

Whereas the region of the ethical is to be explored by literature, moral philosophy should devote itself to the sphere of morality. Here, every individual is constrained by certain rules and regulations, implied by certain basic and non-controversial principles. For instance: do not harm others. These regulations, although we will never quite feel comfortable with them, are necessary, and the outcome of public consensus - there ought to be *some* rules to regulate and control social intercourse. The individual complies to them out of enlightened self-interest. Those issues, however, which belong to the region of the ethical are de-listed from the agenda of ethics proper, or at least from the agenda of its social branch. Small wonder that, all

34

of a sudden, a large number of basic moral issues seems either solved beforehand or reduced to problems that can be easily solved by ethical experts. Indeed, Strawson's proposal is bound to produce the kind of moral philosophy which suffers from what Wittgenstein referred to as a 'loss of problems' - an illness which in my opinion must be considered fatal.[11] In chapter five I will claim that the basic issue of contemporary ethics affects the way the so-called 'public' and the so-called 'private' aspects of moral life remain intimately connected, but this whole matter is 'solved' beforehand by presenting one particular understanding as being self-evident. In Strawson's proposal, all uncomfortable aspects of moral experience are simply considered irrelevant to moral philosophy. He does not seem to recognize the extent to which the meaning of these apparently residual aspects is significantly reduced by transferring them to some 'private' realm.

Another albeit more elaborate example of the ethics of compartmentalization is furnished by Richard Rorty (1989). In 1980, Rorty had accused Plato of being the first philosopher to try to transform ethics into a science by introducing a standard or master vocabulary that would allow for the disqualification of all existing vocabularies incompatible (or, to use the phrase preferred by Rorty, *incommensurable*) with it, excluding them from philosophical discourse. These vocabularies were referred to as sophistry and were considered to be at odds with science. The demand of commensurability with the standard vocabulary as advocated by Plato was rejected by Rorty. Instead of producing commensurability, philosophy should be considered a practice of self-formation or *edification* of individuals. Rorty sided with the 'marginal' philosophers who, rather than contributing to the transformation of moral philosophy into a science, participate in an endless conversation. The point of 'edifying' philosophy is not the quest for truth. Rather it is a continuous effort to keep the conversation going. Rorty opted for a multiplication of language games. His philosophical hero was Socrates - not, of course, the mutilated Socrates as he is presented to us by Plato, but the original Socrates still recognizable in some of the dialogues in spite of Plato's continuous effort to discipline, subdue and rectify his master. This is the Socrates who, mastering several vocabularies or language games, participates and excels in a conversation which remains under the sway of exciting disagreement, surpassing others in discursive flexibility, remaining tolerant towards the incommensurable.

Social intercourse was considered by Rorty a *forum* in the true sense of the term, a hermeneutical scene where protagonists of incompatible vocabularies meet and exchange their constructions of reality. The aim of their hermeneutical encounter is

---

[11] 'Manche Philosophen ... leiden an dem, was man "loss of problems", "Problemverlust" nennen kann. Es scheint ihnen dann alles ganz einfach, und es scheinen keine tiefen Probleme mehr zu existieren, die Welt wird weit und flach und verliert jede Tiefe; und was sie schreiben, wird unendlich seicht und trivial' (1984, § 456).

not to constrain or discipline but to understand the other's language game, allowing him to take the floor. 'Heteroglossia' (the Bakhtinean phrase to indicate a plurality of language genres) is encouraged, a 'centrifugal' attitude towards social discourse affirmed. Allow me to elaborate a Rorty-like position by means of a famous passage, taken from *The Acts of the Apostles*. In Athens, Paul was challenged by some epicurean and stoic philosophers to defend his doctrine in public, as all the Athenians seemed to spend their time in nothing but philosophical debate. On the Areopagus he was subjected to mockery when he came to speak about the resurrection of the souls, but others seemed willing to continue the discussion.[12] The Epicureans and Stoics, although weary of their interminable dispute and eager for something 'new', still opted for a hermeneutical position and were willing to allow the unknown vocabulary or language game to make its appearance on their discursive *forum*. Attention was given to the unprecedented and incommensurable. The *agora* was a locus for discursive exchange in which all free-born Athenians seemed eager to participate. Paul's performance, however, is ambivalent. It can be considered an intensification of pluralism. He is challenged to appear on the Areopagus so that his teachings could be judged and considered more carefully. Although his message is ridiculed by some, others seem interested in carrying on the conversation. Paul himself, however, is not. On the contrary, his objective is to establish a truth regime, a standard vocabulary, abolishing polytheism. After his encounter with the Athenians, he prefers a restricted audience, for instead of joining

---

12 'Now while Paul waited for them [Silas and Timotheus, his companions] at Athens, his spirit was stirred in him, when hee saw the city wholy given to idolatrie. Therefore disputed he in the Synagogue with the Iewes, and with the devout persons, and in the market dayly with them that met with him. Then certaine Philosophers of the Epicurians, and of the Stoikes, encountered him: and some said, What wil this babbler say? Other some, He seemeth to be a setter foorth of strange gods: because hee preached unto them Iesus, and the resurrection. And they took him, and brought him unto Areopagus, saying, May we know what this new doctrine, whereof thou speakest, is? for if thou bringest certaine strange things to our eares: we would know therefore what these things meane. (For all the Athenians and strangers which were there, spent their time in nothing else, but either to tell or to hear some new thing.) Then Paul stood in the mids of Mars-hill, and said, Yee men of Athens, I perceive that in all things yee are too superstitious. For as I passed by, and beheld your devotions, I found an altar with this inscription, *To the unknowen god*. Whom therefore yee ignorantly worship, him I declare unto you. God that made the world, and all things therein, seeing that hee is Lord of heaven and earth, dwelled not in Temples made with hands [And Paul proceeds to explain the christian articles of faith. Finally,] when they heard of the resurrection of the dead, some mocked: and others said, Wee will hear thee againe of this matter' (*The Actes*, 17:17-21).

the philosophers' interminable dispute, Paul withdraws among his fellow spirits.[13] What must be emphasized is that the mockery of the Athenians, after paying attention to Paul's remarkable speech, is not simply a private event, nor mere irony. Rather it is an instance of public agonistic laughter resounding on an ancient market-square, the effect of an intense discursive struggle among incommensurable speech genres, incompatible forms of moral subjectivity.

In *Contingency, Irony and Solidarity* Rorty (1989) tries to further elaborate this hermeneutical attempt. Once again, he claims to renounce the quest for a master vocabulary that would solve all differences and pacify social and philosophical discourse. Yet he recoils before the social implications of such a gesture, and finds himself obligated to take refuge in the strategy of compartmentalization we already encountered in Strawson's article - that is: *he takes refuge in the master vocabulary of liberal etatism*. In fact, he sets out to draw a picture of what he refers to as a liberal utopia, which requires a rigid separation of the private and the public realms.[14] Philosophers like Nietzsche, Heidegger and Foucault are referred to as 'ironists', and their writings are of significance only for the private realm. They

---

13 Nietzsche considered the Renaissance to constitute an Athenian *agora* on a European scale, whereas he considered Luther's attitude towards the Renaissance as reminiscent of Paul's attitude towards ancient Athens. Up to a certain point, there is some truth in Nietzsche's view, although, undeniably, there are other, more 'centrifugal' aspects at work in Luther as well, challenging official discourse, introducing popular linguistic modes, resisting 'monoglossia' (Bakhtin), allowing the Word to be released instead of being disciplined and rectified by clerical scholarship, etcetera. (cf. Chapter 4). Furthermore, we somehow still discern an astonishing continuity between first century - that is: Hellenistic - Athens, visited by Saint Paul, and ancient Athens as it must have been in the fourth century B.C., inhabited by Socrates. In the Plato dialogues, we already encounter the typical Athenian, eager to hear something new, and we already witness the crowd of philosophers involved in their interminable disputes, for ever mocking and challenging each other. Somehow, christianity really managed to impose its truth regime, to abolish paganism and polytheism. Paul succeeded where Plato had failed (cf. Chapter 3).

14 He writes for instance: 'The social glue holding together the ideal liberal society [...] consists in little more than a consensus that the point of social organization is to let everybody have a chance at self-creation to the best of his or her abilities, and that goal requires, besides peace and wealth, the standard "bourgeois freedoms". This conviction would [...] be a conviction based on nothing more profound than the historical facts which suggest that without the protection of something like the institutions of bourgeois liberal society, people will be less able to work out their private salvations, create their private self-images, reweave their webs of belief and desire in the light of whatever new people and books they happen to encounter. In such an ideal society, discussion of public affairs will revolve around (1) how to balance the needs for peace, wealth, and freedom when conditions require that one of these goals be sacrificed to one of the others and (2) how to equalize opportunities for self-creation and then leave people alone to use, or neglect, their opportunities'.

merely aspire to attain personal autonomy and 'criticize' established morality by means of irony. Mill, Habermas, Rawls and others, however, address the issues of public life. Their work tries to answer the question of how we could succeed in establishing a just society, with the aim of inflicting as little pain to others as possible - these philosophers are fellow citizens rather than ironists. Insofar as irony claims to be of some significance beyond the private realm, it must be considered a failure. The ironic perspective on the human condition is valuable on a private level, but it cannot advance the social or political goals of liberalism.

Rorty's book tries to show how things would look if we dropped the demand for a theory which unifies the public and the private and are content to treat the demands of self-creation and of human solidarity as equally valid, yet for ever incommensurable. Rorty's new hero is the *liberal ironist* who behaves like Nietzsche in the private realm, while remaining a J.S. Mill in the public realm, and who agrees that there is no such thing as truth, that there is nothing beyond vocabularies, that these vocabularies do not refer to an internal or external reality which could be considered a standard of truth. Some vocabularies are more promising than others, but no single vocabulary can be rejected in an argumentative way because every argument derives its persuasive power from (and therefore remains dependent on) the vocabulary to which it belongs. In other words, the unit of argumentation is a vocabulary, rather than a proposition. Hegel is praised for being a philosopher who mastered several vocabularies and was able to switch from one vocabulary to the other, but he is blamed for having suggested that his ironic narrative had any significance for public life and could contribute to answering the question of how a just, tolerant and peaceful society could be established. The books by Hegel, Heidegger and others are nothing but autobiographies.[15] Their irony is devoid of any social implication and any effort to apply their ironical game to real life is pointless and futile, even dangerous.

According to Rorty, all human beings carry about a set of words which they employ to justify their actions: their 'final vocabulary'. An ironist is someone who has continual doubts about the final vocabulary he currently uses, doubts which cannot be solved by argument. Therefore, he is someone who is never quite able to take himself seriously. He is aware of the contingency and fragility of his description of the world. A liberal, on the other hand, is someone who considers cruelty the worst thing possible, and therefore takes pains not to be cruel towards his fellow individuals. A liberal ironist is someone who refrains from cruelty, yet simultaneously affirms that any account that tries to consolidate liberalism into a moral principle merely appeals to *platitudes* - i.e. views which happen to be

---

15 The only 'ironist' who, up to a certain point, would perhaps agree with Rorty's 'redescription' is the later Nietzsche who, in *Ecce homo*, contends that his *Untimely Considerations* '...im Grunde bloß von mir reden' (§ 3).

commonly accepted, but remain open to doubt or ridicule. According to the ironist, established moral criteria are never more than platitudes which define the terms of a final vocabulary currently in use, and ironical doubts cannot be overcome by argument. In order to be convinced by a particular argument, one has to accept the vocabulary to which it belongs. Philosophy is about *re*description rather than argument, and dialectic is the attempt to play off vocabularies or redescriptions against one another. Indeed, Rorty claims that a more up-to-date word for dialectic would be literary criticism. Hegel is considered the founding father of ironist philosophy, someone who helped turn it into a literary genre.[16]

Now an obvious 'argument' against Rorty's ironic redescription of philosophy would be that this redescription is grounded in a platitude, indeed the platitude of platitudes, the one apparently most in need of creative and ironic redescription, namely, the quasi self-evident compartmentalization of moral life into a private and a public sphere. Yet Rorty would probably be all but embarrassed by such a remark, and would readily admit it. Still it is a platitude Rorty's redescription cannot do without, for it postulates liberal irony's basic condition. I will claim, however (notably in chapter five), that this platitude, shielded against ridicule by Rorty, severely hampers our understanding of the present moral condition. In the next section I will already suggest that the best way to abandon it is to return to Rorty's previous philosophical hero, Socrates, and the kind of laughter he represented. But first, I would like to illustrate how Rorty himself defends his position against two possible lines of criticism.

Rorty discerns or anticipates at least two basic objections to his own views. One is the sense that the liberal ironist's willingness to respect his fellow citizens seems to imply that there is something within human beings which deserves respect and protection quite independently of the language one happens to speak. Yet Rorty maintains that a universal ethics, grounded in the imperative that we are not to inflict any pain upon each other, would be incompatible with ironism simply because it is hard to imagine stating such an ethic without some doctrine about the nature of man - a doctrine which is bound to remain vulnerable in the face of private laughter. Such an appeal to real essence would be the antithesis of ironism.

---

16 'I want to defend ironism, and the habit of taking literary criticism as the presiding intellectual discipline, against polemics such as Habermas's. My defense turns on making a firm distinction between the private and the public. Whereas Habermas sees the line of ironist thinking which runs from Hegel through Foucault and Derrida as destructive of social hope, I see this line of thought as largely irrelevant to public life and to political questions. Ironist theorists like Hegel, Nietzsche, Derrida, and Foucault seem to me invaluable in our attempt to form a private self-image, but pretty much useless when it comes to politics... Habermas [however] shares with the Marxists... the assumption that the real meaning of a philosophical view consists in its political implications' (p. 83).

The second objection seems even more problematic. There is clearly something anti-social and irresponsible, even cruel and offensive in irony. The ironist is bound to destroy some value cherished by his fellow citizens, and will depict anyone who attaches himself to such a value as being prejudiced, foolish or vulgar. Rorty agrees that irony humiliates, but feels that it does so in a rather modest way. Instead of aiming at mastering and submitting other vocabularies (the basic objective of metaphysics) it contents itself with presenting an ironic redescription for the sake of those who happen to be susceptible to it. It is a redescription which does not force itself upon those fellow citizens who maintain their personal commitment to certain ideals, but remains a redescription for private purposes only. The ironist contents himself with redescribing the world; it is not (or rather, should not be) his ambition to transform it. Irony in the strict sense of the term does not imply any harm to others. The writings of Foucault, for instance, are to be considered merely an effort of the philosopher himself to gain personal autonomy. They do not really incite us to derive any implications for public life. The political impact and content of Foucault's work need to be subdued, in order for him to pass as an ironist. Perhaps the philosophers involved would be hesitant, to say the least, to accept Rorty's redescription and rectification of their work as ironical, but we simply are not to accept the anti-liberal implications of some of the ironist's writings. According to Rorty, Foucault is an ironist unwilling to be a liberal, whereas Habermas is a liberal unwilling to be an ironist. But we should recoil from encouraging the private discontent addressed by irony to express itself within the public realm.

Now what happened to Socrates, Rorty's initial hero? In *Contingency, Irony, and Solidarity* he occupies a rather moderate position and is replaced by new heroes like Derrida and a few others. Rorty admits that Socrates is not a liberal ironist but a 'liberal metaphysician', someone who still cherishes the hope that one day the inner and the outer man will become one and that irony will no longer be necessary, someone whose metaphysics falls subject to rigid redescription by Rorty's new philosophical hero Derrida, turning the metaphysical into the merely private and idiosyncratic.

Both Strawson and Rorty aim at compartmentalization. Although Rorty, unlike Strawson, is quite willing to consider ironism a branch of moral philosophy in its own right, it is a philosophy of a rather private and literary nature, carefully separated from public discourse. The philosopher is either to provide some guidelines for public behaviour, or to embark on a private, ironic exercise. In my view, such a conception of philosophy is indeed quite at odds with the philosophical practice of Rorty's one-time hero Socrates, as he in fact came to realize himself. In the case of Socrates, philosophy meant contesting public consensus and established conviction, revealing the vulnerability of the apparently self-evident. Socrates' objective was not consensus, but truth, and this truth was not of a merely private nature. In his famous apology, when Socrates finds himself confronted with the accusation that his teachings constitute a threat to public life and established conviction, he appeals to a higher sense of duty, a divine mission, a responsiveness to a divine inner voice. Any compromise is to be rejected, for one is to obey the divine powers rather than one's fellow citizens. Never will he adapt his behaviour or abandon what he considers his proper duty: to question, to irritate, to expose to laughter, regardless of the consequences for public life. He remains unwilling to accept the basic rules of established moral discourse, considered himself appointed by a divine power who commanded him to interrupt the very discursive logic to which he refuses to comply: 'Sentence me or set me free, but never will I refrain from my mission'.

In my view, the quintessence of Rorty's ethics of compartmentalization is his understanding of laughter. There is clearly an awareness that laughter poses a threat to public regulation and that public mockery might imply political risks with regard to solidarity. Therefore laughter is subdued and reduced to irony, excluded from the *agora*, the market-square of unrestricted public discourse, and dispelled into the private sphere. Laughter is fundamentally transformed, and in the course of this transformation a certain form of moral subjectivity (the compartmentalized Self) is established. Rorty's new hero is someone who manages to split himself into Nietzsche and Mill (cf. Rawls' personal and institutional identity), someone who considers established morality quite unconvincing but still accepts that one is not allowed to laugh in public. In short, laughter is bereft of its public and political implications and the postmodern hero, the compartmentalized individual is supposed to laugh only in private. True laughter are reduced to irony. This picture of moral subjectivity either implies a rejection or a far-reaching rectification of Socrates as a philosophical hero, a mutilation and adaption far more drastic than the one undertaken by Plato (and apparently deplored by Rorty). Let me therefore allow Socrates to take the floor, and let us pay special attention to his laughter so that we may acquire a rough idea of what is lost in Rorty's account, in order to prepare ourselves for a more careful and elaborate *re*reading of Socrates' philosophy of laughter in the subsequent chapters.

4. THE CASE OF SOCRATES, OR: A BUFFOON WHO HAD HIMSELF TAKEN SERIOUSLY

In chapter three, I will emphasize the importance of final words, but first sentences are also important. The sentence with which Socrates, in Plato's *Apology*, makes his appearance on the stage (i.e. the court of law at Athens) already abounds in mockery and wit: 'I do not know what effect my accusers have had upon you, gentlemen, but for my own part I was almost carried away by them - their arguments were so convincing. On the other hand, scarcely a word of what they said was true' [17a]. Indeed, in the course of his speech, Socrates piles jest upon jest - 'I was astonished ... when they told you that you must be careful not to let me deceive you - the implication being that I am a skillful speaker... I have not the slightest skill as a speaker - unless, of course, by a skillful speaker they mean one who speaks the truth' [17b].

Plato's *Apology* is a vivid picture of the man Socrates must have been: straightforward, confident and, above all, someone who 'always views the world of men with a bit of humor... whose argument is always mingled with amusement' (Treddennick 1961). He prefers to make his appearance in the open, public places of his city [17] and claims to speak in an inartificial tone of voice. He strongly rejects the accusation that he is one of those philosophers who have acquired the professional competence to 'make the weaker argument defeat the stronger' and whom he ridicules by means of irony [18b].[18] Yet the basic mode of laughter at work in Socrates' plea before the court is not of an ironic nature. Basically, his plea is parodical, a magnificent parody of the court plea as a speech genre. At first glance, all elements of this genre are represented in Socrates' speech, but it does not escape the majority of his audience, the members of the jury, that they are in fact being mocked and ridiculed, and perhaps this is their main reason for convicting him and passing a death sentence on him. Let me give a few examples, although a thorough rereading would reveal that his speech simply abounds in parodical jest.[19]

Socrates starts at the beginning, with the charge. But instead of considering the charge at hand, he immediately turns over to another, previous and anonymous

---

[17] Cf. Nietzsche, who refers to him as a street philosopher, lingering wherever an opportunity for idle conversation presents itself (*Human, All-to-human I*, § 433).

[18] 'I think that it is a fine thing if a man is qualified [to educate people and charge a fee], I should certainly plume myself and give myself airs if I understood these things', p. 6.

[19] Although the difference between parody and irony will be further clarified elsewhere, perhaps it is wise to start with a provisional definition of both modes of speech. Irony basically means: saying the opposite of what one has in mind (cf. the example just mentioned: 'It sure is a fine thing to be able to educate people and charge a fee'). Furthermore, it applies to the level of a sentence, a speech act, or a phrase, rather than to a genre, a vocabulary, like parody. Parody can have two meanings. Originally, it was the effort to respond (not necessarily in a comical vein) to an already existing word or work of art in such a way that it produced a kind of revival, a work of art in its own right. Subsequently, it came to be considered a primarily comical device, exposing a serious genre to ridicule by meeting its conventions in an exaggerated or distorted way, or by straightforwardly applying them to a totally absurd topic, thus creating a comic double. Whereas irony is considered a refined and individualistic kind of mockery, parody is commonly associated with vulgar farce.

charge, already taxing the patience of his audience. And then, apparently in response to their signs of impatience and anger, Socrates suddenly inserts the following line: 'Perhaps some of you will think that I am not being serious, but I assure you that I am going to tell you the whole truth' [20d] - certainly a stock line in the mock speeches of all time. After this, Socrates relates a series of scenes that also belong to the comical genres of all times, involving a wandering buffoon who puts ridiculous questions to the wise, which they are unable or unwilling to answer and than draws the conclusion that he is wiser than they are, because while it is an established fact that he himself understands absolutely nothing, they apparently understand even less.[20] This 'pilgrimage' or 'occupation', undertaken in obedience to his deity, kept him 'too busy to do much either in politics or in my own affairs. In fact, my service to God has reduced me to extreme poverty' [23b]. At a certain point, Socrates succeeds in parodying the genre of philosophical dialogue and that of judicial plea simultaneously by introducing the particular truth game that made him famous (the Socratic Dialogue) in court. However, his strategic device is somewhat impeded by the fact that on this occasion his partners are even more reluctant than usual to participate in his game and more than once Socrates is forced to come up with the answers himself.[21] Meanwhile, the continuous laughter of the audience is almost audible.

But of course, like any other genius of comedy, his performance is not *merely* comical. The claim that God has appointed him to the duty of leading a philosophical life, examining himself and others, is serious up to the point of serenity.[22] And also his ridicule of the fear of death eventually implies a serious insight. Laughter recurs, however, when he claims in a most straightforward manner that, according to himself and quite unlike what is suggested in the official charges, no greater good has ever befallen the city of Athens than his relentless service to his God:

---

20 'But how is it that some people enjoy spending a great deal of time in my company? You have heard the reason, gentlemen; I told you quite frankly. It is because they enjoy hearing me examine those who think that they are wise when they are not - an experience which has its amusing side' (p. 19). Later on, he claims to expect that death will be 'rather amusing' (p. 25) provided he is allowed to continue the Socratic truth game with the inhabitants of the underworld.

21 'Is not this the case? Of course it is, whether you ... deny it or not'; 'If you do not want to answer, I will supply it for you'; 'Is not that so? It is. I assume your assent since you do not answer' (p. 13).

22 Cf. Nietzsche, who refers to the 'wonderful seriousness' with which he maintained his divine calling even before his judges (*The Birth of Tragedy, § 13*), although elsewhere, when he comes to talk about Socrates' self-awareness as a divine missionary, he adds that it is difficult to tell how much Attic irony, jest and love of mockery is at work even here (*Human, All Too Human II*, 'The Wanderer and his Shadow', § 72).

For this reason, gentlemen, so far from pleading on my own behalf, as might be supposed, I am really pleading on yours, to save you from misusing the gift of God by condemning me. If you put me to death, you will not easily find anyone to take my place. It is literally true, even if it sounds comical, that God has specially appointed me to this city, as though it were a large thorough-bred horse which because of its great size is inclined to be lazy and needs the stimulation of some stinging fly. It seems to me that God has attached me to this city to perform the office of such a fly, and all day long I never cease to settle here, there, and everywhere, rousing, persuading, reproving everyone of you. You will not easily find another one like me, gentlemen, and if you take my advice you will spare my life [30d/e].23

This is not someone who is begging the jury to spare his life the way he would have been expected to do under the circumstances (given the conventions of the genre), but rather someone who pursues his sheer mockery, his parodical mode of speech at all costs, regardless of the consequences. Although (in accordance with the official genre conventions) he does include a line about sparing his life, he formulates it in such a way that it becomes an 'advice' rather than an entreaty.24

But the summit of mockery is reached at the very moment of decision. After Socrates has been found guilty of the charge, a fitting penalty must be determined - and the death penalty has been demanded. And this is the moment in which Socrates reveals himself as the kind of man he is - the perfect jester who simply will not stop at anything. To begin with, he impudently and explicitly skips the part where the accused is expected to make passionate appeals, but proceeds directly towards the final question. What penalty would be appropriate for having been the man he is and having lived the only life he considered to be of significance? Free maintenance at the state's expense! Once again, a roar of laughter is almost audible - it is Socrates'

---

23 And this is how he continues: 'If you doubt whether I am really the sort of person who would have been sent to this city as a gift from God, you can convince yourselves by looking at it in this way. Does it seem natural that I should have neglected my own affairs and endured the humiliation of allowing my family to be neglected all these years, while I busied myself all the time on your behalf, going like a father or an elder brother to see each one of you privately, and urging you to set your thoughts on goodness?' (p. 17).

24 The picture of Socrates as jester, the way he emerges for instance in the novels of Rabelais, was again discerned by Nietzsche. Under certain historical circumstances, he claims, where authority still presides over reason, the critical philosopher is a buffoon. Socrates was a remarkable case, because he was a buffoon who managed to have himself taken seriously and put to death: 'Überall, wo noch die Autorität zur guten Sitte gehört, wo man nicht begründet, sondern befiehlt, ist der Dialektiker eine Art Hanswurst: man lacht über ihn, man nimmt ihn nicht ernst. - Sokrates war der Hanswurst der sich ernst nehmen machte: was geschah da eigentlich? - ' (*The Twilight of the Idols*, § 5).

44

greatest comic performance. But he is still not finished with his antagonists. What other proposals could be made? Imprisonment and exile are out of the question, for it would impede him to pursue his life of ruthless examination. Perhaps a fine? At this point, when one would expect Socrates to try to save his own life, he comes up with his final joke: 'You will not believe that I am serious', he exclaims [37e] as he continues to persist that a life, not of public responsibility, but of permanent examination is the best thing a man can do, whereas life without it is not worth living. In view of his way of living, Socrates claims that he is not accustomed to think of himself as someone deserving punishment. Therefore, he ends up suggesting (in view both of his innocence and of his poverty, resulting from his way of life) the lowest possible fine: a mina. 'I suppose I could probably afford a mina. I suggest a fine of that amount' [38b]. After Socrates' final jest, a ruthless parody of court plea as a serious genre, his fate is sealed.

Kierkegaard (1989) refers to a contemporary expert on Socrates called Ast who felt indignant over the vulgar, ludicrous manner Socrates behaved himself in the *Apology* as well as over the bold confidence with which he spoke, apparently merely aiming at ostentatious self-exaltation. Indeed, he seemed to debase himself in order to indirectly exalt himself even more, expressing his contempt for others with the vain intention of exalting himself. According to Ast, he even 'slipped into the comical' [!] when he declared himself to be ignorant yet at the same time wiser than all others. In the eyes of Ast, the summit of ridicule is reached when Socrates explains that the death penalty holds no punishment for him because it will not keep him from questioning those dwelling in the underworld. And Kierkegaard adds: 'It is undeniable that here Socrates almost lapses into the ridiculous in his zeal ... and who can keep from smiling when he imagines the somber shades of the underworld and Socrates right there in the middle, indefatigably interrogating them' (p. 40).[25] Instead of suggesting that Socrates is 'slipping into the comical' or 'lapsing into the ridiculous', however, it must be stressed that he is being ridiculous on purpose. Rather than exalting himself he is able to *laugh* at himself by including himself, as well as his famous truth game (the Socratic dialogue), in his mockery. The straightforward application of the conventions of a certain genre (such as the Socratic dialogue) to a ridiculous situation is one of parody's basic techniques. As will be explained more carefully in chapter two, Socrates applies the parodical strategy of overcoming fear (for example, fear of death) by transforming the terrible (for

---

25 Bakhtin points out that such a scene is a stock element in the popular tradition of carnivalization of the nether world ('gay hell') where representatives of different sections of society and different historical periods meet on equal terms and enter into familiar contact with each other (1968, p. 109). Bakhtin also points out that this comic scene of Socrates' visit to the underworld was used (and exaggerated, of course) by the Cynics later on: 'In the comic afterlife visions of Menippean satire, the heroes of the [past] and living contemporaries jostle with one another in a most familiar way' (p. 26).

example, the somber prospect of a life to come) into something completely ridiculous.

Due to the vivid and life-like performance of the brilliant parodist presented to us in Plato's dialogue, we find that his basic technique is not irony but parody. Whenever Socrates is considered primarily an ironist, his laughter is subdued and reduced. Irony is a case of reduced laughter. It is negative, individualistic, furtive, dissatisfied with itself. Parody, however, is gay, a laughter that really laughs. It is public laughter, and travesty. A serious genre is ridiculed, ruthlessly reversed, turned upside down, in public, before a life and laughing audience. All stock elements of the serious genre are systematically abused. It is straightforward, challenging and irresistible. Its effect on official discourse is devastating. In the next chapter, where several philosophies of laughter will be reviewed, the difference between irony and parody will be explored more carefully. Moreover, as I already announced, in chapter three the case of Socrates will be subjected to a more thorough *re*reading. Yet there still is one issue that has to be dealt with here. Socrates is not a *liberal ironist*, and Rorty was quite right in admitting this, for two reasons.

To begin with, he is not an *ironist*. Although it is beyond doubt that irony is one of the ingredients in his comic speeches, he is basically a parodist - but this will be explained more adequately elsewhere. The second reason, the one that will be dealt with here, is that he is not a *liberal* either. And any effort to present him as a supporter of liberalism would imply a rectification and adaption of Socrates with the intention of attuning him to the standard account of contemporary ethics. Even in the *Apology*, although apparently the one dialogue which lends itself most easily for a liberal redescription, the compartmentalization of moral life is not at all respected. Even here, where the personal, idiosyncratic aspects of the Socratic truth game are so strongly emphasized, its public and political aspect still manifests itself.

In section 31c, Socrates' plea suffers a somewhat unexpected turn. 'It may seem curious', he says, 'that I should go round giving advice like this and busying myself in people's private affairs, and yet never venture publicly to address you as a whole' [31c]. He explains that it is his *daimonion* or inner voice which bars him from entering political life and office. And rightly so, for no man who opposes public wrongs and illegalities can possibly escape with his life. 'The true champion of justice, if he intends to survive even for a short time, must necessarily confine himself to private life and leave politics alone' [32a]. Now if anything, these lines appear to contain a perfect articulation of the Two Worlds Theorem of liberalism, and Socrates' *daimonion* appears to be perfectly in tune with a compartmentalization of moral life into a public (political) and a private (ironical) sphere. Socrates' ethic seems to have accepted the compartmentalization of ethics and to settle for ironism long before liberalism was born. True virtue can only be acquired in private life, while irony does not apply to public life. Such an understanding of the Socratic truth game, however, is thoroughly misguided.

Socrates' basic claim is rendered meaningless should it be considered an articulation of liberal ironism, the one in which he justifies his behaviour by appealing to his God: 'It is literally true, even if it sounds rather comical, that God has specially appointed me to this city' [30e]. An ironic reading is bound to reduce this claim to a mere rhetorical phrase. And yet, it is a perfect and revealing articulation of Socrates' basic position. Although Socrates is clearly not an etatist, the nature of his guardianship is political. Let me explain once more what I mean by etatism. It entails a top-down perspective on politics as the art of exercising public power. Plato is a perfect example of a top-down, etatist perspective. In order to reform the individual, the state has to be reformed beforehand. In order to educate the individual, one must constitute a state and regulate public life. Now there are several historical forms of etatism, ancient despotism being one of them, while the Roman empire, notably during its final, Christianized epoch, is another one. It goes without saying that socialism is a kind of etatism as well, but today the most important form is liberalism, a version of etatism which seems to correspond to present historical conditions most adequately. For as was explained above, although liberalism is often associated with a distant and reserved kind of public policy, in reality it has produced the omnipresent modern megastate, penetrating public life in all its aspects and regulating social intercourse in a most severe manner, in order to allow the individual certain eccentricities in the private sphere. It is, clearly, a top-down perspective on the art of government. A state has to be constituted in order for the individual to become an autonomous subject.

Socrates is not an etatist, neither of the totalitarian nor of the liberal kind. Rather, his perspective is bottom-up and his starting point is the reformation of the individual. The individual, however, is not considered an end in itself by Socrates, and he does not consider the saving of souls to be his mission (Socrates is not at all a Christian). The individual is to be reformed in order to make a better politician. His bottom-up perspective is of a aristocratic kind, and the individuals he is particularly interested in are the ones who are bound to become the politicians of the future. They are the ones who are to be reformed, not for the sake of their private lives or happiness but for the sake of the future well-being of the city state of Athens. Indeed, Socrates' God is not of a Christian but of a pagan kind. He is not concerned with individuals, but with political unities, and that is the reason why He, according to Socrates, appointed him, in order to effect a major change.

In fact, Kierkegaard also considered Socrates primarily an ethicist who wanted to improve the individual rather than the state, someone who considered the state a 'necessary evil'. But at the same time Kierkegaard agreed that this did not imply that he distanced himself from *public life*, and this is an issue of significance. Socrates considered the public space as an *agon* and the fact that he refrained from taking active part in political affairs did not at all imply that he was unpolitical or that he considered his philosophy a matter for private use only. Unlike the politician in an etatistic sense he was not so much concerned with the *well-being* of individuals as with the kind of person (or politician) they would *be*. He exemplified a certain way of living, a certain form of moral subjectivity (the examined Self) which was shortly to become important, ethically as well as politically.

It has been suggested by Nietzsche that perhaps the Athenians were right to sentence him to death, and that apparently Socrates did succeed in corrupting their youth.[26] No doubt the etatists at that time recognized that his performance indeed entailed a basic challenge to established morality, a basic contestation of the moral foundations of the state. Socrates himself was quite frank in this respect. The basic objective of the Socratic truth game was to transform established moral subjectivity,[27] preparing the way for the emergence of quite different political regimes, less attached to those forms of life or moral subjectivity which grounded power relationships in ancient Athens.[28] Socrates' ethics was a political ethics, but of a bottom-up, non-etatist kind. His basic objective, the reformation of moral subjectivity, was not effected by the establishment of a certain political regime, but grounded in the experience of laughter which ruthlessly undermined the serious and

---

[26] *Beyond Good and Evil*, Introduction. Cf. Kierkegaard (1989): 'Whether the Athenian state committed a glaring injustice in condemning Socrates, whether we are right in voluntarily joining the scholarly professional mourners and the crowd of shallow but lachrymose humanitarians whose blubbering and sighing because such a good man, such an honest human being, paragon, and cosmopolitan all rolled into one, became a victim of the meanest envy, whose blubbering and sighing, I say, still echo through the centuries; or whether the Athenian state was completely justified in condemning Socrates [...] all this we shall not discuss further here' (p. 167-168). According to Kierkegaard, the *Apology* testifies to Socrates' negative relation to the established order, his inability to contract any real relationship to it, having totally emancipated himself from it and refusing to accept any kind of public responsibility. Instead of being a citizen in the Greek sense, he hung about the streets and boulevards, exempting himself from carrying the burdens of civil life. Yet he did not distance himself form public life as such but remained in very lively contact with it. He was a virtuoso in casual contacts. By lifting others out of their natural position, he actually did do evil. He truly was a seducer of the youths, awakening certain longings in them without assuming any responsibility for their later life.

[27] How he managed to achieve this, and what the 'established form of moral subjectivity', as well as the 'unprecedented, Socratic one' consisted in, will be explained in the next two chapters.

[28] The basic feature of moral subjectivity in ancient Greece was the attachment to life and Socrates' redescription of Greek life, apparently the summit of health, as an illness was a remarkable, subversive act indeed (cf. chapter two and three).

established moral truths. His fellow Athenians who sentenced him to death knew perfectly well what they were doing. His laughter would have resisted any strategy of containment, and his followers - the gay, idle, aristocratic Athenian youth - had already been infected by it.

Chapter 2

Laughter as a State of Mind

Was ich *finde, was ich suche -,*
Stand das je in einem Buche?
Ehrt in mir die Narren-Zunft!
Lernt aus diesem Narrenbuche
Wie Vernunft kommt - 'zur Vernunft'!
(F. Nietzsche, *Human, All Too Human II*, Prelude)

1. DESPOTIC LIBERALISM, *RE*READING AND GAY LAUGHTER

In the previous chapter I explained how a certain moral regime (referred to as 'liberalism' or the 'method of avoidance' and grounded in what Rorty would refer to as its basic platitude: the compartmentalization of moral life) managed to impose itself on contemporary moral discourse and to immunize itself against possible criticism, either by rejecting all instances of fundamental contestation as fundamentalistic, immoral or ridiculous, or by reducing them to private laughter or private embarrassment, in short: to irony. In contrast to these established moral platitudes, I advocated the idea that the basic objective of moral philosophy should remain a Socratic one, namely contestation rather than justification or consolidation. Instead of presenting the established consensus as non-controversial, experiences of discontent are to be articulated, its basic vulnerability is to be revealed, and its basic platitudes are to be contested. But what would such a Socratic strategy amount to under the present circumstances? I have already referred to Nietzsche who recognized the comic nature of Socrates' verbal performance. In § 5 of *The Twilight of the Idols*, Nietzsche refers to the despotism of ancient Greek morality which succeeded in rendering critical arguments futile, irrelevant and impotent. In order for established morality to be challenged, another more effective discursive strategy had to be pursued - laughter.

Indeed, to the question that Nietzsche raises - 'What happened in the case of Socrates, the buffoon who had himself taken seriously?' - I would propose the following answer, one which will be reconsidered and elaborated in subsequent sections. Socrates was not at all the serious philosopher who was so unfortunate as to find his critical arguments ruthlessly ridiculed by moral authority. On the contrary, he himself was the one who recognized and utilized the strategic potential of ridicule. Whenever a certain moral regime has turned despotic, has successfully immunized itself against critical argument, that is, against a particular discursive strategy called criticism, the moral philosopher has to take recourse to another discursive strategy, namely parody or laughter. This is a strategic insight which was perfectly realized by Socrates, whose seriousness was of a gay and merry nature and whose wisdom abounded in knavery.[1] But a similar line of reasoning might hold for the present despotism of ethical liberalism as well. Unlike irony (or reduced laughter), parody (or gay laughter) is much more difficult to contain and poses a much more 'serious' challenge to any established set of platitudes.

In chapter three, a thorough *re*reading of Socrates' mode of speech will reveal that gay laughter was indeed his basic tool. As has already been indicated in the introduction, *re*reading is the philosophical method which I will employ, a way of reading which is aware of the fact that established morality has biased (or 'guided') our reading of certain parts of the philosophical (or theological) corpus for too long, and that the established way of reading, which has dominated our reception and current understanding of discursive events like Socrates, not only conceals important aspects of the modes of speech involved but also constitutes an important stronghold for the established moral regime itself. The subsequent chapters will contain a similar *re*reading of Luther and Ibsen, focussing on the way their laughter challenged established morality in the sixteenth and nineteenth century respectively. In the present chapter, however, our philosophical understanding of laughter, and notably the difference between reduced and gay laughter, will be deepened. The *philosophies of laughter* that will guide my subsequent *re*reading of Socrates, Luther and Ibsen will be introduced, starting with the one elaborated by the Russian philosopher and literary scientist Bakhtin already mentioned in the previous chapter.

Although philosophers have increasingly come to recognize the philosophical importance of his work, Mikhail M. Bakhtin (1895-1975) was first of all an expert in the field of literature. His most important books were on Dostoevski and Rabelais. This section will chiefly summarize the Rabelais book and the philosophy of laughter it contains. Bakhtin's account is both historical and systematic. His objective is to gain a thorough understanding of laughter as a basic mode of thought as well as to produce a description of the way gay (or: popular) laughter came to be subdued and reduced by the serious genres of modernity. His philosophy of laughter is a basic ingredient of his 'agonistic' theory of discourse, elaborated throughout his writings, a theory which I consider to be fundamentally congenial with those of Nietzsche, Bataille and Foucault, although there are important differences as well.

---

[1] Cf. Nietzsche, *Human, All Too Human II*, 'The Wanderer and his Shadow', § 86.

2. TOWARDS A PHILOSOPHY OF LAUGHTER : BAKHTIN

According to Bakhtin's 'agonistic' theory, a discourse, either social or moral, is a strategic field of genres, mutually mocking, parodying, intimidating, challenging and influencing each other. Furthermore, Bakhtin emphasizes the basic ambivalence of every word that makes its appearance in such a strategic field. There are, according to Bakhtin, no neutral words, only artificially neutralized ones. This basic conviction, elaborated throughout his writings, also dominates his book on Rabelais. To understand Rabelais, Bakhtin (1968) claims, one must recognize his basic affinity with the popular culture of laughter of the medieval and Renaissance market-place. Rabelais' work is an encyclopedia of popular genres, idioms, dialects, proverbs and abuses. Its strategic field was constituted by the basic opposition between the established, official genres (serious and dogmatic) and the popular, unofficial genres (relying on parody and laughter). During the Middle Ages, popular laughter was tolerated, within certain boundaries, by official discourse. In the sixteenth century official discourse collapsed and popular laughter temporarily gained the upper hand, only to give way to the establishment of the new official and serious discourses of modern rationalism and Protestantism during the Counter-Renaissance. Popular laughter continued to exist, however, as an indestructible undercurrent, time and again exposing the vulnerability of what was presented as self-evident and beyond contestation by official discourse.

This popular culture is referred to by Bakhtin as 'carnivalesque', although we find its basic principle (gay laughter) at work in many other manifestations besides carnival proper. Gay laughter defies ('carnivalizes') all instances of authoritarianism, dogmatism, seriousness and narrow-mindedness, and its basic device is parody. Even the most serious genres of official discourse were parodied by the laughing people of the Middle Ages, and found themselves accompanied by a comic double. The predominant, official truth, held to be eternal and indisputable, was time and again exposed to ridicule or comic imitation and exaggeration. Moreover, there were no clear demarcations between seriousness and laughter, no ideologically reliable words or genres, and medieval monks and abbots produced learned treatises as well as *parodia sacra*. The number of manuscripts parodying ecclesiastical, philosophical or juridical genres is immense. For the medieval parodist, everything without exception was comical, and everywhere the world seemed to manifest its gay and festive aspect. In modern times, however, parody ('gay laughter') is subdued and transformed into irony ('reduced laughter') - a laughter that does not laugh. Or it is considered a *merely* comical and, above all, merely *negative* phenomenon. In gay laughter or parody proper, however, a basic positive force is at work, and its basic aim is renewal and affirmation rather than destruction. Furthermore, whereas modern reduced laughter is a private phenomenon, gay laughter is a collective experience, a laughter of all the people. True parody is basically ambivalent: it both mocks and affirms, defies and unites.

To understand the positive force at work in parody, one has to recognize its basic affinity with the grotesque. The popular culture of laughter was closely connected with bodily life, notably the body's lower stratum, with food, drink, defecation, procreation and intercourse. In the grotesque conception of the body, emerging in the writings of Rabelais, the needs, appetites, extensions and potentials of the body are grossly exaggerated. The grotesque body is fertile, abundant and grandiose. Official discourse is carnivalized and degraded by transferring it to material, bodily existence. Not a single saying of the Scriptures was left unchallenged if it could provide some hint of equivocal suggestion that could be travestied and transposed into the language of the material bodily lower stratum, that is, reinterpreted in terms of eating, drinking, sweating, urinating or sexual intercourse (p. 86).[2] The Word is made flesh, and attention is concentrated on the mouth, the belly and the reproductive organs, on swallowing, defecation, copulation, pregnancy and birth. This 'degradation', however, is basically an ambivalent phenomenon. Again, its ultimate aim is not degradation as such, but renewal and affirmation.

Gay laughter defies any pretention to absolute, extra-temporal truth, and reveals the origin and limitations of such a truth.[3] The representatives of established truth are referred to by Rabelais as 'agelasts': they cannot and do not wish to laugh, are unaware of the inevitable, namely that time is bound to turn their speeches into ridicule and that they *are* in fact already ridiculed by their laughing audience. The Sorbonne (i.e. official, serious knowledge), for instance, is represented in *Gargantua* by a character called Janotus, although Rabelais was forced to replace the word 'Sorbonnite' by 'sophist'. His oration is an excellent parody of the Sorbonnite's method of argumentation, while the diction suggests and imitates the sounds of coughing, spitting, and shortness of breath.

In early modern times, the grotesque conception of the body was rejected by the canon of classicism, by the aesthetic of the beautiful and the sublime, and regarded as hideous, disproportionate and deficient. We ceased to understand the grotesque 'logic' long ago and came to accept the pejorative use of the word 'grotesque' as self

---

[2] Cf. for example Christ's last words in the Gospel of John: 'Sitio' ('I thirst') and 'consummatum est' ('it is accomplished'), deliberately distorted into 'consumatum est' ('it is consumed'), a minor change (the ommision of merely one letter) and yet a debasing transposition that successfully transforms a solemn tragedy into a jovial scene - 'Postea sciens Iesus quia omnia consummata sunt, ut consummaretur scriptura, dixit: Sitio... Cum ergo accepisset Iesus acetum, dixit: Consummatum est' (19:28-30).

[3] In his discussion of Aristophanes' comedy *The Clouds*, Kierkegaard (1989) also claims that parody (or 'laughter for laughter's sake') is a 'corrective element' that makes the phenomenon at hand (either a person or a situation) intelligible through exaggeration, cf. chapter three.

evident. The grotesque did not die, however, but was merely expelled from the sphere of official art and confined to the non-canonical, popular and burlesque genres. At the same time, the state encroached upon popular festive life, and either turned it into an official parade or transferred it to the private sphere.

In the second half of the eighteenth century, however, a literary controversy broke out in Germany about the character of Harlequin, a constant participant in dramatic performances at that time. Some demanded his expulsion, being at odds with the demands of the sublime, but others recognized that the parodical and the grotesque have their own criteria of perfection. From that time onwards, Europe witnessed a revival of interest in medieval parody, with its *festa stultorum*, its Societies of Carefree Lads and its *risus paschalis*. Parody and the grotesque were rehabilitated by the Romantic canon. Yet Bakhtin emphasizes the basic difference between medieval or gay laughter (parody proper) and modern or somber laughter (the Romantic versions of laughter, notably irony and sarcasm). In the case of gay laughter, something terrifying (for instance, the gloomy and intimidating eschatology of late medieval ecclesiastical discourse) was transformed into something gay and comic (the grotesque monsters of the carnivalesque parade). The devil was presented as a gay and jovial fellow, and the buffoon-like in him eclipsed the terrifying and alien. In the case of Romantic or somber laughter, however, something frightening is revealed. A terrible vacuum, a nothingness lurks behind the grotesque-Romantic mask. The devil is presented as melancholic and sarcastic. Romantic laughter is the sardonic laughter of a lonely eccentric. It is purely destructive, lacking the positive, regenerating element.

A somewhat similar development occurred with regard to the discourse on women. In late medieval discourse, women were either idealized (the chivalrous tradition) or associated with the devil and presented in a negative way as an object of fear (the ascetic tradition). In the popular, comic tradition, however, women are presented in an ambivalent way. Womanhood is connected with both the principle of debasement and the principle of renewal, and both aspects merge in the popular theme of cuckoldry: the festive uncrowning of the old husband. According to Bakhtin, the modern, satirical view on women is more akin to the ascetic than to the popular tradition. It has lost its positive tone and has become purely negative.[4]

Furthermore, in order to understand gay laughter - the basic principle at work in the parodical and the grotesque - it must be clearly distinguished from the merely satirical and negative laughter of the, predominantly Protestant, pamphleteers who were Rabelais' contemporaries. These pamphleteers, often referred to as 'Grobianists', used the parodical and the grotesque merely as rhetorical devices to support a serious, abstract idea. Their satirical mockery served a serious goal and was

---

4 Nietzsche's view on women constitutes a perfect example of this: it is modern, negative and ascetic, rather than gay.

aimed at moral condemnation of 'vices' like gluttony, idleness and excess. In the writings of Rabelais, however, laughter is not merely a device. Rather, it has a deep philosophical meaning in itself. It is one of the essential forms of truth concerning man. Certain aspects of the world are only accessible to laughter (p. 66). Gay laughter is a universal philosophical principle, revealing a basic truth, and fundamentally akin to both the philosophical laughter of Democritus and the eternal laughter of the Gods. No one can resist the truth of laughter.

Laughter as a philosophical principle was associated by Rabelais with Hippocrates ('the gay physician') and Democritus ('the gay philosopher'), and also with Aristotle's famous formula that of all living creatures, only man is endowed with the faculty of laughter.[5] But the most prominent ancient protagonist of philosophical laughter was Socrates, whose critical philosophy is presented by Bakhtin as devoid of narrow dogmatism, and as capable of being tested in the crucible of laughter (p. 121). According to Bakhtin, carnival forms of antiquity fertilized the Socratic dialogue and freed it from one-sided rhetorical seriousness. True seriousness fears neither laughter nor parody, even demands it as its corrective and complement. In the prologue to *Gargantua*, the gay ambivalent discourse of abusive praise and praiseful abuse in which nothing is stable or reliable, is merged with humanist scholarship and a parody of Plato's *Symposium*. Alcibiades' comparison of Socrates with Silenus was popular among humanists and cited by Erasmus in three of his works. Socrates is depicted as an ill-shaped, ridiculous figure with the face of a fool and ways that mark him as a simpleton, hopelessly unfit for public office, forever laughing, forever drinking. And yet, his mockery contains lucid knowledge and divine understanding. Rabelais transfers the ancient *Sileni* to the drug-stores in Paris streets: statuettes containing popular drugs and remedies, quite familiar to his readership. Almost every word in this prologue is ambivalent, an instance of the praise/abuse which characterizes parody as a genre. The reference to the *Symposium* emphasizes the gaiety and freedom of philosophical table talk. Rabelais boldly states that he writes only while eating and drinking and his articulation of gay truth is the exact opposite of the gloomy serious tone and gothic darkness of late medieval philosophy, while the immense interest in food and dishes is the exact opposite of medieval asceticism. The emblem on Gargantua's hat portrayed 'a man's body with two heads facing one another, four arms, four feet, a pair of arses and a brace of sexual organs, male and female. Such, according to

---

5 'The fact that human beings are susceptible to tickling is due ... to their being the only creatures that laugh'. Aristotle (1937/1961) *Parts of Animals*, Book 3, chapter 10 (673a) - and not in *De Anima*, as is suggested by Bakhtin (p. 68). As a matter of fact, his references to philosophy are somewhat careless at times, due no doubt to the difficult circumstances in which he worked.

Plato's *Symposium*, was human nature in its mystical origins'.[6]

Elsewhere, in his book on Dostoevski, Bakhtin points out that the Socratic dialogue, together with the Menippian satire and other ancient literary forms, belongs to a series of genres referred to as *serio-comical* (Bakthin 1973, p. 87 ff.). They originate from the age-old popular traditions of carnival and are permeated by a carnival attitude to the world through and through. Unlike epic and tragic genres, their subject matter is the present, and they persistently convey an atmosphere of freedom, jolly relativity and familiarity. Due to the absence of epic or tragic distance, their themes and figures are dealt with in a crudely direct and familiar way. Even persons of eminence become *familiarized*. In the case of historical figures, behavioural peculiarities are emphasized and peculiar features of their bodily exterior are rendered visible.[7] Moreover, in defiance of the demand for generic unity, the serio-comic genres usually contain a vivid mixture of seemingly incompatible generic elements, a mesalliance of comic and serious modes of speech. Although as a literary form it came to be identified with Plato, the Socratic dialogue was a widespread genre in its time, and Socratic dialogues were not only written by Plato, but also by Xenophon, Antisthenes, Aeschines, Phaedo, Euclid, Alexamenos, Glaucon, Simias, Criton and others, although only those of Plato and Xenophon have survived. Unlike official monological modes of speech, the Socratic dialogue does not claim to be in possession of an already discovered and indisputable truth. Rather, it conveys the sense that truth is of a dialogical nature and that only in the course of a dialogue it can be discovered (although later on Plato's dialogues degenerate into monological pseudo-dialogues so that the rather mechanical and predictable answers of the pupil fails to contribute anything whatsoever to the course of the argument). Also the localities in which the Socratic dialogues are set (the *Protagoras* and the *Symposium* in a stately Athenian mansion, *Phaedo* in a prison cell, etc.) are in accordance with serio-comical genre conventions. Like the Menippian satire, moreover, the Socratic dialogue serves a philosophical end. Its objective is to put a philosophical idea, a philosophical issue of the day, to the test (for instance the issue of whether virtue is teachable in the *Protagoras*). For this reason, the Socratic dialogue is referred to by Bakhtin as a form of 'moral-psychological experimentation' (p. 95).

In short, the Socratic dialogue constitutes an important episode in the history of philosophical laughter, and this explains its prominence in the world of Rabelais. Early Christianity, however, tried to condemn laughter in order to establish an intolerant mood of seriousness and asceticism. Humanity ceased to laugh from the fourth century onwards, but wherever the fever of fanaticism subsided, men began to

---

6 *Gargantua*, Book 1, Chapter 8; cited in Bakhtin 1968, p. 323.

7 Pericles, for instance, is stripped of his helmet so that his egg-shaped head is revealed (Plutarch 1959, 5).

laugh once more (1968, p. 73, p. 92). In the popular strata of society, the culture of gay laughter, of travesty and merriment (often relying on ancient local pagan celebrations), persisted with a remarkable obstinacy and stubbornness, notwithstanding increasing limitations, restrictions and prohibitions. Gay laughter as well as frank and unrestricted speech could never be silenced completely, but continued to exist, for instance in the laughing freedom and gay vocabulary of philosophical table talk and prandial discourse. Gay laughter made its appearance in official medieval manuscripts as *chimeras* or *drôleries* - comic, grotesque scenes, involving devils, jugglers, and popular figures. These illustrations are not to be considered cryptograms which secretly convey a 'repressed' message. Rather, they are the products of a gay and carefree mood.[8] Finally, the Renaissance indicates the collapse of the gloomy late medieval eschatological discourse that had managed to establish its regime of terror and intimidation. It was the victory of gay laughing, liberating public discourse from seriousness and fear. Gay laughter is not a camouflage of a serious truth that would have been formulated in a more serious vein had there been no 'repression'. It reveals a basic, comic aspect of the world, coexistent with and fundamentally equal to the serious one. True laughter is devoid of the moralizing and critical tendencies of 'Grobianism'.

The seventeenth century was marked by stabilization and seriousness, by the establishment of monarchical power, rationalist philosophy, and classicist aesthetics. As to Rabelais, his novels were either rejected as coarse and crude or reinterpreted in allegorical terms, with the implications that all its characters and images represented (and could be replaced by) real historical figures and political events. This tradition of deciphering the 'hidden meaning', of reducing the text to a series of cryptograms, a rather prominent technique of containment in the eighteenth century, failed to understand that the grotesque had its own logic and content. In this same period, the grotesque concept of the body was replaced by a mechanistic conception of bodily life. Rabelais was appreciated mainly for his anticlericalism, but was no longer venerated as the author who claimed to write only while eating or drinking. In his *Temple du Goût* , Voltaire describes an ideal library, referred to as God's library, in which nearly all books are abridged and revised by the muses, stripped of their dialect and their indecencies, of everything considered superfluous, residual and incomprehensible. According to Bakhtin, Voltaire's own famous laughter does not really laugh, but is merely satirical and almost entirely deprived of

---

[8] *Drôleries* (fanciful marginal designs) are 'a characteristic feature of Northern gothic manuscripts ... Their subject matter encompasses a vast range of motifs: fantasy, fable, and grotesque humor, as well as actually observed scenes form everyday life, appear side by side with religious themes. The essence of *drôlerie* is its playfulness, which marks it as a special domain where the artist enjoys almost unlimited freedom. It is this freedom, comparable to the license traditionally claimed by the court jester, that account for the wide appeal of *drôlerie* during the later Middle Ages' (H.W. Janson 1962/1986, p. 354).

its regenerating and renewing element. All that is positive is placed beyond the sphere of laughter and represented by an abstract idea. And although in Rococo literature the gay tone of carefree speech is preserved, it is at the same time subdued by transferring it to the boudoir atmosphere of chamber intimacy and erotic frivolity. During the French Revolution Rabelais was (mistakenly) considered an enemy of royal power and a conscientious propagandist of systematic atheism. His grotesque exaggerations were either considered a device to gain popularity among the masses or once again confused with moralizing satire - the enormous amount of food, drink and clothes spent on Gargantua, for instance, were understood as criticizing the royal expenses imposed upon the people. In short, the grotesque was reduced either to political (that is, serious) satire, or to the merely amusing literary genres of reduced laughter. Contrary to this distorted and misguided reading of Rabelais, Bakhtin emphasizes the general tone of laughter at work in Rabelais' novels, constituting a ground which allows particular comic utterances or images to emerge. It cannot be reduced either to humanism or anticlericalism, since it is the expression of something more primitive and elementary. Bakhtin emphasizes the intrinsic connection between laughter and truth. Laughter is a basic mood or mode of thought that allows a basic aspect of the world to emerge. It is not a satirical camouflage of an abstract idea or serious truth. Rather, the comical and the rational are two basic conditions of human reflection. A century later, however, Spinoza saw the path of truth as demanding that the human mind purge itself from laughter: *non ridere [...], sed intelligere* was his motto (p. 141).

At this point, a brief comparison of Bakhtin's understanding of laughter with the one articulated by Bergson (1940/1969) may help to clarify the singularity of Bakhtin's view. Bergson starts his analysis of laughter with three basic observations: (1) the comical is a human phenomenon (to laugh, or to be laughable, is human); (2) laughter presupposes indifference towards its object and (3) laughter is always the laughter of a certain group, it reverberates, is eager for response - it is a phenomenon of complicity. Yet, although Bergson intends to deal with laughter and the laughable *as such*, it is nonetheless clear from the very outset that he focuses on the laughter of one particular era, the seventeenth century, the world of Descartes and Molière (much like Bakthin focuses on the laughter of Rabelais). Molière is Bergson's model and although Descartes himself is never mentioned, he tends to read Molière from a Cartesian perspective. One has the impression that he latter's philosophy provides Bergson with his one basic image: the machine-like aspect of human behaviour, notably of our bodily movements. Like Bakhtin, Bergson contends that comedy is intrinsically connected with the body and with bodily life, but in a way quite different from how they are connected in the world of Rabelais. According to Bergson, not the grotesque but the mechanical is comical. We laugh whenever the body gives the impression of functioning automatically and in a mechanical manner, like a puppet or a machine. We laugh when someone's movements or speech acts become mechanical and resemble the dull, obstinate patterns of machines (p. 38 ff.). We laugh whenever a human being seems to be transformed into a thing, an *automaton*. The moral function of laughter is to remind us of the fact that we human beings run the risk of loosing our responsiveness and flexibility, of becoming a machine. Laughter corrects certain 'mechanical' forms of discourse, for instance, by introducing an absurd element into the mechanism. In such a case, what is laughable is not the absurd element as such, but the obstinate, inflexible way the established mechanisms are applied to it. Like Bakhtin, that is, Bergson credits laughter with a moral function, but once again, its functionality is quite different from what it amounts to in Bakhtin's view. According to Bergson, laughter is a correction of the individual, a penalty for being stubborn and inflexible, for relying excessively on one's routines. By means of laughter, society urges the individual to adapt himself, to recover his alertness and flexibility, instead of relying on his conditioned reflexes, and in that manner society forces him to modify his maladjusted, eccentric behaviour. From a Bakhtinean point of view, such an understanding of the moral functionality of laughter would rather seem an adaptation of laughter to the demands of modern bourgeois forms of life. In Bakhtin's view, laughter sides with the individual rather than with society. What is 'corrected' is not the individual, but certain mechanical aspects of established culture and its representatives (like the mechanical discourse of the Sorbonnites). Laughter is a phenomenon of resistance rather than adjustment.

In the world of Rabelais, Bakhtin claims, gay laughter is in opposition to the official and the canonical. It is omnipresent in the unpublished spheres of speech, where the dividing lines between objects and phenomena are drawn quite differently than in the prevailing picture of the world. In these unpublished spheres of speech there are no indifferent or neutral words. Gay laughter is in permanent opposition to the stabilizing tendencies of the official and monotone discourse, to the official, sufficiently neutralized and generalized nomenclature. It transfers the official to the material and prandial. The grotesque banquet image conveys an affirmative mood and its gross exaggerations adhere to the universal and utopian. Therefore, they constitute the very opposite of ascetic criticism or moralistic satire.[9]

And yet, to the embarrassment of at least some of his readers, Bakhtin does not seem very consistent in his rejection of a reductive reading of the Rabelais novels. Notably in his final chapter (chapter seven) but in earlier passages as well, he

---

[9] For instance, Bakhtin rejects the interpretation of the German academic critic Schneegans who in his *Geschichte der grotesken Satire* (published in 1894) explains the grotesque as a conflict between the displeasure caused by the impossible and improbable nature of the grotesque image and the pleasure caused by moral satisfaction at finding depravity degraded. He rejects this view because it considers exaggerations and excess as something negative and condemnable, ignoring its positive aspect.

himself has recourse to a strategy of reading which seems to reduce the parodical and the grotesque to the status of vehicle for a line of thought which is in itself serious, abstract and progressive. Already in Chapter one, it is suggested that during the Renaissance gay laughter became the *form* of a 'critical historical consciousness' (p. 97). And on page 113 Bakhtin claims that during the French Revolution 'Rabelais's deeply revolutionary spirit' was well understood. Rejecting the misguided opinion that Rabelais was an enemy of royal power, he corrects it by explaining that 'Rabelais was never an enemy of this power but on the contrary perfectly understood its progressive meaning in his time' (p. 119). On page 208 it is claimed that during the Renaissance the parodical and grotesque forms, developed over a period of thousands of years, came to serve 'the new historic aims of the epoch' (p. 208). Claims such as these seem to suggest something like a progressive historical scheme supported by Rabelais.

Toward the end of his book, these ideological reconsiderations, putting laughter in the service of progress, become increasingly problematic. On page 380, for instance, it is claimed that certain carnivalesque gestures of Gargantua prepared the soil for a new, bold, free, sober and human *seriousness*, as well as for the development of free, experimental and materialistic knowledge. On page 406 it is claimed that Herder's concept of human progress elaborated on the idea for which a letter written by Gargantua was the theoretical basis. On page 438 it is claimed that, although Rabelais never adopted any official point of view, he appreciated the 'relative progressiveness' of royal policy and that, although Rabelais did not speak in a 'conceptual language', he did 'prepare the soil for a new seriousness' (p. 439). On page 446 it is suggested that *Gargantua* is intimately connected with the political events and problems of its period and that there is even 'an element of straight satire against the emperor's aggressive policy' at work in it, while at the same time being in support of the rights of nations to fight for their independence and of the distinction between just and unjust wars. Finally, on page 452, Bakhtin claims that:

> In the political conflicts of his time Rabelais took the most advanced and progressive positions. Royal power was in his eyes the expression of the new principle to which the immediate historic future belonged, the principle of the nation state. Therefore, he was equally hostile to the claims of the papacy and to those of the empire seeking supranational power. In the claims of both Pope and emperor he saw the dying past, whereas the national state reflected the new, youthful, popular and political historic life (p. 452).

All kinds of political avant-garde positions are suddenly attributed to Rabelais, whereas it is claimed that in certain chapters of *Pantagruel*, we hear 'a direct and an almost entirely serious speech... a new form of speech, a progressive speech, the last word of the epoch and at the same time Rabelais' completely sincere opinion' (p. 453). Moreover, gay laughter is suddenly reduced to the prudent insight that there are limits to seriousness and progress, although at the same time Bakhtin admits that Rabelais always leaves a gay loophole, allowing even relative seriousness and progressiveness to be ridiculed - for 'Rabelais ... never exhausts his resources in direct statements' (p. 454).

Now it seems clearly inconsistent to claim, on the one hand, that gay laughter is in itself an 'essential form of truth' and, on the other hand, that laughter merely 'prepares the soil' for a progressive, serious truth which is eventually to be formulated in a serious and direct, more adequate mode of speech. As Bakhtin formulated his views under the watchful eye of an extremely repressive regime (his book on Rabelais was written in Stalinist Russia in 1940), it might be suggested that inconsistencies such as the ones just cited are to be considered as superficial efforts to accommodate his views to the established, official 'truth' of dialectic materialism (while remaining basically at odds with this dogmatic truth), rather than as reflecting a basic ambivalence or uncertainty in Bakhtin's own mind. Subsequently, it would still be possible to maintain that Bakhtin's recognition of the philosophical significance of laughter as an 'essential form of truth' is to be regarded as his basic achievement - even if the subsequent elaboration of this basic insight happens to strike us as inconsistent at times. Also Bakhtin's own work is a strategic, agonistic field in which incompatible discursive forces compete with each other. Although the latter claim is undoubtedly true, the effort to account for the inconsistencies just mentioned simply by regarding them as resulting from Stalinist censorship cannot be considered as highly satisfying. Although the difficult question as to whether Bakhtin's view of laughter, while apparently in opposition to the repressive truth of Stalinism, can also be considered as congenial to it in some respects (that is, the question as to what extent the Stalinist regime can be considered as popular and grotesque in its own right) need not be answered here, the relationship between the official truth regime of Stalinism and Bakhtin's analysis of popular laughter is less equivocal than is sometimes suggested.[10] Therefore, instead of arguing that Bakhtin is either being inconsistent or simply adapting himself to external circumstances, I will contend that there is yet another possibility, namely that we still fail to grasp what 'the truth of laughter' really means, that we still fail to grasp the basic difference between the truth of propositional logic (i.e. the truth of

---

[10] Bakhtin's ambivalent relationship with his Stalinist environment is suggested by phrases like 'the triumph of the people as a whole' (p. 302). On page 341 he writes: 'The body ... has nothing to fear. Death holds no terror for it. The death of the individual is only one moment in the triumphant life of the people and of mankind, a moment indispensable for their renewal and improvement'. I guess Bakthin's reading of Rabelais must be considered both as a criticism and as a product of the Stalinist era, much like Luther is both a foe and a product of late medieval Catholicism.

science) and that of laughter. Therefore, I suggest that we will now reconsider Bakhtin's view on laughter as a basic form of truth somewhat more carefully. Subsequently, in the next section, I will compare Bakhtin's view on the grotesque with Marx' 'official' judgement of what he refers to as 'Grobianism'.

Bakhtin basically claims that, whereas reduced laughter lacks philosophical depths, true laughter is a universal philosophical principle (p. 16, p. 66, p. 70). Due to laughter's peculiar 'logic' (p. 11) - that of the inside out and upside down - the entire world is seen in its droll aspect, in its gay relativity. The serious narrowness of official truth is rendered untenable by the irresistible and indestructible principle of laughter which allows us to escape the 'truth of this world' in order to look at the world with eyes that are free from this truth (p. 49). Consequently, we are liberated from all forms of narrow seriousness that direct the prevailing understanding of the world. This understanding finds itself uncrowned and reduced to the relative and the limited. The principle of laughter destroys all forms of limited seriousness and all pretense to extra-temporal meaning. It frees human consciousness, thought and imagination for new potentialities. 'For this reason', Bakhtin claims, 'great changes, even in the field of science, are always preceded by a certain carnival consciousness that prepares the way' (p. 49). Yet, laughter is *not* an external defensive form of some abstract truth or other in the sense that, if there had been no repression, truth would have cast off the clown's attire and would have spoken in serious tones (p. 93). On the contrary, 'laughter is essentially not an external but an interior form of truth; it cannot be transformed into seriousness without destroying and distorting the very content of the truth which it unveils' (p. 94). Laughter is 'another truth' (p. 94, p. 95), a form of truth in its own right. Laughter liberates, not from censorship, but from 'the great interior censor', fear. Laughter is not a camouflage of some abstract tendency or idea, but contains 'something else, something far more meaningful, profound ... the comic aspect of the world' (p. 134).

In order to determine what *kind* of truth Bakhtin has in mind whenever the phrase 'the truth of laughter' is used, Heidegger's distinction between truth as revelation ('aletheia') and truth as representation ('adequatio') is indispensable. 'Adequatio' refers to truth in the scientific sense of the term: a certain proposition or doctrine is regarded as true insofar as it adequately represents an actual state of affairs. But this, Heidegger (1927/1986) tells us, is a secondary form of truth. In order for reality to be represented adequately, it has to emerge, has to be brought out first. This original event of *re*vealing or bringing out, of *Entdecken, Aneignen* or *Erschliessen* is something which cannot be brought about by science itself.

Contrary to scientific discourse, the *experience* of laughter does not contain a systematic and propositional representation of reality. The definition of truth as the *correspondence* (adequatio) of propositional knowledge with its object, does not apply to laughter. Rather, the experience of laughter allows reality to appear and to emerge in a certain light.[11] In terms of Heidegger's distinction, therefore, the truth of laughter is an experience of revelation. Bakthin likewise refers to laughter as a state of mind that allows reality to appear, rather than being a propositional or doctrinal form of truth (i.e. a truth that could be captured in the form of a doctrine, a theory, a sequence of propositional claims). Certain basic aspects of the world are revealed, rather than represented, by laughter.

This might be clarified somewhat further by an important passage in Bakhtin's book on Dostoevski. Laughter, Bakhtin tells us, is 'a specific ethical attitude toward reality, untranslatable into logical language, a specific means of seeing and seizing the world' (1973, p. 137). Laughter seizes a phenomenon in the process of its transition, stressing its relativity and inconstancy, remaining incompatible with the basic will to power at work in scientific seriousness, that is, with the permanent effort of science to represent the world, that is, to secure and determine it by means of theories, definitions and laws. Certain aspects of the world are revealed by laughter in defiance of the official representation of the world produced and sustained either by theological seriousness (the medieval situation), or by scientific seriousness (the present situation).

In short, laughter allows the world to become visible and accessible. A scientific understanding of the world is rendered possible by laughter because laughter produces the kind of subjectivity presupposed by science, it produces the kind of subjectivity which no longer feels intimidated by the boundlessness of reality, by its unfathomable depth. Reality is familiarized by laughter and 'persuaded' to reveal itself. Therefore, the truth of science is preceded by, and rendered possible by the truth of laughter, but this does not imply that laughter is merely a temporary truth, to be replaced by science, or that it is merely a rough and intuitive grasp, to be clarified by systematic observation, propositional representation and appropriation. Laughter remains a world-revealing force in its own right, and a way of escape, even from the very truth-game rendered possible by it. Likewise, laughter does not contain some *moral* doctrine or other, nor can it be reduced to any particular set of moral propositions. Under specific circumstances, certain forms of moral responsiveness are rendered possible by it, but it remains a basic form of 'answerability', a basic possibility to respond in its own right, a principle moral force which, under different circumstances, will manifest itself in different and, above all, unpredictable ways. Laughter allows the kind of moral subjectivity presupposed by the ethical discourse of a certain epoch to become established. Although laughter, under certain historical circumstances, will support a particular scientific, moral or political view, it will nevertheless retain its awareness of the relative and temporal nature of this truth, and the alliance is broken off as soon as the scientific, moral or

---

[11] Thus preserving and humanizing the ancient pagan conviction that the creation of the world is to be attributed to the laughter of the gods (Bakhtin 1968, p. 71).

political view involved starts presenting its truth as absolute and extra-temporal. The gay and festive aspects of all scientific, moral and political transformations must not be taken to imply that laughter as a philosophical principle can be instrumentalized for all eternity. Whenever the principle of laughter seems to be in support of any particular policy, and in opposition to another one, it remains unreliable and unstable. Laughter's affinities remain short-lived, she does not sell her birth-right for a limited amount of progress. Laughter always leaves a gay loophole, allowing even 'relative' and 'limited' seriousness and progressiveness to be ridiculed - and this is laughter's 'final' word.

3. MARX, OR: JUDGING GROBIANISM

Apart from having greatly influenced Bakhtin's compatriots - notably the authorities - Marx' judgement of sixteenth century 'Grobianism' is of some interest in itself. Bakhtin at times referred to it and - at least implicitly - challenged, or even rejected it, because basically Marx sides with science and critical argument, denying laughter the claim to being 'an essential form of truth' in its own right. Laughter is instrumentalized by Marx as a temporary means to achieve an abstract and serious objective.

In his polemical essay *Moralizing Critique and Critical Morality: a Contribution to the History of German Culture*[12], Marx (1847/1972) enters the ring against the German writer Heinzen who rehabilitated and promoted a certain literary style referred to by Marx as *Grobianism*. He describes it as a crude, popular genre emerging shortly before and during the Reformation, which even at that time provoked aesthetic repugnance. The grobian genre, Marx claims, is unable to please anyone whose aesthetic taste has acquired at least *some* education. As the nineteenth Century, much like the sixteenth Century, was an age of transformation, Marx expected its temporary resurgence.[13] He described it as vulgar, coarse and simplistic, expressing semi-educated plebeianism, abounding in references to bodily life and bodily features, with a predilection for the excessive and the giantesque, siding with ordinary life against learning, contaminated by the physical agitation that had

---

12 *Die moralisierende Kritik und die kritisierende Moral: Beitrag zur Deutschen Kulturgeschichte.*

13 'Kurz vor und während der Reformationszeit bildete sich unter den Deutschen eine Art von Literatur, deren bloßer Namen frappiert - die Grobianische. Heutzutage gehen wir einer dem 16.jahrhundert analogen Umwälzungsepoche entgegen. Kein Wunder, daß unter den Deutschen die grobianische Literatur wieder auftaucht. Das Interesse an der geschichtlichen Entwicklung überwindet leicht den ästhetischen Ekel, den diese Sorte von Schriftstellerei selbst einem wenig gebildeten Geschmack erregt und schon im fünfzehnten und sechzehnten Jahrhundert erregte' (p. 331).

somehow infected the whole epoch, raging with the same excessive ferocity against progressive, as it did against conservative political forces. Due to lack of other talents, it relied heavily on abusive language. It had all the characteristics of a puppet show taken from the medieval market square and put into print. The subtitle 'Contribution to German *Cultural* History' must no doubt be taken ironically, for he thought of it as *cul-the-sac* rather than as culture. He considered Thomas Murner, nicknamed 'Goose-preacher' by his contemporaries as the writer who represented the genre *in optima forma*; most likely for political reasons since Murner had sided with, and put his 'talents' in service of the catholic establishment against Luther. The genre was later refined, however, and put to use by Shakespeare. In *Troilus and Cressida*, it is personified by the knave Thersites, who mocks and ridicules one of the tragic heroes (Ajax), calling him a peacock and an ass who is suffering from excessive wit but is unable to discharge it.

Some aspects of Marx' essay are worthy of our attention. In the first place, although it is clearly his objective to ridicule his opponent Heinzen, the larger part of his essay is remarkably boring and of little substance. And although he too relies heavily on abusive language, his laughter does not laugh but merely displays a cynical grin. That is, although he relies on a technique apparently borrowed from the very genre he rejects, Marx' language is not grounded in a gay and laughing mood but in a modern, cynical one. Furthermore, for someone who pretended to side with the popular strata of society, he displays a remarkable contempt towards what he refers to as a plebeian genre, the expression of semi-education and popular wit. On further consideration, however, his judgement is quite consistent with his political metaphysics. In the sixteenth Century the modern working class was still to emerge on the scene and this explained the political ambivalence bound to raise the suspicion of anyone devoted to the cause of socialism and progress. The grobian literature excelled in squandering energy without accomplishing or changing anything. It aimed at exposing the world by means of ridicule, but with no intention of changing it. It abounded in indignation, but was bound to thwart any effort to translate its plebeian discontent into a political program. Instead of promoting the resurgence of such a genre, therefore, a consistent politics should be developed that would allow for the seizure of state power and the systematic exploitation and transformation of the vital, popular forces grobianism represented but unfortunately left fallow. Such a top-down and etatistic intervention, which came to be referred to as 'proletarian' dictatorship, would no doubt put an end to popular laughter once and for all and would allow for an effective mode of exercising power to become established.

In view of Marx' canonical judgement, Bakhtin's effort to rehabilitate grobianism in Stalinist Russia was a rather delicate one indeed, although others, notably Gorki, had paved the way. Apparently, it challenged Marx' basic claim that interpretation should be put to the service of political progress or change. Laughter is appreciated by Bakhtin for its peculiar ability to reveal a basic moral truth and perceive reality in a certain light. It serves neither as a hinge for the class struggle of marxism, nor for that matter will it contribute in any way to solving the social problems of liberalism.

This does not imply, however, that true laughter - as opposed to sarcasm, cynicism or irony - is devoid of historical or political significance. On the contrary, by exposing a basic moral truth, the established forms of moral subjectivity are challenged or even crushed, and this prepares the way for unprecedented forms of moral subjectivity to constitute themselves. In other words, true laughter defies one of liberalism's basic platitudes, namely the understanding of politics as a technology for exercising public power, as a technology for governing and regulating the public behaviour of individuals - an understanding which I referred to as etatism. Although laughter does not provide any devices for solving policy problems, its political impact can be astonishing. In fact, all the major historical transformations (such as the decline of the Greek city state or the dawn of modern Europe) were accompanied by laughter. Laughter's political impact, however, is bottom-up instead of top-down, and therefore quite unlike the political technologies provided by Marxism, liberalism and other versions of etatism.[14]

In his own writings, most notably the early and polemical ones, Marx himself used to rely on comical and abusive language to a considerable extent. He was clearly aware of the fact that criticism is basically a comic genre. Marx basic strategy was to refute his opponent's point of view by means of ridicule. In *The Holy Family*, *The German Ideology* and other polemical works a comic mode of speech is used. In *The German Ideology*, for example, Marx and Engels tell us that it is their aim to 'ridicule' the philosophies as well as the philosophers of their time (5, 23) and to bring out the 'tragicomic' contrast between their illusions or pretensions and their actual achievements (5, 28). In fact, they act as if attending a Christian church fathers' council, the 'Leipzig Council', an allusion to the fact that the works of the two 'church fathers' criticized in this section, Bruno Bauer ('Saint Bruno') and Max Stirner ('Saint Max'), were published in Leipzig. The whole section abounds in ironical allusions. Marx and Engels consider the philosophers of their time to be comic, parodical, pseudo-Hegelian imitations of Hegel's serious

---

14 I consider Marxism a kind of despotic etatism considered indispensable by Mill whenever the transformation of moral subjectivity presupposed by liberalism (that is, by sophisticated etatism) has not yet been realized due to specific historical circumstances. Marxism's basic objective was to establish a just society by seizing state power and 'temporarily' opting for a proletarian dictatorship, although it was admitted that this dictatorship implied 'governing-too-much' and that eventually the state was to disappear. Although Marx takes credit for its political metaphysics, Lenin, notorious for his chronic sarcasm, elaborated its political technology.

discourse. They admit that if, like Hegel, one designs a certain system or pattern of explanation for the first time, one cannot do so without great energy, keen insight and positive knowledge. But if one is satisfied with using an already existing pattern and applying it in a mechanical manner, like Bauer and Stirner had done, the result 'inevitably becomes comic' (1846/1976, p. 176). [15] The strategy of Marx and Engels basically comes down to keeping close track of their opponent's reasonings, incessantly ridiculing it, for instance by comparing it to famous lines or sections taken from the Scriptures. The opening lines of *The Holy Family*, for example, contain a parody of the language of the Gospels: 'And Criticism [i.e. the philosophy of Bauer, Stirner and other Hegelians) so loved the mass that it sent its only begotten son, that all who believe in him may not be lost, but may have Critical life', etc. (1845/1975, p. 9). [16] Or Marx and Engels will isolate a peculiar phrase and repeat it time and again, until the reader is thoroughly convinced that it is indeed a rather ridiculous thing to say. Stirner, for instance, had used the following line somewhere: 'Robespierre, for example, Saint-Just, and so on'. As Marx and Engels feel that both Robespierre and Saint-Just were unique historical personalities, individuals beyond comparison, Stirner's line strikes them as odd - '"Robespierre, for example", (for example!), "Saint-Just, and so on" (and so on!)'. They repeat it again and again until everybody agrees that it is a tremendously funny phrase, a perfect exemplification of the stupidity of its author. Although the bulk of their critique is rather tedious, it is nonetheless comical at times. Still another comic technique used by Marx and Engels is comic reversal, which they notably applied to titles, for example: *The Holy Family, or Critique of Critical Criticism* and *The Poverty of Philosophy. Answer to the* Philosophy of Poverty *by M. Proudhon* (1847/1976).

Moreover, the humour of Marx (or Marx and Engels) is more than just a figure of speech or rhetorical technique. Their philosophical convictions really allow them to discern the comic aspect of books, persons or historical events that appear to be serious at first sight. Take, for example, another opening line, a famous one often cited: 'Hegel remarks somewhere that all facts and personages of great importance in world history occur, as it were, twice. He forgot to add: the first time as tragedy, the second as farce' (1852/1979, p. 103). The revolution of 1848 was a parody, a comic replay of those of 1789 and 1793 and, he adds, the same goes for Luther who 'donned the mask of the apostle Paul' (11, 104). Marx' basic objective is to bring about something of a reversal, and to turn Hegelian dialectics 'upside-down' by acknowledging that the basic facts of history are those concerning food and drink and

---

[15] Bergson (1940/1969) likewise points out that the mechanical application of certain established patterns of interpretation in an inflexible, obstinate manner is always comical.

[16] The title of the book itself is, of course, ironical.

68

bodily existence rather than the lofty themes of German idealism. Still it is clear from the very outset that his laughter is far from gay. It is cynical and sarcastic, similar in many respects to the 'negative laughter' of the Protestant pamphleteers who were Luther's contemporaries. Although parodical devices such as comic reversal and comic repetition are used by him, Marx' basic mood remains cynical, and his humour is jeering rather than jesting. While writing with a cynical (sometimes comical) grin, his basic objective was to initiate a serious discourse that would put an end to the ridiculous balderdash of his opponents once and for all. Although Marx makes extensive use of laughter's peculiar logic, the logic of the inside out and upside down (most notably in his early writings), laughter eventually remains a purely negative phenomenon, instead of being considered a world-revealing force in its own right.

In chapter 1, I already pointed out how Marx, in *The Capital, Part 1* explains the emergence of the massive reservoir of labour power presupposed by the kind of society that was coming into existence in the early nineteenth century (1962/1979). The starting-point of the whole process, the 'original accumulation' of capital, was usually explained by means of 'an anecdote from the past', told with 'sovereign earnestness', but really a comic reversal of the theological account of original sin. Whereas the Biblical story tells us why we human beings have to labour in the sweat of our faces, the accumulation-anecdote explained how some human beings came to be exempted from this scourge. In times long gone by, it was told, there were two sorts of people; one, the diligent and intelligent; the other, lazy rascals, spending their substance in riotous living. Thus it came to pass that the former sort accumulated wealth, and the latter had at last nothing to sell except their own skins. And from this original sin dates the poverty of the great majority that, despite all its labour, still has nothing to sell but itself, and the wealth of the few, the one time diligent, that increases constantly, although they have long ceased to work (p. 741). In Marx' counter-account, however, the true history of this 'original' accumulation is revealed. It proves to be a history of violence, plunder and terrorism which, notwithstanding its astonishing amount of cold-blooded cynicism, provides a 'comic mirror' which reveals the ideological nature of the 'standard account'.

Indeed, the historical chapters of *The Capital, Part 1* tell about the excessive exploitation and slaughter of human lives, the unrestrained vampirism that determined the real living conditions of the working classes during the terrible epoch known as the industrial revolution and for which Dante's inferno provided the literary model (p. 261). Subsequently, Marx points out how the working classes, although completely overruled at first, gradually learned to put up some resistance. Yet, the truly popular (that is, parodical) forms of resistance are hardly taken into consideration by him. When quoting from dialogues between child-labourers and a party of officials investigating working conditions in England, for example, he is startled by the children's remarkable lack of education. Apparently, the comic nature of their responses, the mockery of their retorts escapes him. One of the interviewees, a twelve year old boy, did not know what country he lived in, did not know anything about England, believed God to be a little bird, the devil a good person and Christ a wicked fellow, believed the king to be a queen (p. 274).

4. *INCIPIT PARODIA*: NIETZSCHE

Freie Geister: Gesellen mit denen man lacht...[17]

Both Bakhtin and Nietzsche have recognized a philosophical insight of crucial importance: that there is truth in laughter. This section sets out to explore the basic affinity as well as the basic tension between Bakhtin's concept of *parody* - elaborated in the Rabelais book - and Nietzsche's concept of *gay science*. It is my contention that both Bakhtin and Nietzsche draw attention to parody or gay science as a basic philosophical technique or mode of thought that enables the philosopher to contest the apparent self-evidence of an established truth-regime and to reveal hidden aspects of moral existence. There are other basic techniques or modes of thought such as argument or irony, but under certain conditions, parody becomes indispensable. Both Bakhtin and Nietzsche emphasize the negative as well as the positive aspect of laughter. On the one hand, laughter exposes the vulnerability of a prevailing truth, a predominant rationality. This aspect of laughter becomes important when we find ourselves confronted with an official truth-regime which presents itself as indisputable and beyond contestation. Laughter serves to reveal the lack of self-evidence, the fundamental vulnerability of such a truth.This is its negative aspect. There is, however, a positive aspect to laughter as well. As Bakhtin phrases it in his book on Rabelais, laughter has a deep philosophical meaning, being one of the essential forms of truth. Certain essential aspects of the world are accessible only to laughter (1968, p. 66).

In the previous chapter I pointed out that the gay and popular aspect of Socrates' performance was certainly recognized by Nietzsche. Section 190 of *Beyond Good and Evil*, for instance, is one of the occasions where the relationship between Plato and Socrates is defined in terms of the aristocratic versus the vulgar. According to Nietzsche, Plato desperately tried to give Socrates' performance some eminence by boldly redescribing a basically vulgar way of reasoning, which he (Plato) picked up from the streets like a popular song or theme,[18] and transformed into something

---

[17] *Human, All Too Human I*, Preface, § 2.

[18] According to Nietzsche, Socrates' way of drawing conclusions 'smells plebeian' (l.c.).

serious.[19] Of crucial importance, however, are the remarks on Socrates in the book in which Nietzsche elaborates his own philosophy of laughter, *The Gay Science.*

In the introduction to *The Gay Science* Nietzsche defines 'gay science' as follows: it is the *saturnalia* - a term, of course, of some prominence in the Bakhtinean vocabulary - of a mind who has patiently resisted a persistent pressure of long standing. It is a kind of recovery, almost like a state of drunkenness, where many a foolish and unwise thing will emerge.[20] According to Nietzsche, gay science reveals the basic connection between truth and laughter (I, §1). To be able to laugh at oneself is the summit of wisdom.[21] Laughter is an instant of truth and revelation, where a basic liberating insight is finally gained.

In *The Gay Science* Nietzsche draws a basic opposition between gay science on the one hand and morality on the other. Morality is an established truth, supposedly beyond contestation, whose basic vulnerability is nevertheless exposed by laughter. Morality's basic claim, according to Nietzsche, is: Thou shalt not laugh. The true philosopher, however, laughs at the basic values of morality. He perceives reality as a playful comedy, full of jest.

Yet, in *The Gay Science*, Nietzsche draws a second opposition, namely between morality and scientific truth, an opposition which seems to moderate the previous one between morality and laughter. It is Nietzsche's hope that, eventually, morality will give way to scientific truth. The truth of science is bound to maintain itself, even in the face of laughter (I, § 46). If, through laughter, we recover from the illness of morality, we will finally be able to think scientifically - and one cannot laugh at science. Science seems to be regarded by Nietzsche as an end in itself (III, § 123), whereas laughter appears to be merely a path to truth, a kind of purification. We need gay science to recover from morality and Christianity, but ultimately laughter is to be subordinated to science. Real science is no longer 'gay' but serious. We need the fool, the jester, to recover; it is a path to truth, toward science, but ultimately Nietzsche seems to agree with Spinoza: *Non ridere... sed intelligere*: we should not laugh, we should think.[22]

In this respect Nietzsche disagrees with Bakhtin, who considers laughter ultimately irresistible. The view elaborated in *The Gay Science* can be found in other

---

19 Kierkegaard (1989) also presents Socrates as someone who belonged to crowded and noisy city life, not at all disturbed by the bustling work of the artisans, the braying of the pack-asses or the boisterous noise of the marketplace, someone who liked walking around and talking with all sorts of people, an ever quick-witted ironist who could begin anywhere and whose attention could be triggered by any subject or situation.

20 Introduction, § 1.

21 Cf. De Unamuno (1954): 'It is necessary to know how to make ourselves ridiculous, and not only to others but to ourselves' (p. 306).

22 IV, § 133; cf. Bakhtin 1968, p. 141.

writings of Nietzsche as well. In *The Antichrist*, for instance, Nietzsche blames Christianity for having prematurely destroyed the formidable effort of the Greek and Roman elite to establish and foster a scientific understanding of reality. Christianity is blamed for having discredited reason, knowledge and enquiry, the will to perceive things as they truly are. Christianity (or the medieval epoch) is the victory of the faulty moral sensibility of the great majority of vulgar fools over the scientific sensibility of a rational elite[23].

And here, a second basic tension between Bakhtin and Nietzsche emerges. For whereas Bakhtin appreciates parody as a popular medieval genre, Nietzsche throughout his writings displays a chronic contempt of all things medieval, popular and vulgar. In fact, he considers it one of Christianity's great merits and achievements to have done away with a lot of vulgar, medieval rubbish, with a lot of popular heroes and popular lore. Indeed, he considers this to be Christianity's one great contribution to Enlightenment (III, § 122). The Middle Ages are referred to by Nietzsche as the great alcohol poisoning of Europe (III, § 134). Even Faust and Mephistopheles, two great figures of medieval popular culture, are considered by Nietzsche as representing a basic prejudice against knowledge, and therefore to be exorcised on behalf of the will to truth. In this regard, Nietzsche's views seem quite at odds with the basic attitude and sensibility of Bakhtin, who instead affirms parody and laughter as basic elements of medieval life and thought.

Bakhtin and Nietzsche do not seem to share the same aesthetic taste. Whereas Bakhtin appreciates medieval culture as a grotesque combination of a variety of heterogenous elements, Nietzsche praises unity of style, as can be found in Provencal poetry, the very opposite of the medieval public square, which is considered the principal locus of laughter and resistance in Bakhtin's work. In the Rabelais novels, the Provencal idiom is merely one of the linguistic elements put to work, besides all sorts of popular devices, proverbs, school farces, *soties*, abuses, and sayings from the mouths of fools and clowns. Indeed, his novels are democratic rather than aristocratic. It is the very culture of the market square that Nietzsche, because of his aristocratic taste, despises. He reproaches the German culture of his time for being merely an aggregate of influences and subcultures - too pluralistic, chaotic, even 'grotesque' - and refers disapprovingly to it as a popular fair.[24] The one

---

[23] A view confirmed by Luther who claims that the truth of faith is ridiculous from the point of view of reason and contrary to actual experience.

[24] In *Untimely Meditations*, volume 1, German culture is reproached for excelling in 'Stillosigkeit oder dem chaotischen Durcheinander aller Stile', and he complaints about the 'Jahrmarktlärme der modernen Ideen'. True art implies mastering chaos. As to Hellenism, however, although far from constituting a unitarian style, it was not a mere aggregate of influences and subcultures either. Nietzsche argued that Hellenism had succeeded in organizing the chaos. It was not a mere mixture, but rather a contest of styles, organized in such a way that it had to be appreciated from an artistic point of

basic feature of true culture, Nietzsche claims, is unity of style. In other words, a strong tendency towards asceticism and purification appears to be at work in Nietzsche's writings, something that is quite absent in the popular 'grobianism' of Rabelais. Whereas the Rabelais novels renounced the demands of classical literary taste, condemned by the classical canon in the seventeenth and early eighteenth century precisely for this reason, Nietzsche clearly appreciates the effort of classical French literature to conform to the rigid canons of unity to which the classicist poets subjected themselves, thereby removing all burlesque and *buffo* elements from the theatre as 'crude' and 'barbaric' survivals. With regard to the problem of truth we encounter the same tendency towards purification, restriction and expulsion in Nietzsche's writings. After having profited from Christianity's effort to do away with a lot of barbaric insanity in the name of 'truth', it is now time for European culture to do away with a lot of Christian insanity as well in the name of *scientific* truth.

Yet at the very moment *we* are convinced that the scientific will to truth is Nietzsche's basic commitment, he himself withdraws from such a conclusion, emphasizing that even science itself is constituted by a basic, moral conviction, ultimately without foundation (V, § 344). There seems to be a basic ambivalence at work. The final entries of *The Gay Science* are devoted to laughter and parody rather than to science. Here Nietzsche formulates the ideal of a more-than-human state of well-being, the final parody of all earnestness. In *Ecce Homo* Nietzsche indicates that *The Gay Science* was written out of a certain 'physiological state', referred to as 'great health', which seems to be not merely a path but rather an ideal, a prospect. The summit of wisdom is the mood of laughter itself. In the introduction he had called his book a bit of merrymaking after long deprivation. Indeed, Klossowksi (1963) is basically right when he claims that Spinoza's classic formula *Non ridere, non lugere, necque detestari, sed intelligere* enabled Nietzsche (albeit in a negative manner) to acquire a deeper understanding his own mode of thinking as a philosophy of laughter, mourning and profanation, a philosophy which evolved out of a *reversal* of Spinoza's maxim, instead of identifying itself with it.

Already in *The Birth of Tragedy* Nietzsche had pointed to a basic form of truth that came to be neglected and obscured but should be regarded as more profound than the limited truth of reason. In fact, he claims that Greek tragedy evolved out of the perpetual struggle between two basic principles, the Apollinian and the Dionysian. The Apollinian is the *principium individuationis*, the principle of Self, of measure and self-constraint, while the Dionysian refers to a state of excessive physical excitement (the 'glow of pleasure'), exemplified by the time-old image of a gay, wandering and boisterous crowd. It is the principle of fraternization among men as

---

view. In fact, Bakhtin shared this positive judgement and referred to Hellenistic culture as a 'living novel'.

well as of reconciliation with the forces of nature.[25] In ancient Greece, Nietzsche claims, Dionysian unruliness and excess was checked and balanced by the moral, Apollinian principle of measure and self-constraint. Whereas the Apollinian principle provided a superficial veil, a reassuring *picture* of the real, the Dionysian principle was regarded as a higher, more profound truth that allowed man to discern the real as such. Due to Euripides and Socrates, however, the Apollinian principle was replaced by the Socratic principle of criticism and reason, while the Dionysian principle was no longer considered as a basic form of wisdom. Instead, it was rejected as irrational and banished from the realm of rational truth (§ 19). Nietzsche, however, longed for the recurrence of the dionysian truth of tragedy. Yet in his later writings he will put his hopes in the recurrence of a gay rather than a tragic 'science'. Indeed, there is a shift in Nietzsche's work from the tragic (*The Birth of Tragedy*) to the comical (*The Gay Science*). Still, although tragic truth eventually gives way to the truth of laughter, both serve as a remedy to counter the one-sidedness of scientific truth (cf. chapter 3). Like Bakhtin, Nietzsche eventually discerns that laughter is a basic form of truth, a philosophical principle whose truth cannot be reduced to, or identified with that of science.

In the next chapter, which is on Socrates, both the basic affinity and the basic difference between Bakhtin's and Nietzsche's philosophy will be further elaborated and clarified by drawing attention to one particular entry in *The Gay Science*, where Nietzsche refers to Socrates' famous final words cited by Plato in *Phaedo*. In this section, however, I want to pursue my reading of Nietzsche's own philosophy of laughter by drawing attention to some comments on it.

In his article on Nietzsche the jester - *Nietzsche Narrentum* - Walter Bröcker (1972) recalls several passages where Nietzsche emphasizes the importance of jest with regard to truth. On 4 May 1988 for instance, in a letter to Brandes, Nietzsche presents himself as someone who is mocking the most serious things.[26] And in *Ecce Homo* he confesses that he wants to be considered a buffoon - in German: a *Hanswurst* - rather than a saint. I am a buffoon, he claims, and yet I am a spokesman of truth. However, even in earlier writings, when he took science's claim

---

25 And Nietzsche adds: 'Auch im Deutschen Mittelalter wälzten sich unter der gleichen dionysischen Gewalt immer wachsende Scharen, singend und tanzend, von Ort zu Ort: in diesen Sankt-Johann- und Sankt-Veittänzern erkennen wir die bacchischen Chöre der Griechen wieder ... das glühende Leben dionysischer Schwärmer. Unter dem Zauber des Dionysischen schließt sich nicht nur der Bund zwischen Mensch und Mensch wieder zusammen: auch die entfremdete, feindliche oder unterjochte Natur feiert wieder ihr Versöhnungsfest mit ihrem verlorenen Sohne, dem Menschen ... [Jetzt] fühlt sich jeder mit seinem Nächsten nicht nur vereinigt, versöhnt, verschmolzen, sondern eins ... Singend und tanzend äußert sich der Mensch als Mitglied einer höheren Gemeinsamkeit' (§ 2).

26 Ich hänge den ernstesten Dingen einen Schwanz von Posse an...

to knowledge more seriously than during his final episode, Nietzsche recognized that the buffoon had a special task as a herald of new truths. When he refers to the first volume of his *Human, All Too Human* as a fool's book, *ein Narrenbuch*, he does not consider the fool someone who is denied access to truth. On the contrary, it is in the fool's discourse that new truths first make their appearance. The fool is granted the privilege of uttering them for the first time. While being excluded from the old established truths, the fool's cap allows him to introduce new unprecedented ones.

Although Nietzsche's style is often associated with an ironic attitude, he in fact shared Bakhtin's negative appreciation of irony. He considered it a negative, pessimistic and even decadent mode of speech (Behler 1975) and insisted on moderate use (Bräutigam 1977). Furthermore, like Bakhtin he rejected the sense of complacency conveyed by it. For although he considers himself superior to others, the ironist remains unable to come up with anything positive or affirmative, he merely rejects. Another reason for Nietzsche's aversion was the fact that, in the nineteenth century, irony was generally associated with romanticism whereas Nietzsche, faced with the dispute between Romantic and classicist aesthetics, claimed to be in favour of classical taste. However, Behler and others point to the fact that, notwithstanding his apparent rejection of romanticism and its aesthetic devices, Nietzsche was 'infected' by it to a much larger extent than he himself was willing to admit or recognize. He was both a Romantic and a self-avowed anti-Romantic (Del Caro 1983). I will return to this issue in depth in my review of Nietzsche novel *Thus spoke Zarathustra*, but I do agree that there is a good deal of irony or complacent laughter at work in Nietzsche's own writings. As pointed out by Behler, his rejection of Romanticism was an aesthetical demand, quite in tune with some of his basic theoretical views, but rather at odds with his personal literary inclinations. Moreover, there is a fundamental affinity between irony and one of Nietzsche's basic devices - the use of masks. Van Tongeren (1989), Behler and others have stressed the fact that, although Nietzsche sometimes uses the term irony in a 'pejorative' sense, on other occasions he emphasizes the original meaning of irony as *eironeia*, or *dissimulatio* - that is, irony as an adopted veil covering one's true insights.[27] If one conceals one's noble character and intellectual depths in order to spare others the painful recognition of their inferiority, irony (or *dissimulatio*) is a manifestation of strength and sovereignty rather than of weakness and decline. Such an ironical attitude is part of the 'pathos of reserve' which Nietzsche considers a mark of

---

[27] According to Kunnas (1982) eironeia had a negative, moral connotation and referred to insincerity, whereas dissimulation was a far more neutral, technical term indicating a rhetorical device.

personal superiority and distinction.[28]

Yet Nietzsche's *basic* mode of laughter seems to be parody, rather than irony (Van Tongeren 1989). This is also suggested by Gilman (1975), although he restricts himself to the importance of parody in Nietzsche's poetry.[29] Gilman points out that, in Nietzsche's appreciation and use of parody, two incompatible conceptions of this genre compete with each other: the classical or aesthetical one (formulated by Goethe) and the Romantic or psychological one (formulated by Schopenhauer). The classical conception indicates that, unlike mere negative 'parody', true parody is not *merely* comical or degrading. Rather, it is a successful reconstruction of the original and becomes an independent and valid work of art in its own right. The perfect example of parody in the classicist sense of the term is *Troilus and Cressida*, Shakespeare's magnificent parody of Homer. Although parody is bound to generate laughter, the comical effect is not its main objective. This classicist conception of parody profoundly influenced the aesthetic sensibility of the young Nietzsche and inspired several parodical, but certainly not degrading, adaptions of Goethe's poems. In 1865, however, while still a student, Nietzsche discovered Schopenhauer, who articulated a Romantic view on parody, stressing its comical and degrading aspect. Schopenhauer's understanding of parody made Nietzsche abandon the classical approach, although he never *completely* estranged himself from it, in favour of the psychological one expressed in *Beyond Good and Evil*. Here, Nietzsche's understanding is considered 'psychological' because its psychological *function* is emphasized: parody is presented as a psychological device that meets certain psychological needs. Moreover, the sections concerned - notably § 40 and § 223 - once again reveal Nietzsche's basic inconsistency or ambivalence, time and again swaying between a positive and a negative appreciation of the phenomenon at hand.

In § 40, Nietzsche claims that everything profound desires a mask. Some mental events are delicate to such an extent that they are in need of some crude concealment or other. I can even imagine, Nietzsche claims, that some people, in order to hide something vulnerable, roll crudely through life like a mouldy old barrel of wine, refusing to communicate their true content even to those who are quite near to them. Every profound mind is in need of a mask. According to Behler (1975) this aphorism implicitly refers to Socrates. Although he is not mentioned explicitly, Behler

---

28 Cf. for example *Human, All Too Human II*, 'The Wanderer and his Shadow', § 175 where he explains that mediocrity may well be the mask of a superior mind who does not want to offend his less gifted fellow-men and for this reason takes on an outward posture that is not very likely to give the impression of actually being a mask (since mediocrity is what the great majority of individuals happen to have in common by definition).

29 'It is in his lyric poetry that the use of the mode of parody is initially and most clearly presented. It is to this specific aspect of Nietzsche's writings that the critic can turn prior to promulgating a general theoretical statement of the development of Nietzsche's understanding of parody and its application in other contexts' (p. 53).

considers the barrel-image as a hint to the passage in Plato's *Symposium* which became a famous *topos* in world literature from the sixteenth century onwards (notably in the writings of Erasmus and Rabelais): Alcibiades' comparison of Socrates with the *Sileni*, little wooden statues with a grotesque exterior but containing articles of great value, a comparison which implied that Socrates, notwithstanding his buffoon-like ways and appearance, was really the summit of wisdom and sober-mindedness. In the case of Socrates, so it seems, parody is to be regarded as a mark of superiority.

In § 223, however, Nietzsche's appreciation of parody is much more negative. Instead of concealing some *profound* content, it is instead a camouflage for *lack* of content. Yet there is something positive in parody as well. According to Nietzsche, the European *Mischmensch*, an ugly plebeian, is in need of some costume or other, and uses history as a store-room of costumes, presenting himself as barocco, classic, romantic, and so on. Ours is the age of carnival, Shrove Tuesday laughter and Aristophanic mockery. Indeed, the realm of laughter is the only realm which allows us to be original to some degree as history's fools and God's buffoons.[30] Bereft of all other talents, we might still excel in laughter. Even with regard to parody, Nietzsche remains basically ambivalent. It can be a mark of superiority or decline, it might suit the intellectual elite as well as the rabble, it can function both as a camouflage of deficiency and as a vehicle of truth.

If we once again try to compare the Nietzschean view on parody and laughter with the Bakhtinean one, it becomes clear that, first of all, both Bakhtin and Nietzsche recognized the importance of the jester as the herald and spokesman of a new truth. Furthermore, they share a negative appreciation of irony and seem to agree - more or less, for Nietzsche remains ambivalent in this respect - that the positive aspect of laughter is of a parodical rather than an ironical nature. Or, to put it in other words, both Bakhtin and Nietzsche recognized laughter's ambivalent nature, but Bakhtin tried to solve the ensuing inconsistencies in Nietzsche's position by clearly distinguishing between gay laughter, or parody, and reduced laughter, or irony. Finally, whereas Nietzsche's position is marked by a chronic dispute between the Romantic and the classical appreciation of laughter - a dispute which he, being an anti-Romantic Romanticist himself, was unable to solve - Bakhtin reverted to a pre-modern conception of laughter which still encompassed both the affirmative aspect, preserved in the classical conception (albeit stripped of its grotesque nature), and the carnivalesque aspect, preserved (albeit in a rather reduced and negative manner) in the Romantic conception. And at the intersection of all these considerations and ambiguities, the image of Socrates emerges. He is both jester and spokesman of truth, both ironical and parodical, both superior and vulgar.

---

30 'Parodisten der Weltgeschichte und Hanswürste Gottes - vielleicht daß, wenn auch nichts von heute sonst Zukunft hat, doch gerade unser Lachen noch Zukunft hat!'

The first four books of *The Gay Science* were written just before *Thus Spoke Zarathustra* and are full of gaiety and wit, redescribing human existence as a comedy. They intend to affirm life, rather than pronounce a moral judgement on it. The time of the supremacy of gaiety, however, is yet to come, for men still live in the time of tragedy, morality and religion. In the fourth book, two aphorisms are devoted to Socrates: § 328 and § 340. In the first one he is considered to represent knowledge in its struggle against stupidity. In the second one he emerges as a mocking pessimist.[31] He is referred to as 'the wisest chatterer there has ever been'. Nietzsche greatly deplores, however, the final words of this man who lived the most cheerful of lives but finally professed his basic pessimism by mockingly depicting life as a kind of sickness. Throughout his life his cheerful appearance had merely been a mask covering a more profound insight, a veiled and hidden experience of life as futile suffering, which manifests itself in his final, disturbing joke.[32]

Nietzsche had already expressed his uneasiness with Socrates' final jest in the first book of *The Gay Science*, where he states that, unlike the Roman emperors Augustus and Tiberius, who died in silence, thus showing themselves *not* to have been comedians, Socrates finally had to strip himself of his mask, unable to refrain from being indiscrete, and uttered his final joke, which amounted to the confession that his gay and merry life - his apparent high spirits and *joi de vivre* - had been a comedy: *comoedia finita est.*[33] Of course, I will come back to this judgement of Socrates in the next chapter.

Book V of *The Gay Science* bears the title *We Fearless Ones*. Here Nietzsche clearly recognizes the basic opposition between gaiety and fear. At the same time,

---

31 'I admire the courage and wisdom of Socrates in everything he did, said - and did not say. This mocking and enamoured monster and pied piper of Athens ... was not only the wisest chatterer of all time: he was equally great in silence. I wish he had remained taciturn also at the last moment of his life; in that case he might have belonged to a still higher order of spirits. Whether it was death or the poison or piety or malice - something loosened his tongue at that moment and he said: "O Crito, I owe Asclepias a rooster." This ridiculous and terrible "last word" means for those who have ears: "O Crito, *life is a disease.*" Is it possible that a man like him, who had lived cheerfully ... should have been a pessimist? He had merely kept a cheerful mien while concealing all his life long his ultimate judgement... *Socrates suffered life!* And then he still revenged himself - with this veiled, gruesome, pious, and blasphemous saying' (Nietzsche 1974, p. 272). Nietzsche is aware of the parody, he puts the genre ('last word') between quotation marks while the phrase 'for those who have ears' is borrowed for the Scriptures, where it is applied to a serious message rather than a joke.

32 'We owe a cock to Asclepias', implicating that life is an illness, and death a recovery for which we ought to show Asclepias, the deity of health and medicine, our gratitude.

33 *The Gay Science*, § 36. Cf. Luther on the difference between the emperor and the jester: 'Wir haben einen frommen keiser... Er ist stille und frum. Ich halte, er redet in einem jar nicht so viel als ich in einem tage' [*Tischreden* 3:3245]

78

however, he maintains that the fearless, laughing ones are confronted with a 'terrible question', one that is not overcome by laughter but already casts a shadow on *The Gay Science*, and an even darker one on Nietzsche's subsequent achievement, *Thus Spoke Zarathustra*.

As our 'final' judgement of Socrates will be suspended until the next chapter, I would now like to continue my comparison of Bakhtin and Nietzsche by subjecting the latter's most important *literary* achievement to a Bakhtinean literary judgement in order to ascertain the extent to which it actually complies to the aesthetics of laughter suggested by his concept of gay science. Or, to put it more frankly, I want to argue that Nietzsche's achievement as a philosopher of laughter surpasses his limited achievements as a poet.

5. JUDGING ZARATHUSTRA

> *I would like to give away and distribute, until the wise*
> *among men will once again have come to enjoy their*
> *foolishness and the poor their richness* (Zarathustra).[34]

I do not share the opinion of Dannhauser (1974) and others that *Thus Spoke Zarathustra* is Nietzsche's greatest work nor the opinion that it is a magnificent work of art from a literary point of view. Rather, I consider it long, wordy and artificial. As to the basic reason for Nietzsche's artistic failure, I believe that he himself did not fully recognize nor consistently exploit the parodical nature of his undertaking, although it is in fact already suggested by the title as such: the phrase 'thus spoke...' is biblical and its German version, *also sprach*, was often used by Luther. The book is studded with allusions to the Bible, particularly the New Testament[35] and Dannhauser adds that 'it is only to be expected that most of these take the form of parody' (1974, p. 244). I have already emphasized, however, that the laughter at work in *Zarathustra* is reduced and negative, rather than gay and parodical. However, before pronouncing a judgement, let us subject the text, greatly appreciated by Nietzsche himself, to a more careful reading.

Several of Zarathustra's acts are indeed reminiscent of those of his biblical Predecessor. Dannhauser refers for example to the fact that at the age of thirty Zarathustra goes into solitude for ten years, thus 'out-doing' Jesus, who spends

---

34 'Ich möchte verschenken und austeilen, bis die Weisen unter den Menschen wieder einmal ihrer Torheit und die Armen wieder einmal ihres Reichtums froh geworden sind' (*Thus Spoke Zarathustra*, Prelude, § 1).

35 Weichelt (1922) listed 107 allusions to the Bible, 78 of which are to the New Testament.

'only' forty days in the desert. It should not escape us, however, that this 'out-doing' is of a parodical nature, that it is in fact a case of grotesque exaggeration, a literary technique used abundantly in Rabelais' novels. Yet the possibilities inherent in parody as a genre are not fully recognized or exploited, neither by Nietzsche himself nor by his commentators. Its laughter is sometimes reduced to sarcasm, at other occasions silenced by seriousness. In general, it suffers from Nietzsche's, or Zarathustra's, persistent effort to preach the serious, cheerless, apparently even gloomy truth of atheism.[36]

The prelude to *Thus Spoke Zarathustra* describes Zarathustra's 'Untergang', an ambiguous phrase which is perhaps best translated as his *descent*, although it contains a more negative connotation as well - a sense of corruption and decline. After an ascetic withdrawal, having lived the life of a mountain hermit for ten years, Zarathustra wants to become human again, to share his wisdom with other human beings. The first person he meets on his way down is a saint. They laugh at each other and at each other's words, but it is a laughter that does not really laugh. Like sarcasm or other forms of 'reduced laughter', Zarathustra's laughter conveys a sense of individual superiority. He laughs at the elderly saint because he has apparently not yet been informed that God has died. It is a laughter that lessens and smoothes something - ignorance. From the very first sections it seems obvious that the book is not written in a gay and merry but in an ascetic mood. Exposure to the world implies risk of corruption. Although there is much talk of abundance and gaiety, Zarathustra's basic experience seems to be an ascetic, averting and defensive one.

This basic ambivalence at work is confirmed in the third section when he finally arrives at the market-square where he encounters not the laughing chorus of Rabelais but a hostile, almost diabolical crowd. The inhabitants laugh at Zarathustra's teachings, but their laughter is a negative, sarcastic one. 'And all the people laughed at Zarathustra', but their laughter lacks the positive element, it merely rejects. After having delivered one of his, albeit rather tedious, speeches, Nietzsche writes, he decides to fall silent due to lack of understanding.[37] It is an experience of estrangement rather than unification.[38] The laughter of the populace, instead of

---

[36] From the point of view of a truly gay science, the truth of atheism would be a gay instead of a gloomy one, a subject for laughter instead of bewilderment - perhaps God has laughed Himself to death.

[37] 'Als Zarathustra diese Worte gesprochen hatte, sah er wieder das Volk an und schwieg. 'Da stehen sie', sprach er zu seinem Herzen, 'da lachen sie: sie verstehen mich nicht, ich bin nicht der Mund für diese Ohren' (§ 5).

[38] Instead of expecting his hero to join in with popular laughter, that is, with the 'wisdom of folly', Nietzsche claims that wisdom is the whispering conversation of the lonely individual with himself amidst the hustle and bustle, the shouts and noises of the market-square (*Human, All Too Human II*, 'Mixed Opinions and Aphorisms', § 386).

revealing a merry truth, refuses Zarathustra's serious, vulnerable, ascetic truth - a truth of purity and ascent, an intimidating, eschatological truth - *Wehe! Es kommt die Zeit...* Ultimately, when Zarathustra's eschatological discourse is interrupted by the cries and laughter of the pack, he claims that the people are full of hatred, even when laughing - in fact, their laughter is cold as ice.[39] It is a negative laughter, full of hatred. But Zarathustra's soul is not corrupted by it: it retains its ascetic purity.

Then, a tight-rope walker makes his appearance, but his performance does not provoke general merriment. On the contrary, it reinforces the atmosphere of hatred and estrangement. Having gotten half way across, he is joined by what at first appears to be a gay and popular market-square figure.[40] But while shouting 'Go on, cripple-foot', he willingly causes the rope-walker's death. His laughter is far from gay, it is sardonic and completely negative. His voice is terrible ('fürchterlich'), and his whole performance dreadful and frightening. This is not gay, but somber laughter. Instead of transforming the apparently frightening and terrible into the comical, as gay laughter does, the apparently comical is transformed into the terrible. Yet many elements of his performance and speech somehow remind us of the gay, popular laughter of the medieval market-square: the verbal abuses - *Lahmfuß, Faultier, Schleichhändler, Bleichgesicht*, etc. - as well as his curvets and pranks. But before long, laughter gives way to gloomy terror and this is reflected in the tight-rope walker's final words before he dies[41]: the comical (the comic devil, pulling people's legs) gives way to the terrible (the gloomy devil, condemning them to hell and damnation). The pied jester reveals himself as the personification of something dreadful and diabolical, lurking behind a quasi-comic veil. A terrible emptiness lurks behind his apparently comic mask. Moreover, dark terror is omnipresent, the town is full of hatred, and Zarathustra only manages to escape because its inhabitants laugh their diabolical laugh at him.[42]

There is a significant difference between the popular heroism of Rabelais and the super-human heroism of Nietzsche. In the case of Rabelais, the 'great man' is

---

39 'Unbewegt ist meine Seele und hell wie das Gebirge am Vormittag. Aber sie meinen, ich sei kalt und ein Spötter in furchtbaren Späßen. Und nun blicken sie mich an und lachen: und indem sie lachen, hassen sie mich noch. Es ist Eis in ihrem Lachen' (§ 5).

40 '[E]in bunter Gesell, einem Possenreißer gleich'.

41 'Ich wußte es lange daß mir der Teufel ein Bein stellen werde. Nun schleppt er mich zur Hölle' (§ 6).

42 Later he regrets having visited the market-square. He now considers it a foolish act - why should the rabble's noise be of any concern to him? 'Als ich zum ersten Male zu den Menschen kam, da tat ich die Einsiedler-Torheit, die große Torheit: ich stellte mich auf den Markt... Mit dem neuen Morgen aber kam mir eine neue Wahrheit: da lernte ich sprechen "Was geht mich Markt und Pöbel und Pöbel-Lärm und lange Pöbel-Ohren an!"' (*Thus spoke Zarathustra*, 'Of Higher Ones', § 1).

profoundly democratic (p. 241). He eats, drinks, defecates, passes winds, laughs, argues, enters a dispute - in short he does all the things we human beings do, but he does so on a grand scale: 'Thus does the heroism of Rabelais' great men differ categorically from all other heroisms, which oppose the hero to the mass of other men as something out of the ordinary due to his lineage, his nature, the extraordinary demands and the exalted value he reads into life and the world (he is different, therefore, ... from the Nietzschean *Übermensch*)' (Bakhtin 1988, p. 241-242).

One of *Thus Spoke Zarathustra*'s highlights is the Feast of the Ass, apparently a comic scene borrowed from popular culture, a copy of one of the medieval *parodia sacra*. All of a sudden he finds his cave full of gaiety and laughter and at first he seems to enjoy the gaiety of his guests, but soon he deplores the fact that the ass's bray will corrupt the cries of jubilation of the 'higher ones'. They laugh, he says, but their laughter is not mine.[43] Then suddenly they fall silent and Zarathustra, to his bewilderment, witnesses the adoration of the ass. 'You rogues, you fools!', he cries, but in the end he seems to reconcile himself with the stubborn human inclination toward devotion - a lenient Moses, so to speak. Kunnas (1982) observes that Nietzsche's parody is negative instead of gay, it is sarcastic jeering, apparently part of an anti-christian campaign, and the opposite of cheerfulness. There is always something spiteful, terrible, denigrating in it. It is, at best, an intellectual kind of laughter, *lächeln* rather than *lachen* (p. 46).[44] Nietzsche is too serious to be truly comical. He is too much of an 'agelast' from a Bakhtinean point of view.

Although the acts of Zarathustra seem to imitate and parody the Gospels at several occasions, the comical aspect is in each case overcome by the constant presence of something negative and frightening. With regard to the speeches of Zarathustra, in *Von den Fliegen des Marktes - On the market's flies -* for instance man is faced with two gloomy options: either the desolate isolation of solitary existence, or the sarcastic laughter of the market-place. And other speeches, like the one on chastity, or the one on young and elderly women, again confirm Zarathustra's asceticism. Womanhood is interpreted in accordance with what Bakhtin refers to as the ascetic tradition, not at all in accordance with the popular, grotesque one. The supposedly abundant and insatiable nature of women is experienced as threatening and corruptive. Zarathustra's verbal abuses - 'the bitch sensuality', 'the ruttish female', etc. - are cynical and vicious rather than gay - *bitter ist auch noch das süßeste Weib*. In *Thus Spoke Zarathustra*, laughter is jeering and derision; its mockery is merely negative, at times even apocalyptical. In short, *Thus Spoke*

---

43 *Awakening*, § 1.

44 Cf. 'Je freudiger und sicherer der Geist wird, um so mehr verlernt er des laute Gelächter; dagegen quillt ihm ein geistiges Lächeln fortwährend auf', *Human, All Too Human II*, The Wanderer and his Shadow, § 173.

Zarathustra is written in a somber rather than a merry key. It conveys the kind of laughter that belongs to the Romantic period, it is 'gothic' in the nineteenth Century sense of the term, but quite incongruous with the gay laughter of the Renaissance it was perhaps intended to equal.

This is quite remarkable because another book, almost written in the same period, was devoted to *gay* laughter - *Die Fröhliche Wissenschaft* ,*The Gay Science*. Although as a novelist Nietzsche's performance is rather at odds with the principle of laughter put forward by Bakhtin, his philosophical position appears to be much more congenial with it, at least in some important aspects. As indicated above, although irony and sarcasm certainly play an important role throughout Nietzsche's writing, several experts on Nietzsche (for instance Van Tongeren 1989) have pointed to the fact that, in order to identify Nietzsche's basic technique of *eironeia* or dissimulation, 'parody' is preferable to 'irony'. Parody, or mockery by means of comic imitation, as a literary technique was refined and deepened by Nietzsche, who used it as a vehicle for self-examination and self-criticism. Indeed, Nietzsche emerges as a philosopher of laughter in the reception of his work in France (cf. notably Bataille, Klossowski, and Foucault).[45]

---

45 Pierre Klossowski (1963) refers to § 333 of *The Gay Science*, devoted to Spinoza's famous line: *Non ridere, non lugere, neque detestari, sed intelligere!* According to this famous phrase, the intellect is to gain prominence at the expense of 'the passions of the soul' - laughter, mourning and profanation. According to Klossowski, however, Spinoza's formula enabled Nietzsche to acquire a deeper understanding of his own mode of thinking as a philosophy of laughter, mourning and profanation. That is, instead of assenting to the predominance of one particular instinct or basic drive - conscious thought, or the will to knowledge - over the others, Nietzsche rather considered philosophical reflection to be a strategic situation in which several rival drives compete with each other - *Triebe, die mit einander kämpfen.* Why not admit that laughter, like seriousness, is a vehicle of truth? Why should the effort to understand something demand the suppression of these other basic motives, rather than relying on them as vehicles of truth of equal standing? Indeed, according to Nietzsche, a truth is nothing but a lie which temporarily manages to impose itself with, for instance, the help of a caste of priests. Indeed, Nietzsche considered the Church the supreme achievement of a caste of remarkably talented imposters, and it took a plebeian buffoon like Luther, the impossible, ridiculous monk, to destroy their masterpiece, the last and final legacy of the Roman Empire. Indeed, Nietzsche's philosophy of laughter is basically connected with his final idea of eternal recurrence. Monotheism resulted from the fact that the other deities, confronted with the ridiculous demand that one of them be regarded as the one and only God, laughed themselves to death. Yet a similar roar of laughter might restore them to life again. Eternal recurrence means the eternal recurrence of the gods - *Le rire est ici comme la suprême image, la suprême manifestation du divin réabsorbant les dieux prononcées, et prononçant les dieux par un nouvel éclat de rire; car si les dieux meurent de cet rire, c'est aussi de ce rire qui éclate du fond de l'entière vérité que les dieux renaissent* (p. 227).

Although Nietzsche's own laughter in some respect preserved its modern, reduced, individualistic vein, it prepared the way for a different and more lucid reading of the Plato dialogues, for an understanding of Socrates' performance, not from a modern perspective but from a Greek. We need Bakhtin to further develop and clarify Nietzsche's concept of 'gay science', much as we need Nietzsche to develop further and clarify Bakhtin's understanding and appreciation of the relationship between laughter and truth. In chapter three, therefore, we will continue our reading of Nietzsche's judgement of Socrates. Before doing so, however, we will look at two other philosophers of laughter.

6. SOLA EXPERIENTIA: BATAILLE

From the very beginning, laughter and parody play a prominent role in the writings of the French philosopher and novelist George Bataille.The opening line of *L'anus Solaire* for instance, claims that the world is thoroughly parodical.[46] Even human life itself is parodical. Indeed, the prominence of laughter is quite apparent in *L'expérience Interieure*, one of Bataille's most important works. According to Bataille, laughter is a phenomenon which still remains a mystery to us, and most philosophical efforts to explain its basic character, notably the one undertaken by Bergson, have failed. Although it is commonly believed that we laugh in order to express our feelings of joy, Bataille emphasizes that we also laugh when we are desperate, or for no reason at all. Indeed, he is considered a philosopher of laughter (Ten Kate 1994).

According to Ten Kate, it is Bataille's principal objective to criticize a philosophical tradition of long standing with Hobbes as its typical modern protagonist - a tradition which merely recognizes the negative, humiliating aspect of laughter, whereas Bataille himself emphasizes laughter's liberating impact and revealing force. Bataille views laughter as a instance of lucidity and revelation. Yet he also perceives a basic connection between laughter and fear, and stresses that both phenomena are genealogically akin - a view supported by Darwin and Freud. According to Darwin, the original function of laughter was to deter, although in the course of evolution it acquired a broader communicative function. There is something ambiguous or even preposterous in laughter, something which defies philosophical or scientific explanation. Moreover, Bataille does not merely *describe* the phenomenon of laughter but uses the language of laughter himself. He is laughing, notably at Hegel, and *L'expérience Interieure* is at times a parody[47] of

---

[46] 'Il est clair que le monde est purement parodique, c'est à dire que chaque chose qu'on regarde est la parodie d'une autre' (I, p. 82).

[47] A 'petite récapitulation comique' (p. 56).

Hegel's *The Phenomenology of the Spirit*. But is his laughter really 'gay', does it really laugh? In *L'expérience Interieure*, the word 'laughter' is said to occur 148 times (Ten Kate 1994), but does Bataille himself really laugh? What is the nature of his own laughter? Let us take a closer look.

L'expérience Interieure is indeed a phenomenology of laughter. Laughter is Bataille's basic 'inner' experience - an experience he claims to share with Nietzsche. Laughter is not merely comical, it is something divine, and Bataille discerns a basic truth or insight to which laughter exposes us. Laughter is an experience of sovereignty, but not of superiority. We do not laugh *at*, or simply humiliate the other, and laughter does not aim at submission or degradation of the other. Rather, it is an experience of connectedness and sympathy.

On the first page of *L'expérience Interieure* Bataille refers to Nietzsche's comment in *Ecce Homo* on *The Gay Science*. Nietzsche tells us that a new ideal presents itself, excessive and divine, which parodies the earnestness of morality and duty and pushes away the curtain of tragedy. Indeed, to witness the somber protagonists of tragedy and laugh, notwithstanding a profound understanding and sympathy, is truly divine.

According to Bataille, laughter contains a basic critique of dogmatism and a profound understanding of tragedy. It transcends and questions the limits imposed on us by a prevalent and established dogmatism, and defies all forms of authority. This is its negative function. But this function reveals a basic truth concerning human existence. Laughter is a non-tragic way of discerning the fearful truth of tragedy. As such, it is not an experience of violence but of sympathy.

Paradoxically, while questioning all forms of authority, the experience of laughter itself becomes our sole authority. Laughter is basically an experience of contestation - laughter *is* contestation. This experience of contestation, however, has to be 'dramatized', has to be lived, for otherwise we would not really be able to laugh.[48] Laughter is primarily a practical or dramatic rather than a discursive phenomenon. It reveals in a dramatic way the actual impotence of dogmatic power. Indeed, practical laughter defies the dogmatism of language itself and silences the established discursive mode. And yet, the revelation of laughter is experienced *suddenly* - it is a sudden, decisive breakthrough in a continuous struggle against dogmatism. A basic truth is revealed, and dogmatism is overcome by the anti-authoritarian authority of this overwhelming experience, which is our sole authority - *sola experientia*. It is the bacchanal, excessive plot of an ascetic effort. The morality of laughter contains a lucid insight regarding a basic, Dionysian truth - *Dionysos philosophos*, the laughter of the true, bacchanalian philosopher that transcends and defies all established limits. This insight is a basic truth, a wisdom of which it is impossible

---

48 cf. 'Une nécessité comique à dramatiser. L'expérience demeurait inaccessible si nous ne savions dramatiser', (p. 136).

to speak without being ridiculed.[49] But this is the negative laughter of ridicule which is completely different from the divine laughter of the true philosopher, who laughs in an unprecedented way, laughing with his whole body, no longer hiding himself behind his discursive mask, rejecting Descartes' device - *Larvatus prodeo* - and actually taking the floor *un*masked. The truth of laughter does not allow for any justification through argument; instead, it justifies itself, being its own authority.

Furthermore, as was already hinted above, there is a basic connection between laughter and fear. Whereas Descartes remains basically fearful, his fear was merely *suspended* by argument, while hiding behind a discursive mask, the philosophy of laughter finally transcends the boundaries of fear. Its gaiety is excessive and generous, and implies the complete loss of certainty.

In *L'expérience Interieure*, Bataille recalls a particular biographical dramatization of true laughter. The dramatic scene occurred when, after an extended period of profound religious piety, his life was shattered by, and dissolved itself in laughter - an experience of revelation, revealing the ground of things.[50] He had read Bergson's treatise on laughter and was about to meet him in London. He was irritated by the book because he felt it failed to explore the true meaning of laughter. He himself considered it a kind of euphoria, providing him with what was to become his key question throughout his philosophical life, but also a depressing and chaotic experience, as if he had been laughing too excessively. It had finally dawned on him that the ridiculous is simply a truth we do not yet dare to recognize and advocate. He eventually rejected Hegel and embraced Nietzsche, who claimed that any 'truth' which does not provoke ridicule and laughter at least once should be regarded as false. Hegel's philosophy of productive labour and discourse was to give way to a philosophy of laughter. Laughter is both a fundamental contestation, exposing the basic frailty of an established truth, and a dawn of day, liberating one from fixed boundaries and ties. Fear is overcome by laughter but remains its origin. Laughter is a sovereign mode of thought, revealing the ground of things (cf. p. 213), and there is no basic difference between laughing at something and understanding its truth. Instead of considering certain scenes or themes are comical and others non-comical, we should recognize that being *as such* is profoundly comical. In the genre of comedy laughter is limited. In philosophical meditation, however, it is limitless (p. 220). And although laughter is considered an experience of sovereignty, Bataille's concept of sovereignty might perhaps be the cause of some misunderstanding. It does not entail the exercise of power, let alone in the sense of etatism. Basically, it is an experience of revolt, of transcending servitude.

---

[49] 'J'ai du divin une expérience si folle qu'on rira de moi si j'en parle' (p. 45).

[50] 'Le rire était révélation, ouvrait le fond des choses' (p. 80).

A substantial part of another of Bataille's works, *Le Coupable*, is devoted to the divine character of laughter, *La Divinité du Rire*, a text which in fact summarizes Bataille's philosophy of laughter. While everyone is at work, he claims, the philosopher is laughing - a laughter which is somehow considered divine, striking us from 'outside'. Whereas the philosophy of labour, i.e. Hegel, aims at suppressing laughter, Bataille (following Nietzsche) aims at identifying philosophy with laughter, at recognizing laughter as philosophy's basic mode of thought. Basically, laughter is lucid contestation, where contestation refers to its negative and lucidity to its positive aspect. Philosophical laughter is a kind of ecstacy, a laughter 'which does not really laugh'.[51] Furthermore, according to Bataille, labour basically means assaulting nature, subjecting it to human objectives. Poetry, on the other hand, means subjecting oneself to nature, it is a kind of idleness and passivity, a submission to divine authority. Like labour, laughter takes a more provocative stance towards nature rather than submitting to it. Its sovereignty and triumph implies questioning nature in a fundamental way. The divine freedom of laughter aims at the subjection of nature rather than submission to it.[52] But whereas labour remains a form of servitude, only laughter is truly proud, sovereign and triumphant. Laughter overcomes not only nature as such but also general human misery being the 'natural' condition of man. He who finally overcomes (human) nature is able to laugh in a divine manner.

Moreover, in *La Divinité du Rire* Bataille recalls another biographical scene of laughter. He describes how as a youth he once climbed mount Etna. As night was already approaching, he entered a mountain hut surrounded by the blackest lava in order to escape from the cold and violent mountain wind. Before going to bed, however, he went outside once more, in order to satisfy a certain physical need - *pour aller satisfaire un besoin* (p. 366). The terrible cold strikes him and he is overcome by fatigue. Yet he longs to climb the mountain slope still further in order to approach its summit, its abyss. Passing the lee that had been protecting him, he is seized by the roaring wind and, finding himself a stone's throw from the crater, the darkness no longer subdues the excessive horror of the sight. At first he shrinks back from it, but then musters his courage. The wind is so violent and the horror at seeing the volcano's summit is so intense, that it is almost unbearable. Never before had the not-me, the inhuman aspect of nature seized him with such intensity. And yet, although his physical exhaustion prevented him from laughing, he was convinced that what had made him climb the volcano's summit was nothing but unlimited laughter. At last, he laughed.

---

51 'Le rire de l'extase ne *rit pas*' (p. 348).

52 'La divine liberté du rire veut la nature soumise à l'homme, et non l'homme à la nature' (p. 356).

This scene is pervaded by what Bakhtin referred to as the grotesque. Terror is transformed into laughter. The terrible and diabolical - the mouth of hell, inhuman nature - is transformed *through* laughter. Still, Bataille's *individual* laughter seems akin to terror, to a greater extent than Renaissance laughter. Although Bataille recognizes that laughter unites and connects, there is still something individual and Nietzsche-like (or Zarathustra-like) in the way he laughs. His laughter has not yet distanced itself from what Bakhtin refers to as the 'sardonic laughter of the eccentric individual'. His laughter is not vulgar but aims at something divine. It is, as Bataille stresses in *Le Rire de Nietzsche*, Zarathustra's laughter, a 'sacred' mode of laughter, revealing something terrible namely the *absence* of God and the basic insight of eternal recurrence.[53] Nevertheless, Bataille adds to our philosophical understanding of laughter, and his insights will prove crucial in subsequent chapters, most notably the one on Luther.

7. UNEASY LAUGHTER: FOUCAULT

As has been emphasized by Michel de Certeau (1994) and others, Michel Foucault, following in the footsteps of Nietzsche and Bataille, was also a philosopher of laughter, someone who wrote in a laughing mood. Yet, although his *philosophy of laughter* shares several basic insights with the ones previously discussed, his *philosophical laughter* seems to be of a peculiar nature - and quite in accordance with his remarkable views and methods. Let us *re*read those passages in his work where his laughter manifests itself, i.e. *The History of Madness* (1961/1972), *Words and Things* (1966) and his essay on Nietzsche (1971).[54]

In *The History of Madness*,[55] Foucault emphasizes that the Renaissance experience of madness differed considerably from the 'classical' and 'modern' ones (cf. Zwart 1995). Madness was considered to be basically akin to laughter - an experience which is retained in the French word *folie*, meaning both madness and folly. Furthermore, madness/folly was held to be omnipresent and inescapable. Another distinctive feature of the Renaissance experience of madness/folly was its fundamental connection with truth. There was something lucid, something revealing in laughter. Madness/folly revealed the futile and ridiculous nature of that which,

---

[53] Note that Klossowski (1963) connected the idea of eternal recurrence and laughter not only with the disappearance but also with the joyful *recurrence* of the gods: both epochal events are accompanied by laughter.

[54] Finally, in chapter five, I will turn to his lecture on frank or unrestricted speech - *Parresia* (1983).

[55] All references refer to the French revised edition: *Folie et déraison: histoire de la folie à l'âge classique*. Paris: Gallimard, 1972.

according to the official established views, should count as serious and important. It was a kind of wisdom that turned official knowledge into mere folly, a profound insight and truth, a striking and revealing view on life. In short, it was an experience of madness/folly that Foucault felt was articulated brilliantly in Erasmus' *Praise of Folly*. Foucault stresses, however, that the Renaissance experience of madness/folly was in itself ambiguous and unstable, containing both a tragic and a critical aspect. Whereas *Praise of Folly* primarily represented laughter's critical aspect ('folly'), the tragic aspect ('madness') notably emerged in the comical/terrible paintings of Jeroen Bosch. The critical aspect indicates that gay laughter reveals certain aspects of the world that are usually neglected and concealed by more serious 'games of truth'. The tragic aspect entails a somber, threatening and violent truth which is subdued by gay laughter. In the subsequent 'classical' and 'modern' experiences of madness, however, this delicate union of the tragic and the gay is lost. According to Foucault, the modern experience of madness is one-sided because the basic connection between madness and folly as well as between madness and truth has been obscured.

Already in the 'classical' experience of madness, which gained sway during the seventeenth century, madness/folly is excluded from official life and discourse. The human subject is forced to abandon his basic ambivalence and to 'choose' between madness/folly and reason, to commit himself to official truth. He is no longer allowed to suspend or ridicule the serious truth of reason. Those who persist, are submitted to certain practices of power, like forced labour, in order to transform them into rational subjects. Moreover, the choice between madness and reason is presented as a *moral* choice, preceding rational discourse as its basic condition, while the houses of correction that emerged during this period are considered 'fortresses of the moral order' (cf. Zwart 1995). Although the threatening, tragic aspect of madness is incarcerated, the critical aspect as such maintains itself, but is radically divorced from laughter: it becomes serious and rationalistic, or satirical and sarcastic at best, but it is no longer experienced as gay, as *folly*. Gay laughter is reduced to satire. During the modern period, the efforts to discipline and normalize madness were intensified due to the emergence of the human sciences, notably modern psychiatry. And yet, Foucault maintains, in the margins of established discourse, some isolated voices manage to retain this experience of the basic connection between madness, folly and criticism which was omnipresent during the Renaissance - authors like Nietzsche and Bataille. Their writings, quite at odds with established truth regimes, are grounded in a basic experience of laughter, transcending the limits of serious, scientific or philosophical discourse and basically contesting established morality. They recognize the basic connection between folly and truth and between the tragic and critical aspects of laughter, and this sense of connection is the basic experience which constitutes the ground and origin of their philosophy. But before turning to 'epistemological' laughter as it emerges in *Words and Things* and to Foucault's appreciation of Nietzsche, let us read some aspects of Foucault's account of the Renaissance experience of laughter in *The History of Madness* more carefully.

At the end of the fifteenth Century, Foucault claims, the grimace of eschatological fear gave way to the cheerful countenance of folly. And until it was finally subjected to reason in the course of the seventeenth century, folly remained connected with all the major experiences of the Renaissance (p. 18). The literary and pictorial image that indicated the emergence of its reign was the 'Ship of fools', depicted by Brandt the poet, Bosch the painter and many of their contemporaries - an image referred to by Foucault as folly's 'satirical vessel' (p. 19). Instead of being caged in prisons and fool's towers, the world's fools were suddenly granted a wandering existence and dispersed all over the country side. In the theatre they acted as guardians and spokesmen of truth while outside the theatre they became the heroes of popular fairs and feasts with their 'spontaneous religious parodies' (p. 25). Moreover, many foolish academical games and disputes -*discours bouffons* - emphasized folly's proximity to truth - indeed, folly seemed closer to truth than reason herself.

Even death was deprived of its seriousness. Fear and death were ridiculed and conquered by permanent irony and laughter. Gay madness succeeded in overcoming death, and terrifying gothic symbolism was demolished. Notwithstanding its absurd features, folly emerged as a form of knowledge, nullifying the diabolic and apocalyptic triumph of the Antichrist that had intimidated the late Middle Ages. The world regained its gay and cheerful aspect, and abounded in folly to such an extent that, as Erasmus phrased it in *Praise of Folly*, a thousand minds like Democritus would not suffice to mock at it. The world's terrors were subdued by an almost superhuman and divine ('Olympic') laughter.

In short, Foucault's account of Renaissance laughter is remarkably similar to Bakhtin's in several respects. Even the Silenus, containing something quite different from what is suggested by its grotesque outward appearance, is mentioned by Foucault (p. 42). Indeed, folly was a paradoxical form of truth, and folly and wisdom were fundamentally akin. Foucault emphasizes, however, that Renaissance folly was not *merely* gay. In itself, it was a form of moral satire, of moral criticism. Folly was a critical, ironical experience, it conveyed a moral lesson (p. 36-37). Renaissance laughter was critical, ironical, even didactic. And its connection to the 'tragic' experience of madness was temporary and unstable. In the course of the seventeenth century folly came to be reduced to criticism and satire proper, whereas the tragic experience of madness was obscured (although never completely abolished) by reason. In short, the Renaissance experience of truth was short-lived and was to give way to the rectitude of rational thought before long. Folly was stripped and disarmed and appropriated by reason. A similar development is described by Bakhtin. Unlike Bakhtin, however, Foucault stresses that even Renaissance laughter was never *really* gay. It never succeeded in standing on its own legs but remained ambiguous and vulnerable, and its final defeat was inevitable - Renaissance laughter was a brief episode in the history of progress and the incessant labour of reason. Ultimately, because of reason's decisive *coup de force* in the seventeenth century (p. 56), the truth of laughter was subjected to the truth of reason as one of its instruments or devices (i.e. satire). It no longer conveyed a truth of its own.

Notwithstanding this deplorable plot, it is important to note that Foucault clearly recognized the *moral* significance of folly. It was basically a form of *moral* criticism. The values of a certain age, a certain morality, were questioned.[56] Moreover, Foucault seems to suggest that, even in a rather delicate position, subdued and instrumentalized by reason and put to the service of reason's objectives, folly's basic irony and playfulness managed to maintain itself. Yet in comparison to Bakhtin's understanding of laughter, the forms of laughter that Foucault portrays are never really gay: there is always something hesitant, something of ironical or satirical at work in them. Unlike Bakhtin's conception of 'true laughter', Foucault's laughter is never simply gay but is always connected with a basic sense of uneasiness. Folly remains unstable and vulnerable and it is ultimately overcome by seriousness and fear rather than conquering them. In fact, reason and seriousness had infected folly from its very beginning. Throughout his work, Foucault remains faithful to this experience of *uneasy laughter* which he already presents in his history of madness.

It is not at all astonishing that laughter (or: folly) gained such a prominent position in a book devoted to the history of madness. It is astonishing, however, that laughter gained such a prominent position in a subsequent book on the pre-history, or rather, the 'archeology' of the modern human sciences. Laughter is the *alpha* and the *omega* of *Words and Things*.[57] It is a basic experience of truth, of revelation and contestation, surpassing the truths of modern sciences and revealing their limited, temporary and vulnerable nature. The very first lines of Foucault's book describe an experience of revelation, of laughter, an experience which is revoked in the final sentence of its decisive, penultimate chapter - the famous one on the death of the modern human subject.

In the very first lines of *Words and Things*, Foucault explains that the book was written because of a text by Borges describing a Chinese encyclopedia which conveyed a way of perceiving and understanding the world quite different from that to which we are accustomed: a perception and arrangement of things which at first glance is bound to strike us as utterly absurd and ridiculous. The laughter evoked by

---

56 'Folie, où sont mises en question la valuers d'un autre âge... d'un autre morale...' (p. 48).

57 All references are to: *Les mots et les choses. Une archéologie des sciences humaines* (Paris: Gallimard, 1966).

the reading of this text, however, is not mere mockery. Rather, it is *uneasy laughter*, for it seems to contest in a very basic manner apparently solid and quasi self-evident practices of perception. It is a kind of laughter that is accompanied by discontent.[58] The taken-for-granted foundation of our language and knowledge, of our 'words and things', proved to be contestable.[59]

This uneasy laughter reflects the general uneasiness that emerged at the beginning of the sixteenth century, when apparently incontestable structures of knowledge and argumentation were suddenly transformed into something basically ridiculous and unconvincing. This event was represented by Cervantes' unsurpassed novel *Don Quixote*. Foucault emphasizes, however, that we now find ourselves on the threshold of another fundamental transformation, affecting the very foundation of knowledge, language and perception. Modern man's 'anthropological slumber' (i.e. the basic conviction that the Cartesian *ego* or the Kantian subject is the ground of knowledge) is on the verge of being interrupted by an epistemological 'dawn of day': the recognition that 'man' as we have come to understand him is but a temporary fold, a recent invention and bound to disappear completely without a trace. Those who remain unwilling to think without presupposing that it is the human subject who does the thinking are to be confronted with a philosophical laughter - *un rire philosophique* (p. 354) - a laughter which interrupts the monotonous, anthropological discourse of the modern human sciences, and forces us to recognize that its ground is absent.[60]

Around 1970, Foucault's *archeology* of medical, psychiatrical, psychological, etc. knowledge is transformed into a *genealogy* of power. This transformation is already apparent in his transitional essay on Nietzsche ('Nietzsche, la généalogie, l'histoire') in which genealogy is presented as a kind of laughter, a form of historical research which *laughs* at the metaphysical quest for lofty and divine 'origins' (Foucault 1971). Instead of searching for the origin of things in the sense of *Ursprung*, genealogy points to their origin in the sense of *Herkunft*. That is, it reveals the vile, ridiculous and accidental features of historical beginnings, degrading the metaphysical, top-down account and replacing it with bottom-up accounts, drawing attention to bodily and material forces and circumstances at work. In *On the*

---

[58] 'Ce texte de Borges m'a fait rire longtemps, non sans un malaise certain et difficile à vaincre' (p. 9)

[59] 'La gêne qui fait rire quand on lit Borges est apparentée sans doute au profond malaise de ceux dont le language est ruiné' (p. 10).

[60] Cf. Nietzsche, *Human, All Too Human I*, § 16 - 'From the point of view of historical philosophy, the *Ding-an-sich* merits homeric laughter', thus expressing the awareness that, once its history, its genealogy is revealed, such an idea, such an effort to save or repair the classical, eighteenth century picture of the world is defenseless against a historical understanding.

Genealogy of Morals, for instance, the ascetic ideal is connected with certain basic, physiological instincts. Unlike *Ursprung* (origin in the sense of ideal foundations) the *Herkunft* of things proves to be something unstable, ridiculous and accidental. Genealogy laughs at metaphysics, just as Nietzsche-the-adult laughed at Nietzsche-the-youth who still bothered himself with the question whether God was to be considered the origin (*Ursprung*) of evil. Historical beginnings are vile and accidental, rather than lofty and divine. When it comes to origins, true history - genealogy - points to the body, to nutrition and digestion, to physical constitution rather than looking for a metaphysical ground. Genealogy is a 'gay', 'coarse', and 'uncivilized' attitude.

Moreover, genealogy is parody: it parodies the attitude towards history referred to by Nietzsche in the second of his *Untimely Meditations* (1874) as the 'monumentalistic' attitude. According to this attitude, history is to be perceived as a series of monumental achievements. The history of philosophy, for instance, is presented as a sequence of astonishing intellectual highlights. By totally neglecting the circumstances that produced them, these highlights are transformed into something incomprehensible and divine instead of being interpreted as the accidental effect or *outcome* of a particular and contingent constellation of forces and conditions. Instead of rejecting this attitude as he had done in 1874, Nietzsche came to parody it, using it in a way that defied its original purpose. At first, he too seems to treat the history of philosophy as a series of astonishing highlights - Heracleitus, Socrates, Plato, etc. Yet he ridicules the very predecessors with which he most intimately identifies himself (such as Socrates and Luther) instead of venerating them as would have been expected in view of the genre conventions of monumentalism. The monumentalistic attitude is degraded and transformed into its parodical counterpart. Furthermore, genealogy is the comic reversal of the nostalgic nineteenth century practice of adopting substitute identities, of feeling at home in historical circumstances long since forgotten, turning history into a fool's game or masquerade. He considers Wagner a perfect personification of such a desperate view on history which Nietzsche exposes to ridicule. History is acted out once more, but is inadvertently transformed into buffoonery. Foucault refers to the famous section 223 of *Beyond Good and Evil* already cited above, where it is claimed that only as history's buffoons, in a carnivalesque mixture of styles and disguises, can modern man hope to attain his share of originality.

In *The History of Madness* laughter emerged as a form of moral criticism and truth (Renaissance laughter) and subsequently as a playful device and instrument of reason (classical or satirical laughter). And in *Words and things* laughter emerged as an epistemological event, an experience of revelation. Subsequently, however, laughter seems to disappear from Foucault's writings. Although genealogy is identified with laughter in the transitional essay on Nietzsche of 1971, parody and gay science seem to be extinguished completely in the genealogical studies that Foucault actually embarked upon during the seventies. *Discipline and Punish* conveys a serious, even gloomy mood. The spectacular punishment related in the first chapter still uses the grotesque language of dismemberment - a human body is treated as fowl or pork in a kitchen, with this difference that the convict suffering such a treatment remains conscious and alive, almost until the very end. He is boiled in tallow and pitch, poached, drawn and quartered, cut to pieces and roasted. Yet, before long the grotesque forms of torture give way to the noncorporal punishment of panoptism. The panoptic society bears a grim countenance and faces grim resistance. Laughter is overcome by the omnipresence of power, and becomes powerless or even absent. The disquieting transformation of human bodies into mechanical, machine-like artifacts is not, as Bergson's analysis would imply, corrected by laughter (perhaps Foucault is implicitly questioning or even rejecting Bergson's view on classical laughter). In Foucault's impressive account of the massive struggle between panoptism and disciplinary power on the one hand and popular or peasant resistance on the other, *the* outstanding manifestation of popular resistance (namely parodical laughter) seems absent.

This twilight of laughter is to last for a decade. In the fall of 1983, Foucault presents a lecture at Berkeley on 'parresia' or unrestricted speech in which modern criticism is presented as a genre whose history was intimately connected with that of laughter for centuries. Special attention is given to one particular tradition of laughter called Cynicism. A similar and simultaneous effort was made by Peter Sloterdijk (1983) in his *Critique of Cynical Reason*. Apparently, several basic genres of laughter can be distinguished. Whereas in the nineteenth century Kierkegaard and others stressed the importance of irony, in this book I side with Nietzsche and Bakhtin who emphasized the importance of parody. I will even contend that, in view of the present moral condition as presented in chapter one, parody must be regarded as the most decisive genre of laughter as far as its moral significance is concerned. In the next chapters I will stress the importance of parodical laughter in three remarkable cases of moral transformation. Finally, in the concluding section of this book (chapter 5, § 4) the relationship between cynicism[61] as presented by Sloterdijk and Foucault, and parody as presented by Bakhtin and Nietzsche will be discussed.[62]

---

61 Or, rather, 'kynicism' (Sloterdijk 1983).

62 'Satire' (or 'classical' laughter) could be mentioned as a fourth genre of laughter in its own right, although it is not taken into consideration here.

Chapter 3

Judging Socrates

He pretends to people and always has his joke with them,
believe me, dear drinking companions! (Alcibiades].

CALLICLES: *Tell me, Chaerephon, is Socrates in earnest or joking?*
CHAEREPHON: *In my opinion, Callicles, he is in deadly*
earnest, but there is nothing like asking him.
CALLICLES: *By heaven, that is just what I am anxious to do. Tell*
me Socrates, are we to consider you serious now or jesting? For if
you are serious and what you say is true, then surely the life of
us mortals must be turned upside down and apparently we are
everywhere doing the opposite of what we should.[1]

1. MOCKING ASCLEPIUS

In the previous chapter I already pointed out a particular entry in *The Gay Science* where Nietzsche refers to Socrates' final words, cited by Plato in *Phaedo*: 'Crito, we owe a cock to Asclepius'. At first these 'final words' seem rather ridiculous, but Nietzsche indicates that they in fact convey Socrates' basic view on human existence - a view quite in accord with the line of argument elaborated in the course of the dialogue. These words imply the view that life is a kind of illness, and death the soul's recovery to a state of health. Socrates, about to die (that is, about to recover from this illness called life) owes the customary tribute to the deity of medicine, Asclepius. His last words contain a jest.[2] He is, in a very fundamental way, a jester, and to jest is Socrates' way of revealing truth.[3] Let us submit *Phaedo* to a more careful *re*reading.

---

1 *Gorgias*, 481b (Plato 1961, p. 264).

2 Cf. De Unamuno (1954): 'Life is ... a comedy for those who think... Those who put thought above feeling die comically... The mockers are those who die comically (p. 315-316).

3 In fact, as Bakhtin points out, the 'gay death' plays an important, liberating part in the Rabelais imagery as well (p. 51).

There are many more instances of parody in *Phaedo* than we might at first expect. For instance, when the cup of poison is handed over to him, Socrates asks the prison guard whether he should poor a libation to some deity from his cup of poison - an act of mocking or even insulting the deity involved - and asks a question which provokes a comical debate with the guard whether the amount spilled by the libation would in fact lessen the effect of the poison, etcetera. Socrates' speech acts, abounding in laughter, represent a genre which may perhaps be compared to 'the language which mocks and insults the deity and which was part of the ancient comic cults' (Bakhtin 1968, p. 16). Indeed, comic pledges and oaths belonged to ancient cultic forms of abuse and derision (p. 352).[4] Socrates is parodying what should have been a tragic scene and therefore, by parodying the conventions of tragedy, Socrates is contesting the predominant view of life and death articulated by this literary genre, for tragedy presupposes the affirmation of life as a value in itself. It presupposes that the hero clings to life, attaching a very positive value to human life, and yet discerns that he has encountered something of more value even than life itself, something for which he is willing to sacrifice his own life - a gesture which would not be tragic at all if he did not sincerely appreciate being alive. Socrates, however, claims that, from a truly philosophical (that is, rational) point of view, the tragic understanding of life must be considered untenable.[5] As Nietzsche writes in *The Birth of Tragedy*, he leaves this world without a trace of the natural 'instinctive' fear of death.[6] Parody is the path toward liberating oneself from this natural fear of death which is presupposed by tragedy[7]. Socrates emerges as tragedy's major foe, where tragedy refers not merely to a certain literary genre but to a certain form of moral subjectivity, to a tragic way of life. Socrates' rejection of tragedy implies a rejection

---

[4] These abuses, Bakhtin claims, were ambivalent: they humiliated, but at the same time revived and are mistakenly considered as indicating that the pagan convictions were losing credibility. In the contrary, these rites and cults of laughter still had to be permitted as a parallel to official christian cults long after the more serious pagan celebrations had vanished.

[5] And this is, of course, deplored by Nietzsche, who initially tended to consider Socrates a spokesman of optimism. Cf. his remark that the death of tragedy was due to Socratic *optimism* (*The Birth of Tragedy*, § 14).

[6] '[O]hne den natürlichen Schauder vor dem Tode... er ging in den Tod, mit jener Ruhe, mit der er nach Platos Schilderung als der letzte der Zecher im frühen Tagesgrauen das Symposion verläßt...' (I § 78).

[7] Cf. Kierkegaard (1989): 'Socrates' death is not basically tragic ... because death has no validity for Socrates. For the tragic hero, death has validity ... Admittedly the tragic hero does not fear death, but still ... it has validity if he is condemned to die' (p. 271). The only punishment Socrates considered appropriate was a punishment that was no punishment, one that amounted to nothing. The death penalty was no punishment for him because he did not know whether death was something to be feared.

of established moral subjectivity, of an unexamined life, affirmed and taken-for-granted life in an unreflected manner, of an 'instinctive' way of living.[8] This contributed to the death of tragedy, allowing for unprecedented forms of moral subjectivity to establish themselves.[9]

There is one particular passage in *Phaedo* where the parody becomes rather obvious:

'You, Simmias and Cebes, and the rest', he [Socrates] said, 'will go hereafter, each in his own time; but I am now already, as a tragedian would say, called by fate, and therefore it is about time for me to go to bath; for I think it is better to bathe before drinking the poison, that the women may not have the trouble of bathing the corpse' (p. 393).

This is parody: Socrates is parodying the tragic conventions in order to reveal the vulnerability of the view of life conveyed by them. That we are in fact dealing with an instance of parody is already indicated by the phrase 'as a tragedian would say'. And indeed, the parodical nature of Socrates' speech acts cannot escape us here. A tragic hero might utter something like 'I am called by fate', but would never add 'and therefore it is about time for me to go to bath' - at least not for this reason. Once we have noticed the jest, the parody, it can hardly escape us. Socrates aims at destroying the persuasiveness of the tragic view of life from which the Athenians (at least some sections of society, notably the youth from the higher social strata) were already distancing themselves at that time. Indeed, there appears to be something parodical in *everything* he says.

And this is rather remarkable, for in his lectures on the history of philosophy Hegel refers to Socrates' farewell-scene as *truly tragic* - 'Das Schicksal des Sokrates ist so echt tragisch' (1971, p. 514; cf. 'Socrates' fate was profoundly tragic', p. 446).[10] Philosophers have been reading Plato's lighthearted dialogues with too much

---

8 With his rejection of an instinctive life, Socrates condemned both the estabished art and the established ethic - 'ebeso die bestehende Kunst wie die bestehende Ethik: wohin er seie früfenden Blicke richtet, sieht er den Mangel der Einsicht und die Macht des Wahns und schließt aus diesem Mangel auf die innerliche Verkehrtheit und Verwerflichkeit des Vorhandenen. Von diesem einen Punkte aus glaubte Sokrates das Dasein korrigieren zu müssen: [er tritt] als der Vorläufer einer ganz anders gearteten Kultur, Kunst und Moral in [die Griechische] Welt hinein' (*The Birth of Tragedy*, § 13).

9 '[D]as, woran die Tragödie starb, der Sokratismus der Moral, die Dialektik, Genügsamkeit und Heiterkeit des theoretischen Menschen...' (*The Birth of Tragedy*, 'Introduction: Essay in Self-Criticism', § 1).

10 His fate was tragic not in the superficial sense of the term, Hegel claims, for instead of being merely deplorable, it constituted the collision between two basic moral forces, each of them to be considered as justified in their own right. Although I agree that

earnestness, so it seems, they noticed the irony, but the parody escaped them. But surely he is joking, even when he seems to be speaking in earnest! His audience, however, did notice it: 'By Zeus, Socrates, I don't feel much like laughing just now, but you made me laugh', says Simmias after listening to one of Socrates' arguments shortly before his death.

The following argument reads like a specimen of Rabelais-like parody rather than of serious rational debate:

SOCRATES: Do you agree [that beautiful things are beautiful through beauty]?
CEBES: I do.
SOCRATES:And great things are great and greater things greater by greatness, and smaller things by smallness?
CEBES: Yes.
SOCRATES: And you would not accept the statement, if you were told that one man was greater or smaller than another by a head, but would insist that every greater thing is greater than another by nothing else than greatness, and that it is greater by reason of greatness, and that which is smaller is smaller by nothing else than smallness and is smaller by reason of smallness. For you would, I think, be afraid of meeting with the retort, if you said that a man was greater or smaller than another by a head, first that the greater is greater and the smaller is smaller by the same thing [the head], and secondly, that the greater man is greater by a head, which is small, and that it is a monstrous thing that one is great by something that is small. Would you not be afraid of this?
And Cebes laughed and said: 'Yes, I should'... (p. 347).

At a certain point in the course of his argument, even Socrates himself laughs and says: 'I seem to be speaking like a legal document, but it really is very much as I say' - a *parodical* laugh indeed, frankly identifying the official speech genre whose figures of speech are borrowed and whose conventions are purposely mocked by its comic double (p. 351).

If submitted to a closer reading, many more instances of parody can be revealed. It is to Nietzsche's merit that he drew attention to Socrates' basic technique: *incipit parodia.* Of course, in *Phaedo* there are many instances of argument, irony, and other modes of thought as well, but parody seems fundamental. Many apparently serious arguments and conjectures, for instance, are bound to strike us as rather ridiculous and unconvincing if we read them carefully and unprejudiced. Moreover, we can discern several instances of irony but they likewise seem less important and do not

---

Socrates was a figure of 'worldhistorical significance' (p. 441) and that his performance exemplified a moral collision, I will contend that this decisive turning point in history was comic rather than tragic, that all crucial moral transformations are brought about by laughter and that Socrates' speech acts belong to a comic rather than a tragic genre.

contain the truly Socratic laugh. Irony implies that one is in fact saying the opposite of what one really wants to convey. It is a kind of 'reduced laughter', as Bakhtin calls it (p. 120), 'laughter without laughter', a 'modernized' laughter *which does not laugh* (p. 45), which has lost its regenerative power and joyful tone (p. 38). It is a mode of laughter directed at utterances rather than genres, merely expressing a negative, critical attitude. Parody, however, implies laughing in a more frank and generous way, contesting the established truth in a more jovial and fundamental way - the truth, not of a certain proposition, but of the speech genre as a whole.

This is how Socrates is presented by Nietzsche in *Twilight of the Idols*: everything he says seems exaggerated, *buffo*, he undermines a certain speech genre by caricaturizing it.[11] His very appearance marks the victory of something popular and vulgar. What was the meaning of this event, Nietzsche asks himself, how could aristocratic sensibility be overcome by vulgarity, disguised as 'dialectics'? According to the aristocratic mind, whatever is in need of justification ought to raise suspicion! Indeed, Socrates was a buffoon who succeeded in having himself taken seriously.[12] What had happened was that the spokesmen of the official moral regime finally came to recognize that the peaceful coexistence between two incompatible forms of moral subjectivity (their strategy of containment, applied to the 'vulgar' truth of popular laughter), had come to an end: established morality was faced with a parodical and apparently overpowering and irresistible intrusion of laughter into the official modes of speech.

At this point, having moderated the importance of irony in Socrates' performance, it nevertheless seems unavoidable that we take up Kierkegaard's reading of the Socratic dialogues. In *The Concept of Irony with Continual Reference to Socrates* he focussed on irony rather than parody as Socrates' basic device. According to Kierkegaard, irony refers to a basic attitude as well as to a certain figure of speech. As a figure of speech, irony basically means saying the opposite of what one has in mind (the 'phenomenon' is the opposite of the 'essence', the 'idea'). For instance, saying something earnestly that is not meant in earnest. As an attitude, it is the expression of a philosophical 'principle' referred to by Hegel as subjectivity.[13] As such, it is absolutely negative, devouring everything without being able to establish anything. It conveys the sense that, in the eyes of the ironic subject, the actual has lost its validity but does not suggest an alternative. Moreover, irony conveys a sense

---

11 'Alles ist übertrieben, *buffo*, Karikatur an ihm' (*Twilight of the Idols*, § 4).

12 'Was geschieht da eigentlich? Vor allem wird damit ein *vornehmer* Geschmack besiegt: der Pöbel kommt mit der Dialektik obenauf... Socrates war der Hanswurst, der sich *ernstnehmen machte*: was geschah da eigentlich?' (*The Twilight of the Idols*, § 5)

13 When Kierkegaard says that *Phaedo*, for example, is ironical rather than tragic, he does not mean the ironic statements or figures of speech as such but rather the basic attitude or ultimate view that permeates the entire dialogue.

of superiority, and by means of ironical speech the ironical subject distances himself from his fellow human beings and from the actual. He does not wish to be understood immediately and looks down on plain and simple talk that everyone can promptly understand. The ironical subject isolates himself rather than wishing to be generally understood ('he relishes his joy in private', p. 249). Kierkegaard points out that irony particularly appears in the higher circles - it is a sophisticated form of speech: 'Just as kings and princes speak French, the higher circles ... speak ironically so that lay people will not be able to understand them' (p. 249). A diplomat's view, for example, is often ironic, and irony can also function as form of political prudence (p. 253).

As a rule, Kierkegaard does not distinguish clearly between 'irony proper' and other modes of laughter. With regard to medieval laughter, for example, he points out that the *parodia sacra* mentioned by him must be interpreted as a kind of irony, indicating that the Catholic faith had apparently lost its validity in the eyes of the individuals concerned: 'in the Middle Ages [the Catholic Church] tended to rise above its absolute reality at certain times and to view itself ironically - for example, at the Feast of the Ass, the Feast of Fools, the Easter Comedy, etc. A similar feeling was the basis for allowing the Roman soldiers to sing satirical songs about the victor... [Likewise] there was much irony in the lives of the Greek deities' (p. 253). Apparently he fails to recognize that parody is a form of laughter in its own right, conveying a different basic mood and even producing comic cults - without the implication that the religious beliefs expressed by them have detoriated. At times, however, Kierkegaard does seem to admit that in particular instances of laughter there might be something more than irony at work. Commenting on the first book of the *Republic*, for instance, he writes: 'On the whole, the irony in this whole first book is so excessive and ungovernable, sparkles so inordinately, frolics with such wantonness and fieriness [that it has] a certain resemblance to the grotesque figures that appear and the equally grotesque leaps that are made in a *Schattenspiel an der Wand* [shadow play on the wall] and it is almost impossible to keep from laughing when Socrates says: Thrasymachus made all these admissions not as I now lightly narrate them, but with much balking and reluctance and prodigious sweating, it being summer' (p. 113-114). Besides the 'grotesque' reference to bodily functions, the 'ironical' relationship between literal meaning and content is indeed absent here. Unlike irony proper, where the phenomenon is at odds with the essence, the literal meaning with its content, this seems to be a case of laughter *for its own sake*, of laughter *per se*, where the phenomenon, instead of being at odds with the idea, simply seems to be 'devoid of any relation to the idea' (p. 114).

Apart from this one reference to the *Republic*, however, Kierkegaard as a rule tends to ignore the parody, the travesty, the parodical play with official genre conventions in the dialogues. As pointed out before, however, I quite agree with

Nietzsche that Socrates' basic attitude is parodical rather than ironical. To begin with, his laughter is plebeian rather than elite. Moreover, apart from its negative aspect, Socratic laughter has a positive aspect as well. It is a form of truth in its own right and in the final section of this chapter I will contend that Socrates, instead of simply devouring or rejecting the actual and the established, exemplified an alternative, a moral 'solution'. Rather than simply distancing himself from ancient Greek culture in which life had become a problem, his basic objective was to make life possible again by exemplifying a cheerful and carefree alternative.

2. THE TRUTH OF LAUGHTER

Nietzsche's rediscovery of the parody at work in *Phaedo* and his understanding of Socrates as *buffo* brings him closer to the Bakhtin of the Rabelais book than his *Zarathustra* does. In the prologue to *Gargantua*, supported by a quotation from *The Symposium*, Socrates is staged as the ridiculous jester whose speech acts nevertheless contain something of great value: gay truth. His ways stamp him as a simpleton, hopelessly unfit for all office in the republic, forever laughing and drinking, forever hiding his divine knowledge under a mask of mockery. Alcibiades' comparison of Socrates with Silenus, Dionysos' vulgar companion, was often used by sixteenth century humanists and cited by Erasmus in three of his works (Bakhtin 1968, p. 169). It contains a combination of abuse and praise which is truly parodical.[14]

'There can be no doubt as to the carnivalistic origins of the Socratic dialogue', Bakhtin claims (1973, p. 108). The 'basis of the original nucleus of the genre', he

---

14 But let me just read aloud the famous first lines of the Rabelais novel: 'Beuveurs tres illustres, et vous, Verolez tres precieux - car à vous, non à aultres, sont dediez mes escriptz, - Alcibiades, ou dialogue de Platon intitulé *Le Bancquet*, louant son precepteur Socrates, sans controverse prince des philosophes, entre aultres parolles le dict estre semblable es Silenes. Silenes estoient jadis petites boites, telles que voyons de present es bouticques des apothecaires, pinctes au dessus de figures joyeuses et frivoles, comme de harpies, satyres, oysons bridez, lievres cornuz, canes bastées, boucqs volans, cerfz limonniers et aultres telles pinctures contrefaictes à plaisir pour exciter le monde à rire (quel fut Silene, maistre du bon Bacchus); mais au dedans l'on reservoit les fines drogues comme baulme, ambre gris, amomon, musc, zivette, pierreries et aultres choses precieuses. Tel disoit estre Socrates, parce que, le voyans au dehors et l'estimans par l'exteriore apparance, n'en eussiez donné un coupeau d'oignon, tant laid il estoit de corps et ridicule en son maintien, le nez pointu, le reguard d'un taureau, le visaige d'un fol, simple en meurs, rustiq en vestimens, pauvre de fortune, infortuné en femmes, inepte à tous offices de la republique, toujours riant, toujours beuvant d'autant à un chascun, toujours se guabelant, toujours dissimulant son divin sçavoir; mais, ouvrans ceste boyte, eussiez au dedans trouvé une celeste et impreciable drogue...' (1919, p. 1-2).

tells us, were the agons of ancient Attic comedy, the carnivalistic-folkloristic debates between, for instance, life and death, permeated with 'the pathos of jolly relativity'. Yet he admits that in Plato's dialogues we find that laughter can be reduced to the extent that, although we can still discern its footprints, we no longer hear laughter itself: 'Thus in Plato's Socratic dialogues ... laughter is reduced (though not completely), but it remains in the structure of the image of the central hero (Socrates) and in the methods of developing the dialogue, and - most importantly - in the genuine dialogicality itself... But here and there in the dialogues of the early period laughter goes beyond the structure of the image and, so to speak, bursts out into a louder register. In the dialogues of the later period laughter is reduced to a minimum' (p. 137-138). Yet, although Bakhtin emphasized the importance of the Socratic dialogue as a serio-comic genre, he himself refrained from analyzing any one of them extensively.

The Socrates of Rabelais (and, by implication, of Bakhtin) is the Socrates of *The Symposium* (Plato 1951), a dialogue conveying a carefree, laughing mood from the outset, where Socrates makes his appearance as the continuously jesting captain of a band of carefree lads. Plato's dialogue presents us with a 'banquet for laughter's sake' (Bakhtin 1968, p. 5), a comic protocol: a set of speeches attributed to some of Socrates' contemporaries which are in fact 'parodies of the styles of their supposed speakers' (Hamilton 1951, p. 12). It is written in a far from serious vein. For example, as Aristophanes is suffering from the hiccups, Eryximachus speaks before his turn. He is presented as a pompous and oracular pedant - 'His analysis is ... mechanical, catalogue-like, and forced, and must have seemed so even to readers to whom the scientific theories on which he relies were living and credible' (Hamilton 1951, p. 15). In fact, he reminds us of the 'gay physician' (Bakhtin 1968, p. 67-68, 179) who restores health by provoking laughter, a practice as can be found throughout the Medieval literature of laughter summarized by Rabelais. Finally, he is deliberately made to misinterpret a famous theory by Heracleitus. When, after this rather absurd performance, Aristophanes takes the floor, he relates 'a humorous fantasy of the nature of the first human beings and their rebellion against the gods, which has often been called Rabelaisian' (Hamilton 1951, p. 16). After Zeus has bisected the impudent, quadruped human rascals, Apollo 'turned round the faces, and gathering together the skin, like a purse with drawstrings, on to what is now called the belly, he tied it tightly in the middle round a single aperture which men call the navel. He smoothed out the other wrinkles, which were numerous, and moulded the chest with a tool like those which cobblers use to smooth wrinkles in the leather..'. And should there be 'any sign of wantonness in them after that, and they will not keep quiet, [Zeus] will bisect them again, and they shall hop on one leg' (Plato 1951, p. 60-61). Yet in the course of his gay-hearted story an important truth is brought to light, revealing a basic aspect of human existence 'only accessible through laughter', as Bakhtin phrases it: we will remain unable to satisfy our fundamental desire. Agathon's speech, taking the floor after Aristophanes, is merely a parody of the conventional rhetoric and diction. Finally, even Socrates' own speech parodies a contemporary genre: the language of the mystery religions of his day, used by Diotima.

The narrative parts abound in jest as well. In the very first lines, Apollodorus (the narrator) is mocked; reference is made to 'a little fellow who always went about barefoot', who happened to be at the party and was considered 'one of Socrates' greatest admirers in those days' (p. 34), whereas Socrates himself - deliberately and jestingly misquoting a citation from Homeros - is introduced in the following vein: 'I met Socrates fresh from the bath and with shoes on his feet, two circumstances most unusual with him'. He arrives late at the party, having taken up his famous position in a neighbour's front porch, where he is said to have made some important discovery. Although many translators have made quite some effort to conceal the omnipresence of carefree laughter, in order to emphasize what they consider the serious aspect of the piece, all participants jest unceasingly and Socrates is presented as the prince of fools who 'spends his whole life pretending an playing with people' (p. 103). A drunken Alcibiades devotes the famous mock-panegyric to him, cited in *Gargantua* in which he compares him to a Silenus, the constant companion of Dionysos, a bald, dissolute old man with a flattened nose, usually riding an ass, and yet considered something of a prophet:

Anyone who sets out to listen to Socrates talking will probably find his conversation utterly ridiculous at first. But if a man penetrates within and sees the content of Socrates' talk exposed, he will find that there is nothing but sound sense inside, and that this talk is [...] of the widest possible application; in fact that it extends over all subjects with which a man who means to turn out a gentleman needs to concern himself (p. 110-111).

A speech that raised general laughter, as the Socratic way of life produced the very reverse of what established morality would consider a perfect gentleman.

The truth revealed by Socrates is *not* the truth of argument or logic - it is the truth of laughter, and dialectics is a comic rather than a serious genre. In *Twilight of the Idols*, Nietzsche again stresses the fact that, unlike many of his disciples, Socrates emerged from the lower social stratum, a fact clearly emphasized by his outward appearance. He was, as Nietzsche phrases it, *buffo*, a term connoting popular jest. With Socrates, vulgarity takes the floor: popular jest, indecent manners and, Nietzsche adds, a vulgar genre, a vulgar mode of thought - dialectics. Socrates indicates the point in history where aristocratic taste is overcome by 'vulgar' genres. But what is dialectics? In Nietzsche's view, dialectics is associated with the lower social classes.[15] To a truly aristocratic mind, whatever has to be demonstrated by means of argument either raises suspicion or is considered sheer knavery, for one has recourse to dialectics only when all other means are lacking: it is a sign of weakness, of being on the defense (§ 6). The dialectician is a buffoon, someone to be ridiculed.

While reading this crucial series of aphorisms, one inevitably gets the impression that Nietzsche is in two minds about Socrates. I would, therefore, propose the following explication. Dialectics is a vulgar mode of speech, I quite agree. But I would add that it relies on laughter rather than 'argument' and 'logic' - unless it is admitted that laughter, as Bakhtin phrases it, has a 'logic' of its own. Perhaps Nietzsche's puritan taste is at work here. As a matter of fact, in *The Antichrist*, the inclination toward reason and argument is considered the expression of an elite rather than a vulgar understanding of life, one supported by the upper classes of society. If one agrees that dialectics is a vulgar genre, this means that it is a comic mode of speech and that laughter (the popular mode of thought) rather than propositional logic is Socrates' basic device.

In the *Symposium*, Socrates is the master of parody rather than serious argument. The dialogue is a carnivalesque scene where members of the upper classes (like Agathon) temporarily become drunk, mingle with the vulgar (represented by Socrates) and engage in parodying the official truth and official rhetoric of their daily routine - they become merry rather than rational. They engage in a comic protocol, subject themselves to an inverted canon, a carnivalesque regime for the sake of laughter (which for example formally defines the amount of alcohol to be consumed and the manner in which the mock-speeches are to be delivered), but they are bound to resume their official life and duties as well as their restricted rhetoric before long. It is a temporary suspension of official routines and moral or aesthetic sensibility, a temporarily sanctioned relapse into vulgarity by way of festive, carefree laughter and affectionate, mutual mockery. Several of the speeches delivered can be compared to the so-called 'grammatical' parodies often practices in learned scholastic circles during the Middle Ages, directed at mocking official genres by exposing their basic grammatical and rhetorical devices. And Socrates, with his persistent claim of being serious, mocks all of them by presenting a parody of what is supposed to be a philosophical discourse or debate. The very persistence of his claim that he is serious ought to raise suspicion because it is a stock line of all comedians. His apparently 'rational' performance is kindred to the carnivalesque debates such as performed by medieval vagrant scholars. His lines of 'argument' are for the most part unconvincing or even ridiculous - although for centuries a large part of his philosophical readership seems to have refrained from reading them in an unbiased

---

[15] '[D]er Pöbel kommt mit der Dialektik obenauf', § 5.

way.[16] A basic truth is revealed by what he says, but it is not the truth of argument, nor is it grounded in argument; it is the truth of vulgar laughter. His philosophy is 'tested in the crucible of laughter', and he himself is 'directly linked with the carnival forms of antiquity that fertilized the Socratic dialogue and freed it from one-sided rhetorical seriousness' (Bakhtin 1968, p. 121). The modern reader notices the 'modern', 'reduced' modes of laughter at work in Socrates' performance, he notices the irony, the cynicism, but often fails to appreciate true, parodical laughter as being Socrates' basic device - a device which reappeared in intellectual discourse during the sixteenth century, was abolished during the ages of Protestant theology and classic aesthetics, of rationalism and Enlightenment, only to be rediscovered by Nietzsche and Bakhtin, for laughter is invincible and ineradicable.

Nietzsche stresses that when Plato (a talented, promising youth from the upper classes of Greek society) met Socrates (a popular buffoon) it changed him completely. It was a change that affected his basic mood and way of life, and was accompanied by a change of genre: he switched over from tragedy to dialogue. Indeed, Socrates transformed young Plato (who had aspired to become a playwright) into a 'novelist', for according to Nietzsche, the Socratic dialogue is the origin, the example and forerunner of the modern novel.[17] Like the modern novel, the Socratic dialogue successfully absorbed many basic elements from all previous genres (such as tragedy and lofty philosophical poetry) into its generic mixture, meanwhile crushing the ancient law of generic and stylistic unification and finally creating a form of art that was subsequently pushed to its ridiculous extreme by the cynics.[18] Like Nietzsche, Bakhtin (1988) argues that the Socratic dialogue constitutes a crucial stage in the genealogy of the modern novel. In Bakhtin's view, the novel has a lengthy prehistory, going back thousands of years. The symposium as a genre was

---

16 A student of mine phrased it thus: 'I came to these works with a similar belief, expecting reverently to find a serious discussion from which I would walk away with profound wisdom, but found instead dialogues I could hardly accept and at times I found simply laughable. And they are laughable... the truth is not in the argument but in the laughter'.

17 Nietzsche considered Plato as someone who mastered all literary styles and whose genre, the Socratic dialogue, assimilated all previous genres. Indeed, his dialogues set the example for the future novel (cf. Verweij 1993, p. 189 ff.).

18 'Wenn die Tragödie alle früheren Kunstgattungen in sich aufgesaugt hatte, so darf dasselbe wiederum in einem exzentrischen Sinne vom platonischen Dialoge gelten, der, durch Mischung aller vorhandenen Stile und Formen erzeugt ... das strenge ältere Gesetz der einheitlichen sprachlichen Form durchbrochen hat; auf welchem Wege die zynischen Schriftsteller noch weiter gegangen sind, die in der größten Buntscheckigkeit des Stils ... auch das literarische Bild des "rasenden Sokrates", den sie im Leben darzustellen pflegten, erreicht haben ... Wirklich hat für die ganze Nachwelt Plato das Vorbild einer neuen Kunstform gegeben, das Vorbild des *Romans*' (*The Birth of Tragedy*, § 14)

the prototype, the ancient precursor of the novel. It was not really a genre but rather a multiplicity of genres, a loosely organized *struggle* of genres (p. 5, p. 7), an art form that successfully parodied other (higher, serious and official) genres, notwithstanding their stubborn effort to preserve their canonical form, by exposing the conventionality of their language.

The speech of Eryximachus mentioned above, for example, which was a relentless parody of ancient medical discourse, might serve as a perfect specimen of parodical dialogue as a literary technique. The genre of the symposia, of which Plato's famous dialogue is just one example among many, is permeated with laughter, irony, parody and self-parody. Its basic feature is its indeterminacy, its open-endedness, its being unfinished. It is a genre that is both critical and self-critical. As Bakhtin points out, the Greek had a feeling for language, for dialects (either local, social, or professional), and this is rather apparent in the Socratic dialogues, where every character has its own accent, its own typical figures of speech, its own professional jargon and class idiom - almost like a nineteenth century novel. Moreover, whereas the 'higher' genres will idealize the past (a feature which gives them something of an official air) the comic genres (like the symposia) will focus on contemporary life, their locality is familiar, their characters are contemporaries, acquaintances and friends. According to Bakhtin, contemporaneity cannot become an object of representation for the higher genres since it is too closely associated with unofficial language and unofficial thought, with familiar speech and profanation (1988, p. 19-20). In ancient Greece, contemporary life (that is, life without beginning or end) was a subject of representation only for the lower, comical genres, rooted in the common people's culture of laughter. Their Self, their contemporaries and their time became the objects of ambivalent laughter, and this applies to the Socratic dialogues as well as to the Roman satire, the Menippian satire and the *Satyricon* of Petronius (p. 21-22).

In the Socratic dialogue, like in these other genres, the subject is portrayed 'without any distance, on the level of contemporary reality, in a zone of direct and even crude contact' (p. 22-23). Or, as Jaspers (1964/1975) formulated it, Socrates is the first philosopher who is presented to us 'large as life'.[19] Distance is essential to all higher genres, and the absence of it is a basic feature of all forms of comedy: 'As a distanced image, a subject cannot be comical; to be made comical, it must be brought close. Everything that makes us laugh is close at hand, all comical creativity works in a zone of maximal proximity' (p. 23). Laughter demolishes fear and piety before an object, before a world, by making it an object of familiar contact, thus clearing the ground for an absolutely free investigation of it:

---

[19] 'Er ist der erste Philosoph, der körperlich leibhaftig vor uns steht. Er war häßlich, die Augen quollen vor. Stülpnase, dicke Lippe, dicker Bauch, gedrungener Körperbau ließen ihn den Silenen und Satyrn ähnlich scheinen' (p. 82).

'Familiarization of the world through laughter and popular speech is an extremely important and indispensable step in making possible free, scientifically knowable and artistically realistic creativity in European civilization' (p. 23). This, according to Bakhtin, was what happened in the fourth Century B.C. as well as during the Renaissance. Due to lack of distance, the object was laid bare, became ridiculous. Indeed, the comic myth told by Aristophanes in the *Symposium* can be considered a perfect condensation of the genre, described by Bakhtin as 'a comical operation of dismemberment' (p. 24). As to the Socratic dialogues, Bakhtin writes:

> We posses a remarkable document that reflects the simultaneous birth of scientific thinking and of a new artistic-prose model for the novel. These are the Socratic dialogues. For our purposes, everything in this remarkable genre ... is significant. Characteristically it arises ... as transcripts based on personal memories of real conversations among contemporaries; characteristic, also, is the fact that a speaking and conversing man is the central image of the genre. Characteristic, too, is the combination of the image of Socrates, the central hero of the genre, wearing the popular mask of a bewildered fool - almost a 'Margit'[20] - with the image of a wise man of the most elevated sort... Characteristic also is the ambivalent self-praise in the Socratic dialogue: I am wiser than everyone, because I know that I know nothing... Around this image, carnivalized legends spring up (for example, Socrates' relationship with Xanthippe), the hero turns into a jester... Characteristic also is the proximity of its language to popular spoken language, as near as was possible for classical Greece... Characteristically, this genre is at the same time a rather complex system of styles and dialects, which enter it as more-or-less parodied models of languages and styles (we have before us therefore a multi-styled genre)... It is, finally, profoundly characteristic - and for us this is of utmost importance - that we have laughter, Socratic irony, the entire system of Socratic degradations combined with a serious, lofty and for the first time truly free investigation of the world, of man and of human thought. Socratic laughter (reduced to irony) and Socratic degradations (an entire system of metaphors and comparisons borrowed from the lower spheres of life)... bring the world closer and familiarize it in order to investigate is fearlessly and freely' (p. 24-25).

Like Kierkegaard, Bakhtin subsequently stresses that 'it is canonical for this genre that even an accidental and insignificant pretext can serve as the ... immediate starting point for a dialogue' (p. 25-26). Finally, he points out that Menippian satire (a Cynical genre) is usually considered a product of the disintegration of the Socratic dialogue, the familiarizing role of laughter being more powerful, sharper and coarser.

---

20 The ancient Greek version of the medieval *Hans Wurst*.

Like the Socratic dialogue, however, its plots and situations all serve one goal: 'to put to the test and to expose ideas and ideologues; these are experimental and provocative plots' (p. 26).

I am in complete agreement of course with most of Bakhtin's observations. Socratic laughter, although often *reduced* to irony, is basically and originally of a gay, cheerful and *parodical* nature rather than being ironic, since it implies playful, degrading criticism of lofty genres - but this, I hope, has been sufficiently substantiated by now. The relationship between Socratic laughter on the one hand and 'free and fearless investigation' on the other, however, still deserves some further consideration since it borders on the difficult question concerning the relationship between the truth of parody and the truth of science, the truth of laughter and the truth of argument.

In chapter two I referred to Nietzsche who, in *The Birth of Tragedy*, explained how (in the fourth Century B.C.) the Apollinian principle of ancient Greek culture (the moral principle of measure and self-constraint) came to be replaced by the 'Socratic' principle of reason, while its Dionysian counterpart (the principle of depersonalization and excess) was suddenly rejected as 'irrational' (instead of being considered a basic form of knowledge in its own right, allowing us to discern a profound and startling truth about human existence). From now on, the wisdom of Dionysian laughter was banished from the realm of scientific truth. Subsequently, however, Nietzsche reconsidered his initial judgement of Socrates many times. In *The Gay Science*, he thought of Socrates as exemplifying 'gay' science rather than 'science', and laughter rather than argument. Moreover, scientific investigation was regarded as *one* particular form of knowledge, a considerable improvement no doubt compared to the Christian inclination toward religious mystification, but the ultimate form of knowledge seemed to be dionysian and gay.

In the case of Bakhtin, a similar ambiguity can be found. On the one hand it is suggested that laughter is a basic form of truth in its own right (certain aspects of the world are 'only accessible through laughter'), while on the other hand it is proclaimed that laughter merely heralds and clears the ground for a serious, rational and scientific mode of speech. Eventually, the truth of laughter is catched up with and overtaken by new forms of scientific seriousness. In my view, however, we should eventually resist this stubborn inclination to consider the truth of laughter as merely a preparation for something else. Laughter is a form of knowledge, indeed, a form of 'free and fearless investigation' in its own right and the basic merit of the Socratic dialogues is the extent to which 'free and fearless investigation' remains intimately connected with the speech genres of laughter. Although laughter will no doubt further scientific investigation by challenging the constraints of dogmatism, its positive truth surpasses its negative function (of overcoming dogmatism) and is not in need of subsequent scientific justification.

This could be the solution to the 'problem of Socrates', as Nietzsche refers to it in *Twilight of the Idols*. His mode of speech, the 'truth game' referred to as 'dialectics' was in fact a *comic* genre - and perhaps even the author of *The Gay Science* is still taking Socrates much too seriously at times. The Socratic dialogues constitute a comic, care-free mode of speech. It is not a serious genre, but rather a comic double of the serious parts of Plato's writings which existed at one time but are lost to us. For some reason beyond our knowledge his comical, 'literary', and - from a 'serious' point of view - less assuming works survived, with Socrates figuring as a buffoon-like hero, although later on the dialogues became more and more serious whereas even the truly 'Socratic' dialogues already contain some hints, some indications of a more serious discourse elsewhere, of another genre in which Socrates is probably no longer needed. In brief, the dialogues constitute a comical, impious, jocular prelude, preparing us for something else, namely Plato's subsequent effort to establish a rationalistic and etatistic truth regime. In those days, serious discourse always needed a comic, parodical double, often provided by the author himself - a procedure quite common in ancient literature, and explicitly supported by Socrates in the *Symposium*. According to Bakhtin, there never was an official genre that did not have its parodic-travestying double, its comic counterpart. The most famous example was the so-called 'fourth' drama, the satyr-play that followed upon the tragic trilogy.[21] All tragedians were writers of satyr-plays as well and Aeschylus (the most serious and pious of them all) was considered the greatest master of comedy (1988, p. 54). Homer himself was credited with a comic work about the fool Margit. Official discourse was always accompanied with 'corrective laughter' (p. 55, p. 59), revealing its limitations and insufficiencies.

Therefore, the basic comic features of the genre - 'dialectics', or 'Socratic dialogue' - should not escape us.[22] Apparently, Plato's appreciation of the significance of laughter differed considerably from that of his teacher. Rather than professing his admiration for Socrates by 'immortalizing' him (that is, by portraying his unmatched comical talents) Plato makes clear that eventually his jocular performance should give way to 'true' philosophy, and that the impious rogue (Socrates) has to give way to the pious guardian of serious reason (Plato). In fact, this is how the Plato dialogues are composed. At first the reader's attention is

---

21 Unlike 'dogmatic' seriousness, tragedy does not fear laughter and parody and even demands it as a corrective and complement (Bakhtin 1968, p. 121).

22 As it did many of his readers - and this not merely applies to philosophers. A perfect artistic example of a neo-classicist, tragic understanding of Socrates, as it was articulated by Hegel and others, is the French painter David's *Death of Socrates*, a painting whose figures are 'as solid - and as immobile - as statues' (Janson 1962/1986, p. 597). Nobody laughs, of course. Whereas the Socratic dialogue as a 'serio-comic' genre aimed at familiarizing Socrates, later on he became elevated, in spite of the atmosphere of jolly relativity conveyed by the dialogues, because of the historical distance.

completely absorbed by Socrates' wit, but eventually he becomes fed up with it, and it is at this point that the comic dialogue suffers an intrusion and is interrupted or even overwhelmed by seriousness, with the implication that eventually gay contest and jolly witticisms are to be replaced by serious monologue.[23] At that point the reader is already entering another genre: serious philosophical discourse - *comoedia finita est; non ridere, sed intelligere*. In defiance of Socrates' own recognition of the truth of laughter, the Socratic dialogues are preparing us for a more serious mode of speech. Meanwhile, it is astonishing that Plato (like Aeschylus) managed to excel in a literary genre he himself must have considered to be of secondary importance.

But are we justified from a methodological point of view to rely on Plato's picture of Socrates to such an extent? Apparently, Plato used his master as a means for achieving a philosophical goal the actual Socrates did not share. In addition to Plato, we have two other sources at our disposal: Aristophanes and Xenophon. From a philosophical point of view, however, Xenophon seems useless. He apparently failed to understand his teacher completely. As Kierkegaard (1989) phrased it, he depicted him as a good-natured, garrulous, droll character who did not stand in anyone's way and uttered sheer nonsense. In his effort to show what a scandalous injustice it was for the Athenians to condemn him to death, Xenophon eliminated all that was dangerous in him, thereby reducing him to absurdity. If Xenophon's understanding of Socrates is correct, Kierkegaard claims, the people of Athens probably wanted to get rid of him because he bored them.

Whereas Xenophon seems inadequate as a source, Aristophanes seems almost too adequate. His play (*The Clouds*) abounds in parody to such an extent that it is difficult to tell whether it really can be considered a basic feature of Socrates' actual performance or must rather be considered a comic device used by Aristophanes in order to *parody* him. The central figure of the play is not Socrates but a 'stupid country yokel' called Strepsiades. He comes to Socrates in order to be educated, but soon shows himself a Simple Simon, quite incapable of being remodeled. Moreover, whereas Socrates' actual practice dealt with abstract concepts, Strepsiades has something definite and ordinary in mind: he wants to learn the 'new' logic taught by Socrates in order to rid himself of his creditors. This 'new' logic is presented to us as a parody of logic proper, a genre quite at home in the market-place and one that can be applied in order to make the wrong seem right. When Strepsiades enters the 'Thinkery' (the locality where Socrates does his teaching) he encounters a group of students in grotesque postures and the first thing we hear about Socrates himself is that yesternight, while gaping at the moon, a lizard befouled him, causing his mental conception to miscarry. This play, abounding in buffoonish knavery,

---

[23] It has often been remarked that Plato's later dialogues are already monologues rather than dialogues since any real conversation is lacking and the dialogical structure of questions and answers has become artificial, superfluous and tedious.

subtleties, slapstick jugglery and practical jokes, as well as references to bellies and paunches, is a comic, parodical rendering of Socrates' actual objective, apparently misrepresenting it on purpose. Kierkegaard refers to this play as 'parodical' and 'truly comic'. The comic situation (the simple farmer Strepsiades coming to Socrates in order to be educated) is a 'parodying shadow' (p. 145), a comic double of what Socrates' actual practice must have been like. As was already pointed out before, Kierkegaard considers the truly comical a 'corrective element' that makes the phenomenon at hand (either a person or a situation) intelligible through exaggeration. According to Kierkegaard, Aristophanes used parody as a device in order to understand the new 'principle' represented by Socrates. Of course, the actual Socrates had many comic sides (he was after all an 'eccentric') but he could only become a truly comic figure for Aristophanes, a target for his laughter insofar as Aristophanes saw in him the spokesman of the new principle of subjectivity, threatening ancient Greek culture with destruction. Therefore, although *The Clouds* contains many examples of parody and basically *is* parodical, this does not prove that Socrates himself used parody as a device. Although Aristophanes' view is important in many ways, too many instances of parody can be found in it and this no doubt indicates that what we are presented with is a somewhat distorted, exaggerated picture of Socrates, one that is biased for the sake of laughter and must therefore be considered too congenial to what I have in mind to count as an unquestionable source. This is why I primarily focus on the way Socrates is presented to us by Plato. The basic objective of my *re*reading is to expose the comical in places where one perhaps would not suspect it, and to reveal the extent to which Socrates' apparently serious discourse is actually comical. Of course, also in the case of Plato the question of the relationship between the 'Platonic' and the 'actual' Socrates remains a difficult issue: what belongs to Socrates and what belongs to Plato? Still, the 'narrative' dialogues (such as the *Apology*, the *Symposium*, the *Phaedo*, the *Protagoras* and the first book of the *Republic*) are generally considered to be more or less 'Socratic': they begin with a trivial situation, pay much attention to locality and circumstances, contain genuine dialogues, and end without a conclusion.[24] Therefore, the narrative dialogues seem to provide us with a relatively trustworthy impression of what the actual Socrates must have been like (although the methodological problem *as such* remains). *Protagoras* counts as Plato's most remarkable achievement from a literary point of view. Therefore, I will briefly discuss the parody contained by it, before proceeding to a final reconsideration

---

24 'The carnival attitude ... is hostile to any final ending, for every ending is merely a new beginning' (Bakhtin 1968, p. 138).

of 'the problem of Socrates'.25

3. THE ABSURD COUPLE AND THE ILL-MANNERED QUESTIONER

From a Bakhtinean perspective *Protagoras* is a dialogue of special interest. In the introduction to his translation, W.K.C. Guthrie (1956) indicates that, although the dialogue is second to none in giving a picture of Greek life, the reader interested in Plato's philosophy as such would do well to pass over a substantial part of it, up to the discussion about pleasure and pain 'when Socrates begins to speak in earnest'. In my *re*reading of *Protagoras* I will emphasize, however, that (1) the preceding part is important from a philosophical point of view as well, and (2) that it is highly questionable whether, in the discussion on pleasure and pain, Socrates really does speak in earnest. Even his apparently 'serious' discourse abounds in comic ambiguities.

From the very beginning it is clear that the dialogue conveys a gay and carefree mood. Note the opening line: 'Where have you come from, Socrates? No doubt from pursuit of the captivating Alcibiades' - a conjecture which happens to be true. The dialogue is, as Guthrie pointed out, 'a little comedy. Plato is amusing himself, laughing at everyone, including his beloved master'. For example, Plato draws attention to Socrates' tiresome passion for verbal distinctions, as well as the fact that, at least to a skilled sophist like Protagoras, not all of his arguments are as valid and convincing as is sometimes suggested - if they are really given unbiased consideration. The main significance of the *Protagoras*, however, is the prominent

---

25 Although the first book of the *Republic* is not discussed here at length, its share of gaiety and merriment is considerable and of a parodical nature. For instance, the dialogue starts with Socrates, Glaucon and Polymarchus in a cheerful mood, returning from a festival in honour of Bendis (the Thracian equivalent of Artemis) that included, among other things, a torch race and an all-night carnival. Moreover, whereas the laughter of Thrasymachos (Socrates' antagonist) is referred to as sarcastic, Socrates' laughter is clearly parodical:

> 'What if I [Thrasymachos] give you a quite different and far better reply about justice? What do you think would be your penalty then?'
> 'The proper penalty of ignorance, which is of course that those who don't know should learn from those who do; which is the course I propose' [Apparently a reference to the provision in Athenian law whereby the defendant, if found guilty, could propose an alternative penalty to that demanded by the prosecution; cf. my discussion of the *Apology*, chapter one, § 4].
> 'You must have your joke', said he, 'but you must pay the fee for learning well'.
> 'I will when I have any cash'.
> 'The money's all right', said Glaucon, 'we'll pay up for Socrates' [377d].

Like in the *Apology*, Socrates applies (in a comical and parodical manner) the official conventions of judicial discourse in order to mock (and annoy) his interlocutor.

role of laughter in the search for truth.

Like in the *Symposium*, the *Protagoras* includes a comic 'doorway scene' in its introductory section - one of the stock ingredients of Socratic comedy.[26] Having reached the doorway of the house where Protagoras is staying, Socrates and his companion just stand there for a while and continue a discussion which had arisen between them on the way in order to reach an agreement. When the porter finally opens the door and discovers them, he cries: 'Ha, sophists!'. The subsequent description of the conversations that take place inside is again remarkably comical. It confirms Plato's excellence in the particular genre to which the dialogue belongs, his peculiar, philosophical version of the comedy of manners.

Protagoras boldly declares himself a sophist. The subject of his teaching is the proper care of personal affairs so that the pupil may learn how to best manage his own household as well as the state's affairs, and eventually may become a prominent person in the city, both as a speaker and as a man of action. This confession immediately provokes a discussion between Socrates and Protagoras as to whether virtue is a subject that can be taught at all. Challenged by Socrates to demonstrate that virtue *can* be taught, Protagoras first decides to tell a story rather than give a reasoned argument. To secure the survival of the human race, the gods bestowed respect for others and a sense of justice on all human beings; for without those civil virtues a city cannot exist. A man cannot exist without some share in justice, or he would not be human at all. Still, justice and moderation are not acquired automatically but through care and instruction and, if necessary, through correction and punishment until the individual is reformed into a virtuous citizen. If a state is to exist at all, then there should be no one who is a layman with respect to virtue. Protagoras' speech is a perfect and elegant example of sophist rhetoric. Socrates subsequent intervention aims at deconstructing his seemingly flawless and convincing speech by asking a series of questions intended to cause embarrassment and doubt. This involves, among other things, an interesting debate on the forms and rules of the subsequent discussion itself. Furthermore, unlike other more complacent dialogues, Socrates' opponent is shown to have the better reason a number of times and Socrates not only occasionally appears to be advocating the worst, but also tedious and tiresome.[27] For example, while discussing courage and confidence, at a certain point Protagoras rightly claims that Socrates is being unfair:

---

26 As Bakhtin points out, the threshold-dialogue or *Schwellendialog* as a generic element was quite common in the serio-comic genres of ancient Greece (1973, p. 91, p. 95).

27 Kierkegaard points out that Protagoras ends with 'the curious turn that Socrates defends what he had wanted to attack and Protagoras attacks what he had wanted to defend'. As far as its philosophical content was concerned, he considered the whole dialogue to be ridiculous.

'No, Socrates, he said. You have not remembered rightly what I said in my reply. When you asked me whether the courageous are confident, I agreed, but I was not asked whether the confident are also courageous...' (p. 342).

The discussion also includes a careful analysis of one of Simonides' poems, but Socrates interrupts it because a conversation about poetry reminds him too much of wine parties. He claims to prefer sober discussion where each of the participants takes his turn to speak or listen - 'even if the drinking is really heavy' (p. 340), remaining aware of the fact that philosophical truth was originally (that is, genealogically) connected with the ancient Greek drinking-bout. Furthermore, the participants occasionally mock, mimic and parody each other's speech - 'Let us, he [Protagoras] replied, as you are fond of saying yourself, investigate the question...'.

At a certain point, however, the discussion, and notably Socrates' part in it, becomes rather tedious and laborious. Socrates himself recognizes this - '"Now my good people", I went on, "if you ask me what is the point of all this rigmarole, I beg your indulgence. It isn't easy to explain the real meaning of what you call 'being overcome by pleasure'"...' (p. 346). Notwithstanding his appeal to indulgence, in the subsequent discourse Socrates continues to switch between seriousness and ridicule. Moreover, laughter becomes Socrates' main argument: 'This position makes your argument ridiculous' (p. 346); 'I fear that if our questioner is ill-mannered, he will laugh and retort: "What ridiculous nonsense"' (p. 346); 'If we had answered you straight off that it is ignorance, you would have laughed at us, but if you laugh at us now, you will be laughing at yourself as well' (p. 348); 'Prodicus laughed and assented, and so did the others' (p. 348). Laughter holds as a refutation, although it may function as an expression of consent as well.

It is the reference to the imaginary 'ill-mannered questioner' just mentioned that seems particularly significant in this respect. Socrates is perfectly aware of the ambiguous nature of his discourse: it is both serious and ridiculous. He is aware that, to a sober-minded spectator, unimpeded by the demands of politeness, by the demands of the genre, his line of argument would be considered ridiculous. There is something fundamentally comical about it, or, in other words, there appears to be a basic connection between dialectics and laughter. Even the dialogue's philosophical 'nucleus' is permeated by laughter, by the carnival attitude to the world. Nothing is self evident or reliable - that is the gay and liberating truth of Socratic dialectics. The importance of laughter is confirmed in the final passage:

It seems to me that the present outcome of our talk is pointing at us, like a human adversary, the finger of accusation and scorn. If it had a voice it would say: 'What an absurd pair you are, Socrates and Protagoras' (p. 351).

This human adversary as well as the 'ill-mannered questioner' remind us of the laughing chorus of ancient popular culture mentioned by Bakhtin, and Socrates is aware that his discourse is open to ridicule; that it still retains something of the gay and festive spirit of laughter that guided the ancient prandial ceremonies. Taking the floor means taking the risk of being ridiculed, for nothing is reliable or stable. Moreover, laughter has the final say: 'What an absurd pair you are'. This does not imply the futility of all philosophical debate, for this would be a merely negative and cynical conclusion. Rather it conveys a basic inside regarding the human quest for truth. The Socratic truth game is agonistic. No discursive option can be considered beyond contestation once and for all. What is to be feared is not so much inconsistency as ridicule; and yet, ridicule seems inevitable.

Although for the most part concealed by the rhetoric of sophistical or rationalistic genres, the vulnerability of human discourse is finally revealed by laughter. Parody or gay laughter, on the other hand, is not simply a rhetorical device but the basic mood in which the dialogue is written. Its basic purpose is to expose the ridiculous nature of complacent discourse. The 'human adversary' reproaching them is a comical rather than a serious figure, and the apparent scorn is nullified by the mood of laughter to which it adheres. It contains both an element of verbal abuse and an element of praise - that is (to borrow a phrase from Bakhtin) the abusive description of Socrates and Protagoras as an 'absurd pair' is basically a *praiseful* abuse, a stock element of all the genres of laughter. Rather than a serious reproach, it is an affirmation of a gay truth, indicating the limits of seriousness as they are recognized by the truly wise. Dialectical logic is 'uncrowned' by gay laughter, and the rest is merriment.

By the way, the *Protagoras* also reveals Socrates' reason for not considering himself a sophist. To begin with, the sophists present their speeches as belonging to a serious genre and try to immunize it against the criticism of laughter by means of lofty rhetoric and verbal decorum. Socrates and the sophists exemplify incompatible verbal practices that can in no way live in peace and quiet with each other. Furthermore, although at first sight the sophists seem to opt for a bottom-up approach, educating the young and talented, etatism is not at all excluded and, should the individual offer serious resistance to the moral transformation required by the state, he must be reformed by force. In the final section of this chapter I will indicate how this differed from Socrates' basic objective. Before passing our 'final' ethical judgement on Socrates, however, let me once again address the question of what *kind* of laughter he relied on.

I guess that the kind of laughter displayed by Socrates in the *Protagoras* and other 'Socratic' dialogues would not meet the criteria of laughter mentioned by Aristotle as befitting a gentleman. In his *'Art' of Rhetoric* he points out that in the course of a debate one will try to confound one's opponent's earnest with jest and his jest with earnest (1926/1959, III 18:7). Yet he adds that, in certain chapters of his *Poetics* that are lost to us, it is explained what kinds of jest there are and which of them can be considered becoming a gentleman. According to Aristotle, irony (eironeia) is more gentlemanly than buffoonery (bomologia).

In his *Nicomachean Ethics*, Aristotle considers jest to be part of the kind of playful conversation that is becoming to a virtuous gentleman, that is, someone who is gifted with a sense of propriety (1926/1982, IV 8:1-11). Those who go to excess in ridicule, however:

> are thought to be buffoons and vulgar fellows, who itch to have their jokes at all costs, and are more concerned to raise a laugh than to keep within the bounds of decorum... Those who jest with good taste are called witty and versatile - that is to say, full of good turns... But as matter for ridicule is always ready to hand, and as most men are only too fond of fun and raillery, even buffoons are called witty and pass for clever fellows; though it is clear from what has been said that wit is different, and widely different, from buffoonery. The middle disposition[28] is further characterized by the quality of tact, the possessor of which will say, and allow to be said to him, only the sort of things that are suitable to a virtuous man and a gentleman; since there is a certain propriety in what such a man will say and hear in jest, and the jesting of a gentleman differs from that of a servile nature, as does that of an educated from an uneducated man (IV 8:4-7).

Civilized wittiness or gentlemanly jest is referred to by Aristotle as *eutrapelia*, usually translated as *urbanitas* in Latin, *urbanity* in English.

Furthermore, Aristotle adds that the difference between both kinds of jest (urbanity and buffoonery) may be clarified by comparison of the old and modern comedies: 'The earliest dramatists found their fun in obscenity, the moderns prefer innuendo, which marks a great advance in decorum. Can we than define proper raillery by saying that its jests are never unbecoming to a gentleman?' Whereas the middle character [i.e. the cultivated, urban gentleman] is called tactful or witty, the buffoon is someone who cannot resist a joke; he will not keep his tongue off himself or anyone else if he can raise a laugh, and will say things a man of refinement would never say.

Now although it would be somewhat inordinate to consider Socrates' laughter vulgar in the sense of being 'obscene', I would nonetheless maintain that in certain respects his laughter is much closer to that of the 'old comedy' than the laughter of Aristotle's gentleman. If Aristotle's criteria are accepted, the kind of laughter conveyed by Socrates in the Socratic dialogues (most notably the *Protagoras*) must be considered as being too buffoon-like and excessive to pass for urbanity. Perhaps

---

[28] I.e. wittiness or 'urbanity', the middle position between boorishness and buffoonery.

we should say that, in the gay and playful atmosphere of ancient Athens, where matter for ridicule was 'always ready at hand', Socrates developed a 'middle position' of his own.

At this point, however, let us once again turn to Hegel who not only considers Socrates' performance as tragic rather than comic (as we have seen), but who also refers to him as a perfect example of the Attic virtue of urbanity - 'ein Beispiel der ausgearbeitesten attischen Urbanität' (1971, p. 454). Socrates is depicted by Hegel as someone who is vivid as well as flexible, loquacious as well as sensible in conversation. In short, he considers Socrates is be a true gentleman in the Aristotelian sense of the term. Besides that, Socrates emerges as a tragic hero - a hero-gentleman. In Hegel's version of him, the comic satyr-like ornament of the *Symposium* is transfigured into a classic statue. Everything comic and grotesque is elevated and overcome by the radiance of the sublime - and exterior gives way to nucleus. Indeed, Hegel refers to Socrates' 'immense stature', mentioning him and Pericles in one and the same breath as 'plastic individuals' and perfect exemplifications of the ancient Greek practice of self-edification. Like Pericles, Hegel claims, Socrates was one of those lofty Greek individuals who transfigured themselves into works of art by means of relentless moral exercise.[29] Subsequently, however, Hegel points out that, according to Plutarch, Pericles ceased to laugh ever since he became involved in politics. Indeed, Plutarch informs us that not only did Pericles have 'a spirit that was solemn and a discourse that was lofty and free from plebeian and reckless effrontery', but also that he had 'a composure of countenance that never relaxed into laughter' (*Pericles*, 5; 1958, p. 13). According to the poet Ion, moreover, Pericles even displayed a presumptuous and arrogant manner of address, containing a good deal of disdain and contempt for others, but Plutarch hastens to add that this view be best ignored because elsewhere this same poet had suggested that, much like the tragic tetralogy was in need of a comic satyr-play, human virtue needed a farcical appendage as well. According to Plutarch, Pericles' habit to avoid all forms of conviviality and familiar intercourse, and to withdraw into ascetic grandeur and turgid diction, testified of his nobility, while his policy of supplying the Athenian populace with a great number of official festivals and processions should be interpreted as an etatistic strategy of encroaching upon popular festive existence in order to diminish the general idleness of Athenian city life. Be this as it may, by mentioning Pericles and Socrates in one and the same breath, Hegel apparently failed to notice that, while Pericles exemplified the grand and lofty

---

29 'Er [Socrates] steht vor uns ... als eine von jenen großen plastischen Naturen (Individuen) ... wie wir sie in jener Zeit zu sehen gewohn sind, - als ein vollendetes klassisches Kunstwerk, das sich selbst zu dieser Höhe gebracht hat... Das höchste plastische Individuum ... ist Perikles, und um ihn, gleich Sternen, Sophokles, Thukydides, Sokrates, usw.' (1971, p. 452).

aspects of ancient Athens, Socrates constituted his comic reversal.

Yet, even Hegel is inconsistent or at least ambivalent when it comes to judging Socrates, for the gay 'exterior' of the actual Socrates is not abolished completely in his account. In the case of Socrates, Hegel tells us, philosophy did not retreat itself from the toils and pleasures of daily life (which was the subject matter of comedy), but flourished while remaining closely connected to it. His philosophy exemplified the Athenian way of life, which basically consisted of idleness and endless conversation, of lingering on the market-square; a way of life, Hegel hastens to add, that would nowadays be considered inappropriate and unbecoming. Socrates, however, strolled along and passed his time with nothing on his mind but verbal entertainment. Neither did he preach, nor could his discourse be considered ironic in the *modern* sense of the term. Rather, his jest exemplified *Greek* gaiety, the gay and merry state of mind that was pushed to its extreme by the eternal laughter of the gods and remains forever incompatible with modern irony.[30] Hegel even admits that, quite unlike Pericles' lofty prose, Socratic seriousness is often tedious and boring (p. 464) - although he fails to add: on purpose. Socrates, he claims, treated moral philosophy in an outspokenly popular manner and his final performance, his *Apology*, was outright 'popular philosophy' - 'Die letzte Unterredung des Sokrates ist Populärphilosophie' (p. 511). Socrates' jest, however, was truly comical instead of being merely funny because it revealed the inner conflicts of ancient moral life (p. 483).

In short, Hegel agrees that Socratic laughter was carefree instead of ironic. His carefree laughter revealed that, as the truly serious, tragic form of life which had flourished in ancient Athens for decades (and which had been idealized by ancient tragedy) had finally outlived itself, the new, scientific seriousness conveyed by sophistic discourse could not avert the imminent transformation of moral life. After the unrivalled tetralogy of ancient tragedy (the artistic achievements of Aeschylus, Sophocles and Euripides), Attic life was in need of a satyr-play. Ancient moral existence was suffering from a general sense of uneasiness, was awaiting a new kind of hero to enter the stage, not a tragic but a comic one. Someone who, by exposing the turgid nature of sophistic discourse through laughter, would not only reveal the hidden inner conflicts of moral life (laughter's negative aspect), but would at the same time present ancient Athens with a moral solution, a new 'middle position' (laughter's positive aspect), allowing moral life to adapt itself to unprecedented circumstances and to flourish once again, although of course this Socratic middle position would fail to meet the established criteria of ancient Attic urbanity summarized by Aristotle just before they were to expire for good, that is, just before moral life became stoic, cynic and hellenistic rather than peripatetic.

---

[30] 'Von dieser Ironie unserer Zeit ist die Ironie des Sokrates weit entfernt' (1971, p. 461).

4. THE PROBLEM OF SOCRATES

In what way do these considerations amount to a final judgement regarding 'the problem of Socrates'? Or should we admit that Socrates escapes us and defies all final judgements? Let us briefly recapitulate what has been said about him in this chapter as well as in the previous one. To begin with, any effort to judge Socrates is impeded by the fact that he is presented to us by someone else. Indeed, one often feels inclined to distinguish between the 'true' Socrates, as he emerges in the apparently more vivid and life-like sections of the dialogues, and the subsequent rectifications and additions by its author. Some dialogues seem more truly 'Socratic' than others, and it is clear that we have been focussing on the more Socratic ones: *Apology*, *Symposium*, *Phaedo*, *Protagoras*, clarifying some of their problems and ambiguities by referring to the ancient popular and comical genres of which these dialogues apparently were a peculiar example. They constitute what Bakhtin referred to as the comic double accompanying a serious genre (one which in this case no longer exists). Instead of being tragic in itself (Hegel's judgement), *Phaedo* must be considered a parody of tragedy and its devices, a speech genre used by Plato to ridicule the tragic view of life, preparing the way for a more 'serious' refutation, a more 'serious' explanation of the rationalistic view of life to which Plato adhered. In short, Plato reduced laughter to its negative function, using it in order to challenge the established tragic 'truth', considering it a preparation, but eventually laughter had to give way to a rationalistic truth regime which was subsequently imposed by him and which came to influence subsequent philosophical thought decisively at the expense of laughter.

Therefore, the Socratic dialogues are to be viewed from a strategic, agonistic perspective. They convey a struggle between comical and serious, popular and aristocratic forces at work, where Socrates represents the popular and comical, and Plato the aristocratic and serious aspects. Whereas Plato eventually sides with the truth of science, Socrates remains a hero of laughter. It is Plato's merit as a literary writer, however, that he retained the truly popular, truly comical aspects of Socrates' performance as a remainder of the culture of true laughter that allowed Socrates to flourish, and as an indication of laughter's positive, affirmative truth he himself apparently rejected. Notwithstanding Plato's efforts at containment, the gay and carefree laughter of the 'true' Socrates managed to retain its regenerative power and joyful tone - its *positive* aspect.

Now the 'problem of Socrates' can be defined as follows. He represented laughter, but at the same time is said to have inaugurated the truth-regime ('dialectics') which aimed at the repression of laughter. The devices put to work by him emerged out of popular culture, conveyed an affirmation of bodily life, but Socrates apparently used them to articulate his final rejection of the value of bodily life in order to establish a tradition of ascetic sensibility from which Nietzsche tried to liberate himself - by means of gay, affirmative laughter. The relationship between laughter and rationality, between popular and official forms of truth remains a problem.

I already pointed out that *Twilight of the Idols* contains an important series of aphorisms on Socrates, reconsidering his final words which are quoted in *Phaedo* and which continued to bother Nietzsche. Apparently Socrates was fed up with life.[31] This caused him to confirm the 'truth' recognized and uttered by the sages of all times: that life is insignificant, that it lacks true meaning and value. Now according to Nietzsche, this remarkable consensus of opinion among the wise - this *consensus sapientium* concerning the value of life - must not be regarded as an indication that the claim involved is actually true but as an indication that the sages of all times are remarkably similar as far as their physiology is concerned. Their judgement with regard to life is a symptom of physical decline, revealing more about their own physical condition than about life itself. What about Socrates? Did he not differ from other, more serious and less popular philosophical heroes in important respects? Socrates was, as we all know, of humble descent: to the Greek mind not really a sign of wisdom.[32] Moreover, he was unattractive: to the Greek mind a sign of retarded physical development and almost a refutation in itself. In Nietzsche's eyes, there is an aspect of exaggeration and caricature in everything Socrates says or does. He was a buffoon, but one who succeeded in having himself taken seriously - what had happened?

At first, Nietzsche suggests that perhaps Socrates' irony was the expression of revolt, of resentment of the rabble toward the higher strata of society, an act of revenge, an effort to render the antagonist's intellect powerless (§ 7). On the other hand, his dialectics seemed to introduce an unprecedented form of *agon*, stirring the ancient Greek instinct for competition (§ 8). Apparently, however, neither one of these judgements grasps the quintessence of Socrates' performance. Rather, Socrates really seemed to have had a remarkably clear sense of what was actually happening at that time: the decline of ancient Greek culture, a process of which he himself was merely a symptom. Human instincts were in danger of becoming excessive and regressive and desperately needed a new 'tyranny', a new form of organization on behalf of self-preservation, and Socrates personified such an unprecedented form of

---

[31] According to Nietzsche, the two great judicial murders of history - the killing of Socrates and Jesus - actually were cases of suicide, both victims wanted to die and choosed to die (*Human, All Too Human II*, Mixed Opinions and Aphorisms, § 94). Kierkegaard (1989) points out that, in the eyes of Socrates', his death was far from tragic since he considered life insignificant, even felt bored by it and doubted whether death really constituted an evil. Apparently, these tragedies were not tragic in themselves but only in the eyes of the beholders.

[32] 'Sokrates gehörte, seiner Herkunft nach, zum niedersten Volk: Sokrates war Pöbel' (*Twilight of the Idols*, § 3).

moral subjectivity - a possible escape from anarchy. Human subjectivity was in danger of being overwhelmed by the tyranny of instincts, and desperately in need of a counter-tyrant: Socrates - that is, of the treatment recommended by him, which consisted of imposing or constituting an unprecedented kind of moral subjectivity. Socrates was the one who, in the face of an omnipresent, advancing anarchy, succeeded in regaining mastery over himself. His case responded to a general experience of distress. In view of the widespread loss of self-mastery, due to the overwhelming anarchy and mutual enmity of human instincts, he represented a solution, a cure (§ 9). He was considered the gay physician of Greek culture.

Nietzsche adds, however, that even this judgement of Socrates is misguided, for that which seemed to be a cure was actually an expression or even an intensification of the decline. Socrates and the morality of amelioration he represented was basically a misunderstanding (§ 11). It was an illness rather than a return to health, but Socrates happened to be the only one who comprehended this. Life had become an illness, he was fed up with it, and wanted to die - 'Death is the physician we are in need of, not Socrates': those were his final words.

Nietzsche's basic strategy consists of exploring several possible interpretations of Socrates, considering him *both* a pessimist and an optimist, *both* a personification of the truth of laughter and a spokesman of the truth of reason. Somehow, these seemingly incompatible explanations are aspects of a final judgement. In those days, established morality as well as the established modes of exercising power suffered a severe decay. This implied that human subjectivity was in danger of being overwhelmed by the tyranny of unorganized instincts. Apparently, they could no longer be contained, neither in a moral nor in a political manner. Laughter not only confirmed the breakdown of established morality but also gave voice to the omnipresence of free-floating energy that allowed for unprecedented forms of moral subjectivity to establish themselves. It allowed for a Socratic, bottom-up solution - a solution, however, which was eventually overcome by rationalism and etatism. Socratic laughter was subjected to a Platonic top-down policy of establishing a new, stable, centripetal and rationalistic moral regime. In other words, Socratic laughter represented an temporary interval, a short-lived flourishing or moral *interregnum* between two etatistic moral regimes. In this respect, the fourth Century B.C. is rather similar to the sixteenth Century A.D., an *interregnum* which likewise witnessed an astonishing discursive event, a roar of laughter produced by someone in some respects reminiscent of Socrates; someone who, like Socrates, was of humble descent and who, like Socrates, was to fascinate Nietzsche throughout his career - Martin Luther.

Before leaping from Socrates to Luther, however, the question may arise as to what happened during the two intermediary millennia. An important epoch in the history of laughter was of course Hellenism, something which Nietzsche and

Bakhtin agree upon, notably the second century A.D. Indeed, the second and the sixteenth century had a lot in common. In comparison to the centuries preceding them, they were a period of prosperity. Their philosophy and literature were of a practical, moral and didactic rather than theoretical nature and permeated by a tendency to imitate.[33] The most prominent spokesman of Hellenistic laughter was Lucian, greatly appreciated and relentlessly imitated by both Erasmus and Rabelais.[34] Indeed, their work conveyed a profoundly Lucian mood (Robinson 1979). Lucian's main genre, satirical dialogue, was a combination of several literary forms that had already existed. The dialogue had gradually become a serious philosophical genre, but Lucian once again stressed its parodical, satirical and burlesque elements, retrieved its comical and popular sources. In fact, Lucian staged the birth of his new genre in one of his dialogues - *The Double Indictment*. In the context of a court room scene he admits, using Dialogue herself as his antagonist, that he adapted the philosophical genre by blending comical elements with it. Dialogue claims to have been wronged and maltreated, i.e. to have been degraded to the comical and average. In other words, she blames Lucian for ridiculing that which had become lofy and serious.

Moreover, what Lucian borrows from Plato is the setting rather than the argument. He transposed the Socratic dialogues into an out-right comic mode of speech. The majority of typical scenes utilized by Lucian (such as the comic banquet, the mock trial, the assembly of the gods, etc.) were second hand. Furthermore, as is the case with other comical writers such as Molière, scenes, settings and characters together with their typical traits, anecdotes and vices tend to recur in subsequent works. They constitute, so to speak, the *topoi* of his writings. To expose the protagonist as a parvenu, an effeminate debauchee or a champion of ignorance are among his favourite 'topoi of vilification' (Robinson 1979, p. 19). In *Lexiphanes*, the protagonist himself claims to be 'counter-banqueting the son of Ariston', that is, parodying Plato's *Symposium*. It is a comic reduction of Plato's dialogue to its extraneous details, nothing serious is said at all. Moreover, like all comic writers, Lucian is highly sensitive towards peculiarities of diction, dialect, and cant. His works abound in parodical devices such as comic exaggeration or the application of serious conventions to totally absurd topics.

One of his most prominent plays, widely read in the sixteenth century, is called *Philosophers for Sale*. It conveys a market-square atmosphere and diction. Zeus and

---

[33] In fact, the Middle Ages were marked by a similar tendency toward appropriating, re-working and imitating materials already available (cf. Lehmann 1922) - an artistic attitude despised nowadays because of the modern emphasis on *being original*.

[34] Bakhtin, however, disliked him: 'Lucian's laughter is devoid of true gaiety' (1968, p. 387). Unlike authors like Rabelais or Shakespeare, he claims, Lucian did not fully exploit and explore the comic potentials of the popular tradition on which he relied.

Hermes are staged as selling philosophers to the public, presenting their (often rather dubious or even deplorable) qualities and condition in a loud voice. In the case of the Cynic, for instance, the buyer is told that he will be taught to consider marriage, children and native land sheer nonsense, to behave impudently in public, using the coarsest language, and to choose the most ridiculous ways of satisfying his lust - he is sold for two dimes. In this manner, all of the philosophical sects are ridiculed. Democritus is presented as someone who laughs incessantly at everything and everyone, as he considers all human affairs laughable and claims there is nothing serious in them. Everything is a hollow mockery, a drift of atoms. And Socrates is presented as someone who is eager to associate with a handsome lad, and to lie with him beneath the same cloak, whereas Plato dwells in a city of his own making where the laws against adultery have been abolished. Epicures is presented as a pupil of the laughing Democritus and the drunk Aristippus - although he himself surpasses his teachers in impiousness. As for Aristotle, reference is made to his remark that man is the only laughing living being, an insight which incites Hermes to conclude that the basic difference between a man and an ass resides in the faculty of laughter. In short, the play is a parody on market-square advertising where the salesmen, instead of boosting about their merchandise, admit and frankly deplore the poor condition and ridiculous nature of their human commodity (an example of parodical reversal) with the possible exception of Aristotle who is able to withstand Lucian's laughter and, in fact, sells for a rather good price - twenty minas. In his subsequent play, the philosophers have returned from the underworld in order to come after Lucian and capture him with the intention of stoning him to death, for having vilified them in his dialogue, until his mockery convinces them that their followers really are as impudent as Lucian had presented them. As is emphasized both by Bakhtin and Nietzsche, however, Hellenistic laughter is finally overcome by the fatal alliance of Christian asceticism and imperial etatism, inaugurating a solid moral regime of seriousness that will succeed to maintain itself up until the sixteenth century.[35]

---

[35] In spite of the fact that the established regime met with parodical popular resistance throughout its reign, at times even in the shape of Christian piety. Religious figures like Saint Francis, for example, challenged established morality by posing as God's simpleton and fool. Bakhtin also refers to his mendicant order whose members referred to themselves as *ioculatores Domini* (1968, p. 57). Unfortunately, the astonishingly rich history of comic medieval resistance is beyond the scope of this book.

Chapter 4

Judging Luther

Aber wohin gerate ich mit meinem Geschwätz... (Luther)[1]

1. PRELIMINARY REMARKS: THE EARLY SIXTEENTH CENTURY AS *AGON*

On the first page of his book on Luther and Kant, Bauch quotes the Luther expert Harnack who claims that, whereas the teachings of the early church, notwithstanding their dogmatic character, still constitute an object for philosophical reflection, no true philosopher will be able to appreciate Luther.[2] Although Bauch shares Harnack's sense of embarrassment with regard to Luther, he nevertheless argues that it is possible to separate the philosophical content from its disagreeable but residual environment[3] - i.e. Luther's impulsive and violent religious drive, his aversion to logic and sound reasoning, his grobian sense of humor, and his lack of proper education ('Bildung'). Now, quite at odds with the position of Harnack and Bauch, the basic objective of my *re*reading of Luther is to show that his philosophical significance cannot be separated from the 'grobian', 'residual' aspects of his achievement. But before turning to Luther himself, I would first like to posit him as a Renaissance figure, and subsequently draw attention to Nietzsche's judgement of him; much like in the previous chapter, I used Nietzsche's judgement of Socrates to further my understanding of Socratic laughter.

Unlike those who (like Nietzsche) try to distinguish the Renaissance from the early Reformation by regarding them as two mutually inimical and basically incompatible historical events, I would rather point out what they have in common. In my view, the Renaissance does not constitute a unity. Rather, it should be considered a strategic, agonistic situation in which several discursive forces compete with one another, at times impeding one another, at times reinforcing one another. Three of the major forces to be distinguished are: (1) sixteenth century humanism,

---

1 'What's the use of all this baloney?'. 'Eine Predigt Martin Luthers, daß man Kinder zur Schule halten solle'. M. Luther. *Werke*, 15 (2), p. 521.

2 'Ein Philosoph vermag die Mittel aufzutreiben, um die Dogmen der griechischen Kirche tiefsinnig und weise zu finden; kein Philosoph aber ist im Stande, dem Glauben Luthers irgend welchen Geschmack abzugewinnen' (Harnack, in: Bauch 1904, p.1).

3 ...das philosophisch Bedeutsame herauszuarbeiten (p. 5).

that is, the rereading and rediscovery of ancient literature on an unprecedented scale and with an unprecedented intensity and satisfaction; (2) a discursive mode that can be considered the completion of certain late medieval tendencies: the literature of parodical (also referred to as 'grotesque' or 'grobian') laughter; and (3) the early Reformation: the translation of the Scriptures into the vernacular and the spiritual resistance against the clergy and Rome. The outstanding individuals regarded as representative of these forces *in optima forma* are of course Erasmus, Rabelais, and Luther. Yet if we read their works more closely, they cannot be considered homogeneous bodies of writing either, but rather constitute strategic fields in their own right. The writings of Erasmus, for example, although undeniably dominated by the humanist objective, laughter is present as well, although its grobianism is subdued and refined compared to that of Rabelais. Likewise, although grobian and parodical laughter is quite prominent in Rabelais's books, humanist and anti-clerical forces are at work as well. Finally, Luther's writings constitute an irresistible mixture of theological seriousness and grobian laughter.

The position taken towards late medieval discourse is not as univocal as is sometimes suggested. Although in all three discursive genres the effort to distance oneself from the medieval state of mind is quite apparent, one should not underestimate the importance of rhetorical exaggeration as a discursive device in the service of self-affirmation. For instance, several basic ingredients of Luther's theology are already present in medieval theological discourse and in medieval mysticism. Of what did the apparent discontinuity with what went on before consist? In my opinion, the discontinuity between the discursive forces mentioned and the late medieval state of mind, lay in what they had in common: their excessive reliance on laughter as an access to truth. For although all the genres or forces mentioned had a significance and identity of their own, laughter somehow constituted a basic mood or state of mind which was present and recognizable in all of them, a general mood or ground which allowed these genres to emerge. Neither Erasmus nor Luther can be fully appreciated if one neglects the basic mood of laughter that is apparent in their writings - let alone Rabelais. Thus the basic mood of laughter allows for the emergence of Renaissance discourse as an agonistic, strategic situation. Yet laughter does not provide a 'ground' in the sense of constituting a stable principle or basic condition of unity. Rather, it is the source of the *instability* which characterizes early sixteenth Century discourse. It is a quasi-ground, temporarily impeding and contesting all efforts to establish a coherent and serious discourse. It is a source of disorder and confusion rather than a constructive, centripetal force (like, for example, the kind of rationality which subsequently came to constitute itself in the writings of Descartes and Kant, aimed at securing a stable and homogeneous discursive field, abolishing laughter.

126

The Renaissance (that is, the early sixteenth century, as far as the North of Europe is concerned) as an epoch must be regarded as a kind of discursive *interregnum* in which the basic mood of laughter temporarily prevents the establishment of discursive unity until modern rationality finally achieves its decisive *coup d'état*, expelling the quasi-principle of laughter to the burlesque undercurrents of official discourse. Subsequently, Renaissance discourse finds itself subjected to a systematic process of rectification and purification with the banishment of laughter as its major objective. Erasmus is appreciated merely as a humanist, while classicist sensibility and Enlightened reason allow only a thoroughly adapted Rabelais to enter their library. In the case of Luther, his grobian laughter increasingly constitutes a source of embarrassment to his followers, who make every effort to separate 'content' from 'residue', serious theology (the serious aspect of his work), from its all-too-primitive environment, Luther's remarkably grobian mode of speech. In my view, however, this has resulted in a profound distortion. My reading of Luther must therefore be considered a *re*reading, an exercise in retrieval, aimed at revealing the philosophical significance of his basic and irresistible laughter. Although *my* reading of Luther is bound to produce a certain one-sidedness as well, it is a bias which is justified as an effort to counterbalance the prevailing one.

In the first chapter I already referred to Toulmin's criticism of the standard account of modernity emphasizing that the ecclesiastical and ideological constraints imposed on public and scientific discourse in the seventeenth Century were much more rigid and intense than the ones in vogue during previous centuries, notably during the Renaissance. Toulmin refers basically to Renaissance writers like Erasmus and Montaigne, Shakespeare and Rabelais, but he hardly mentions their contemporary Luther. Is he to be considered a medieval relic, a spokesman of the Renaissance, or a prelude to seventeenth century rigidity and intolerance? Although many aspects of Toulmin's account are perfectly clear and convincing, the dividing line between Renaissance and Counter-Renaissance remains ambiguous where moral and religious experience is concerned. For instance, Toulmin refers to the artistic expression of seventeenth century Catholicism as 'histrionic and grotesque' and as a way of 'resisting the temptations to disbelief' (p. 54). In this chapter I would like to point out that 'histrionic' and 'grotesque' happen to be the very terms which are used today to indicate the peculiarities of Luther's linguistic efforts to resist the temptations of disbelief. Moreover, as we have seen, a negative understanding of the grotesque which today seems taken-for-granted emerged out of a classical (that is, Counter-Renaissance) aesthetics. What about the histrionic and grotesque features of Luther's language and work? Let us submit some sections of the immense bulk of his writing to a process of *re*reading - notably the ones which appear '*ri*sidual'. Is Luther a Renaissance or Counter-Renaissance phenomenon? Before addressing Luther himself, however, I would like to go into Nietzsche's judgement of him, particularly some remarkable ambiguities or inconsistencies in his judgement, for they seem to constitute a perfect preparation for our own effort to come to terms with him.

2. NIETZSCHE'S JUDGEMENT OF LUTHER

Luther hat es schon gesagt, und besser als ich...[4]

Ich habe nie bis jetzt stärker meine innigste Abhängigkeit von dem Geiste Luthers gefühlt als jetzt...[5]

Although of Lutheran descent, Nietzsche's judgement of Luther does not seem to have been based on a thorough acquaintance with either his work or his life. References to Luther preferably address a limited set of telling anecdotes concerning his (albeit remarkable) personality. As Nietzsche regarded a person's ideas as largely determined by his psychological and physiological constitution, the argument *ad hominem* was not something he would consider improper. On the contrary, meticulous historical or biographical verifications would inevitably reduce its strength.[6] Most, if not all, of Nietzsche's judgements of historical personalities were in fact *ad hominem* evaluations of a psychological and physiological nature - with 'resentment' and 'vulgarity' serving as his basic standards, that is, as the basic items of the Nietzschean 'personality scale'.

Hirsch (1986) and others have pointed to the fact that, in the course of his writings, Nietzsche's appreciation of Luther suffered a remarkable shift. In his earliest writings, notably *The Birth of Tragedy*, Luther was associated with the Dionysian principle, with 'drive', 'music' and 'health'.[7] He emerged as a heroic figure, an intellectual Hercules who put an end to the *vita contemplativa* of medieval asceticism, a Nordic double of the heroes of the Italian Renaissance, a true protagonist of the German soul who could still be of considerable use in the struggle against romanticism and, like Wagner, a prominent spokesman of German gaiety.[8] Underneath the insecure and drifting, 'visible' aspect of German culture, Nietzsche

---

[4] 'Luther already stated it, and better than I did...' [*Dawn of Day*, § 262].

[5] 'Never did I experience my intense dependence on Luther's mind as much as I do now...' [Letter to Erwin Rohde, 28 February 1875].

[6] *Untimely Meditations I*; *Werke I*, p. 254.

[7] *The Birth of Tragedy*, § 23; Cf. *On the Future of our Educational Institutions*, where Nietzsche refers to the 'healthy' mind of Luther-the-miner's-son.

[8] *Untimely Meditations IV*.

suspected there was a vital, healthy, age-old, popular force which during the Reformation emerged suddenly and vehemently from its abyss - an event personified by Luther.[9] He even refers to the Lutheran chorale as a truly 'Dionysian call'.

Of course, Nietzsche recognized that such a picture did not correspond to Luther's own basic objectives. Therefore, a second, apparently incompatible element was added: Luther was basically a plebeian buffoon who *inadvertently* became a hero, and his heroism was at odds with the original intentions of his spiritual revolt. However, due to his insufficient understanding of the art of government (that is, of the techniques and logic of exercising power) he foolishly crushed the basic conditions for what he had in fact wanted to support: Christianity. Indeed, as far as his intellectual talents were concerned, he was rather the opposite of Nietzsche's *real* heroes - the calculating and highly intelligent Renaissance politicians and popes, who were Luther's principal foes. Luther's rejection of the *vita contemplativa*, for instance, did not evolve out of a well-considered judgement, and even less out of dislike for Christianity as such, but rather out of his crude and lumpish, 'peasant' judgement concerning the lives of Saints.[10]

Before long, however, a different picture of Luther emerges in Nietzsche's writings. Although he still considers him a plebeian buffoon, he now recognizes that Luther had in fact saved Christianity from its impending ruin rather than devastating it, by bringing the Renaissance to a halt and provoking the Counter-Reformation with his lumpish and ridiculous stubbornness.[11] Nietzsche now sees him as a grim, violent, retarded and backward mind who succeeded in restoring to life an epoch that had already expired. While the Renaissance is referred to by Nietzsche as the Golden Age of our millennium, the Lutheran revolt is considered its first and foremost foe.[12] In short, Nietzsche's judgement of Luther had become unequivocally

---

[9] *The Birth of Tragedy*, § 23.

[10] *Dawn of Day*, § 88. In a famous letter to Brandes (20 November 1888] Nietzsche refers to the Renaissance pope Cesare Borgia as the summit of Renaissance laughter, the perfect reversal of Christianity ('Cesare Borgia als Papst - das wäre der Sinn der Renaissance, ihr eigentliches Symbol'). Is Luther, the Counter-Pope at Wittenberg, a rehabilitation of Christian seriousness, or the summit of parodical laughter: a grobian, plebeian miner's son for pope!

[11] According to Erik Erikson (1958/1962), it was Jakob Burckhardt who taught Nietzsche to see in Luther the noisy German peasant who waylaid the march of Renaissance man.

[12] 'Dagegen [against the Renaissance] hebt sich nun die Deutsche Reformation ab als ein energischer Protest zurückgebliebener Geister, welche die Weltanschauung des Mittelalters noch keineswegs satt hatten', *Human, All Too Human I*, § 237; Cf. his remarks on 'der Bauernkrieg und Pöbelaufstand, der über den geistigen Geschmack im Norden Europas Herr geworden ist und welcher an dem großen "ungeistigen Menschen", an Luther, seinen Anführer hatte', *Nachlass*, III, p. 465.

negative. Luther becomes the perfect lout, the perfect personification of 'German lumpishness', the spokesman of its crudest instincts.[13] The Reformation is now perceived by Nietzsche as a brutal, peasant version of Christianity, a pointless revolt that emerged out of the primitive indignation of simpletons,[14] the *peasant revolt* in the realm of morality, a ridiculous recurrence of the original 'slave revolt', defying and despising everything more aristocratic, more intelligent, while remaining at the same time eager to obey.[15] Due to a rather coincidental concurrence of political circumstances, Luther was not burned at the stake right away, but was allowed to succeed in preventing the Renaissance from achieving its magnificent goal.

In short, Luther had suddenly become one of the great pessimists whose basic motive was resentment.[16] In a remarkable section of *Human, All Too Human* Nietzsche's revised judgement of Luther is abundantly clear.[17] At times, Nietzsche claims, Fortune's farces become dreadfully visible, like during the negotiations at Regensburg between Luther and Continari. On the verge of a peaceful settlement, Luther's bony head - *knöcherne Kopf* - continued its struggle and resistance, full of suspicion and gloomy fear. For the sake of certain formula which, due to their ideological and theological nature and their lack of correspondence to any real objects or state of affairs, did not allow for any sensible discussion, Germany went up in flames. Forces were put to work whose magnitude remained unparalleled throughout modernity (apparently a symptom of Dionysianism) but they were of a negative, catastrophic and deplorable nature.[18]

Hirsch claimed that this remarkable change in Nietzsche's judgement was caused by his accidental reading of the second volume of Janssen's *Geschichte des Deutschen Volkes*. This controversial claim, although definitely one-sided (Salaquarda 1986), is not without a grain of truth. Nietzsche *did* derive his understanding of Luther from secondary sources, such as Janssen's, instead of studying Luther himself - with one exception. During a decisive episode of his creative life in which he produced *Thus Spoke Zarathustra* and *Beyond Good and Evil*, Nietzsche came to read (and greatly appreciate) the German Bible (Luther's translation of the Scriptures) intensively. In fact, he considered Luther's Bible the

---

[13] Cf.: 'Wenn auf Trunk, Trunkenheit und eine übelriechende Art von Unfläterei auch nur von ferne hingewinkt wurde, dann wurden die Seelen der älteren Deutschen fröhlich - sonst waren sie verdrossen' (*Human, All-Too-Human II*, 'The Wanderer and his Shadow', § 224).

[14] *The Gay Science*, § 358.

[15] *Dawn of Day*, § 207.

[16] *Dawn of Day*, § 3, § 68; *The Antichrist*, § 61; cf. some of his remarks on Luther in the *Nachlass*.

[17] *Human, All Too Human II*, 'Mixed Opinions and Aphorisms', § 226.

[18] *The Gay Science*, § 148.

most splendid German book and, in a way, Luther would have approved of Nietzsche's judgement, for he himself considered his translation of the Bible his most important achievement as a writer. Compared to Luther's Bible, Nietzsche claimed, almost everything else was mere 'literature'.[19] Once again a rather ambiguous picture of Luther emerges. On the one hand, he is still considered a lout and a buffoon. On the other hand, he is the unrivalled master of German prose. The latter judgement was based on Nietzsche's own reading of Luther, the first one at least partly on telling anecdotes, provided by sources such as Janssen.

At the same time, however (and probably because of his intensive reading of Luther's Bible), Nietzsche recognized a basic affinity with Luther - for example when he noticed that, apart from Nietzsche himself, Luther and Goethe were to be regarded the three decisive events in the history of the German language.[20] Hirsch and others pointed to the fact that Nietzsche's reading of Luther's Bible greatly influenced the language of *Thus Spoke Zarathustra*. Allison (1990) emphasizes the extent to which Nietzsche, in *Thus Spoke Zarathustra*, borrowed from and relied on some of Luther's basic rhetorical devices. As I already explained in the previous chapter, however, I quite agree with Hirsch that Nietzsche's imitation did not succeed in equalling the original. On the contrary, compared to Luther's translation of the New Testament (an overwhelming and magnificent literary achievement) *Thus Spoke Zarathustra* is artificial, tedious and decadent. Instead of being *un*timely and anti-romantic, Nietzsche in some respects remains a perfect representative of the nineteenth century, notably of nineteenth century laughter, much like Luther was in many ways a perfect representative of the 'golden' century Nietzsche admired so much but could not equal, let alone surpass.

Nietzsche increasingly came to despise the vulgar, peasant-like aspect of Luther's personality. Yet at the same time he persisted in a rather positive and apparently incompatible appreciation for Luther's comic decorum. For example, he claims that, in the case of great men, the coarse, the impudent and the excessive (the all-too-human so to speak) allows for their influence to be contained within certain boundaries because of the suspicion it is bound to raise.[21] Although at times emphasizing the terrible and tragic events in Luther's biography, Nietzsche recognized that the larger part of it belonged to the comical genre. In *On the Genealogy of Morals* Nietzsche writes that, if one day someone would narrate in a truly psychological manner the 'real Luther', something powerful would emerge (§

---

19 *Beyond Good and Evil*, § 247.

20 [I]ch bilde mir ein, mit diesem Z[arathustra] die Deutsche Sprache zu ihrer Vollendung gebracht zu haben. Es war, nach *Luther* und Goethe noch ein dritter Schritt zu tun'; Brief an Erwin Rohde, 22 February 1884.

21 *Human, All Too Human II*, 'Mixed Opinions and Aphorisms', § 186.

19). But what would this real Luther look like? Elsewhere in the same book (§ 2, § 3) Nietzsche had already explained that Wagner's most cheerful episode had been the one in which he had concerned himself with Luther's marriage. Had he pursued his plans in this direction, Nietzsche claims, he would certainly have produced a wonderful *Luther-comedy*. Instead he created *Parsifal*, the story of the perfect simpleton, but made him a catholic. Was Wagner serious, was *Parsifal* really a tragedy, or rather a farewell to tragedy? Was *Parsifal* with its excesses and wilful exaggerations a *parody* on the tragic genre as such, a comical piece in which Wagner finally reached the summit of artistic creation, being able to laugh at himself[22] with the implication that he had finally recovered from pessimism? In *Human, All Too Human*, Nietzsche included a little scene that reads like a fragment from such a Luther comedy.[23] This comical scene (which in fact resembles or parodies some of the actual conversations between Luther and Melanchton recorded in the *Tischreden*)[24] presents us with the 'real' Luther as perceived by Nietzsche: lumpish and gay, employing grotesque images, transforming the terrible into the comical by connecting it with the material body's lower half and granting that ardent preaching is a symptom of lack of faith.

In Nietzsche's view the bulk of Luther's theology can be explained by his peculiar, folksy logical instincts: his suspicion against arguments and etiquette[25] and, even more significant, his *peasant* conception of truth, considering truth to be something which someone 'has', and someone else does not 'have' - a rather comical and vulgar understanding of the concept of truth according to Nietzsche.[26] Luther-the-peasant, due to a deficient sense of reverence and etiquette, demanded the right to speak with 'his' God directly, without mediation and without embarrassment. Indeed, his resistance against mediation by priest, pope or saint was a sign of peasant

---

22   According to Nietzsche, an artist reaches his summit of artistic creation 'wenn er über sich zu *lachen* weiß', *The Gay Science*, § 3.

23   *Schwarzert* (Melanchton): Man predigt oft seinen Glaube, wenn man ihn grade verloren hat und auf allen Gassen sucht, - und man predigt ihn dann nicht am schlechtesten!
   Luther : Du redest heut' wahr wie ein Engel, Bruder!
   Schwarzert : Aber es ist der Gedanke deiner Feinde, und sie machen auf dich die Nutzanwendung.
   Luther : So war's eine Lüge aus des Teufels Hintern ('What is Truth?', *Human, All Too Human II*, § 66; Schwarzert was Melanchton's original, German name).

24   Cf., for instance, 5:5428.

25   *On the Genealogy of Morals III*, § 22.

26   *The Antichrist*, § 53.

impertinence and rudeness.[27]

From a Bakhtinean perspective, the *Tischreden* ('Table Talks' or 'Prandial Conversations') to which I just referred, collected and published posthumously, constitute a crucial part of Luther's achievement rather than being a collection of raw materials from which the theological content has to be carefully isolated by serious readers at the expense of an enormous residue of grotesque and histrionic waste. Indeed, it is a work where considerable support is found for the picture of Luther as a popular buffoon. The time-old affinity of food with the spoken word, of eating with speaking provides the generic link between Plato's *Symposium* and Luther's prandial conversations. The laughing tone, the carefree vocabulary, the gross exaggerations, the fearless truth can be found in both. Luther's bold (and often abusive) language constitutes a perfect example of what Bakhtin refers to as 'a banquet form of speech, liberated from fear and piousness' (1968, p. 297). Allow me to give a few examples in response to Nietzsche's judgement of Luther as commented on above, notably Nietzsche's remark on the basically peasant-like logic Luther relied on. One remarkable example of this logic is Luther's version of proving the existence of God. According to Luther, the most convincing argument that demonstrates the existence of God resides in the fact that a cow gives birth to a cow, and never to a horse whereas a horse gives birth to a horse, and never to a cow; *ergo*, there must be someone who is guiding this wonderful process of reproduction.[28] Furthermore, Luther at times succeeded in solving some tedious theological issue or other in a rather grotesque and peasant-like manner. Take, for example, the way he responds to a question concerning God's responsibility for the existence of evil in the world, which came up in the course of a discussion on how a certain section of the *2nd Book of Samuel* had to be interpreted. Although in principle God is able to prevent all evil, He sometimes (for reasons that are bound to remain obscure to us) restricts Himself to alleviating or containing its harmful consequences. This is explained by Luther by means of the following example. If

---

27 Luther, diese beredteste und unbescheidenste Bauer... Luthers Widerstand gegen die Mittlerheiligen der Kirche (insbesondere gegen 'des Teuffels Saw den Bapst') war, daran ist kein Zweifel, im letzten Grunde der Widerstand eines Rüpels, den die *gute Etikette* der Kirche verdroß, jene Ehrfurchts-Etikette des hieratischen Geschmacks, welche nur die Geweihteren und Schweigsameren in das Allerheiligste einläßt und es gegen die Rüpel zuschließt. Diese sollen ein für allemal gerade hier nicht das Wort haben - aber Luther, der Bauer, wollte es schlechterdings anders... er wollte vor allem direct reden, selber reden, 'ungeniert' mit seinem Gott reden... Nun, er hat's getan (*On the Genealogy of Morals III, § 22*).

28 'Hoc est optimum argumentum, quod me multum saepe movit, quod ex generatione specierum probat esse Deum: *Ein ku gebür allzeit ein ku, ein pferd ein pferd* etc.; *kein ku gebür ein pferd* nec equus vaccam... Ergo necesse est aliquid, quod ita gubernet omnia' (5:5440).

someone is about to shit somewhere, God may, instead of preventing it, induce him to retreat into some corner or other, rather than emptying his bottom on the table.[29] This is a conversation which reads like a scene borrowed from some primitive popular farce rather than a line of argument in a theological debate[30] - until one recognizes that the transformation of the terrifying (the bewildering thought of God as the omnipotent origin of evil) into the comical is Luther's access to moral truth. It is part of what Bakhtin refers to as the 'specific truth of table talk' (1968, p. 117). Now how could someone who argues in this manner, claiming that our aperture's produce either truth or dung, and consistently comparing his adversaries to arse-holes and sows wallowing in the mire, actually succeed in preparing the way for modern moral experience to emerge? Bakhtin's concept of parody and the grotesque will allow us to further our understanding of this question which was raised rather than solved by Nietzsche. From a Bakhtinean perspective, Luther became the master of German prose *because* he acted as the spokesman of popular laughter; laughter is the basic, vital and 'Dionysian' force at work in Luther's language. This is the hypothesis that will be put to the test in the subsequent sections of this chapter, in which some of Luther's writing will be submitted to a careful *re*reading. I will discard the standard and 'pious' account, which can be found in almost every introduction to his writings and which holds that the quintessence and truth of Luther's work must be carefully separated from those elements which seem *merely* anecdotical as well as those which nowadays are considered disturbingly grotesque - in short those elements which have been 'over-emphasized' by ill-disposed (notably Catholic) readers.

---

29 'Cum autem Semei male agere vult, *so sagt Gott: Dem thues und sonst niemandts! Als, wenn einer scheissen will, das kann ich nicht weren, aber das ers hieher thue auff den disch, das will ich weren und sprich: in winckel!'* (V, 5225). Of course the comical effect is intensified by Luther's tone of voice, his perfect mastery of the grotesque mode of speech, which remains unsurpassed, provided his language is judged according to the standards of the genre. Notice also yet another basic feature of parodical discourse, the 'macaronic' mixture of languages, of fragments in Latin as well as in the German vernacular (Cf. Bakhtin 1968, p. 150).

30 Simons (1990) points out that, whereas in the case of a sermon scenes form every life provide a clue which enables one to focus attention on the spiritual (that is, the lower is connected with the higher), in the case of parody it is the other way around: the higher is degarded and reduced to the level of the lower (p. 74). Many prandial conversations are difficult to subsume with certainty either under the genre of parody or under the genre of the sermon - their generic identity remains ambivalent.

3. LUTHER 'LIE-GENDS'

In the previous section I pointed out that Nietzsche partially based his understanding and appreciation of Luther on anecdotes. Even during his life-time Luther was surrounded by a host of biographical or quasi-biographical legends - he himself referred to them as *lie-gends* ('Lügenden'). Some of them are incorrect, even malicious. Others, however, are at least partially true, or focus attention on certain significant aspects of his achievement which might otherwise escape us. In short, we should not reject them altogether. Moreover, the basic characteristics of the time-old carnivalistic tradition will apply to them as well. Carnivalistic legends, Bakhtin tells us, debase the hero and bring him down to earth. They familiarize and humanize him and bring him up close, but they do so 'without harming the genuinely heroic core of the image' (1968, p. 109).

Among the most obstinate of these Luther lie-gends[31] is the claim that he descended from a line of notorious drunkards and superstitious simpletons, while he himself appreciated what he euphemistically referred to as a proper drink.[32] It has often been claimed that the many physical ailments that disturbed him in his later years were caused by excessive food and drink,[33] and that he died from hitting the hay with an overburdened stomach. Another lie-gend holds that he firmly believed in the existence of devils, while others suggest that he encouraged gross sensuality and libertarianism (*pecca fortifer!*) and that his basic motive for starting the Reformation was his personal inability to hold on to celibacy.[34] All of these lie-gends support the image of Luther as a popular buffoon, an impious, gluttonous, 'impossible', ridiculous monk, a character such as can be encountered in early modern novels and popular farces. Furthermore, there is another set of lie-gends that persistently portray him as a hard-headed, stubborn peasant wilfully blocking serious possibilities for

---

31 See, for example, Van Bakel (1946).

32 'Wer nicht liebt Wein, Weib und Gesang, der bleibt ein Narr sein Leben lang' is one of his most famous lines. In case one is tormented by temptation or nausea, or falls short of faith, Luther recommends sexual intercourse and substantial drinking ['thue einen guten trunk'], for a Christian ought to remain a gay sort of person, while the devil will attempt to turn him into a melancholiac: *Ein christen soll ein frolich mensch sein* [*Tischreden*, 3:3298].

33 'Fressen und saufen'. Cf. the passage in the *Tischreden* where he calculates what is consumed by him each year in view of his growing too fat, and is embarrassed and astonished at the result [Sedens et edens in mensa dixit... 3: 3258].

34 In fact, one of the reasons for Luther's father to object to his son becoming a monk was his prediction that Martin, in view of the inherited, innate physical temperament of the Luders, would not be able to endure a monastic regime (Luther's original family-name was Luder).

consensus and mutual settlement. Although these images of Luther are (at least partly) deplored and considered incorrect by many Luther experts, these experts do admit that (albeit most unfortunately) they are encouraged and fostered by some peculiar (but apparently inessential) features of his achievement - notably the fact that his writings display and at times even excel in coarseness and verbal abuse, while in some respects he remained attached to 'gothic' remnants which before long came to be considered offensive to reason, such as his rather traditional and 'gothic' opinions on devils, and even his understanding of the Communion. When he claims just a few days before his death to have spotted a devil sitting on a rainpipe, in the shape of a black dog exposing his behind, one is indeed reminded of the gothic, demonic ornaments still to be seen on the roofs and drains of gothic cathedrals, borrowed from late medieval popular imagination.

All his biographers agree that the picture of Luther as a person contains several astonishing contradictions. During his student years, someone referred to him as *musicus et philosophicus*, a description often cited as it already seems to point to the *clair-obscure*, the gay and gloomy aspects of his personality. At times he was quite gentle and indulgent, but at other times he was ferocious and inflexible. He was both a revolutionary and a conservative, both a scholar and a prophet, both a national figure and a *pater familias*. In short, he seemed to exemplify *in optima forma* the energetic but politically unreliable, early modern temper referred to by Marx as 'grobian'.

There was already something remarkable in his physique, in the architectonics of his body. Instead of bowing his head while walking, as he was taught in the convent, he strode along with his head facing the sky. His face bears the expression of peasant firmness, stubbornness and humor. We are told that in his youth his glance was uncanny, almost unbearable. During the examinations at Worms, his adversaries shuddered before his ghastly, demonic aspect and one of them, Nuntius Aleander, describes how Luther made his appearance with an idiotic expression of laughter on his face, which seems to have suggested something like a blustering fire or a raging storm. Cajetanus, it is said, refused to continue the dispute at Augsburg because he felt intimidated by the gloomy profundity of his eyes. But at other occasions, notably during his later years, he emerges as a gay, merry, laughing figure whose physical appearance marks the rejection of medieval asceticism. We are also told that he moved his members vividly while preaching or praying. His devotion was of a merry nature,[35] and he actually coined a special term for it: *Friedigkeit*, indicating gay recklessness or merry audacity. As Preuss justly noted, one cannot separate Luther from his sense of humor (1947, pp. 54-55). His merriment was as abundant as his rage. His verbal aggression was as ferocious as it

---

[35] Cf. his first spiritual: 'Nun freut euch, lieben Christen g'mein / und laßt uns fröhlich springen'.

was gay. There is irresistible wit at work in the way he keeps comparing his enemies to hogs, goats, snails, asses, dogs and others farm animals.[36] Luther's language clearly excels in carefree humor - *Iß und trink, auf einem vollen Bauch stehet ein fröhlig Haupt*. He is not gay and merry on occasions, but intrinsically merry, writing in a basic mood of laughter, whereas it is the devil's basic objective to turn us into melancholiacs.[37]

In most biographies, Luther is presented as an unstable intermediary figure, a transition between the world of medieval dogma (unable to retain him) and that of modern philosophy (unwilling to admit him), something like an obedient rebel or a brisk neurotic, both restoring and adulterating the Word of God. All biographers, however, unanimously point to his astonishing gift for language as well as his vulgar humor, his folksy manners, and his excessive reliance on verbal abuse. Erik Erikson (1958/1962) has drawn a very famous psychological portrait of him as a young man. The 'folksy' aspects of Luther's personality are explained as remnants of his rather humble descent: his nostalgia for the hard simplicity of peasant life, his vulgarity and blockheadedness, his preoccupation with saws, mud, soil and fertility, his stubbornness and rebelliousness, as well as his 'gothic' preoccupation with devils. Erikson's book is primarily on *young* Luther and he discerns a marked difference between the young Luther, a fascinating, highly gifted neurotic, and the old Luther, a sturdy, voluble table-talker who looked back on his past as a mythological auto-hagiography, indulging himself in florid self-revelations with a 'histrionic' flair, contributing selected memories to what was about to become his official identity. Erikson expresses his distaste for those histrionic 'after-dinner exaggerations', those 'folksy exaggerations of his table-talk vocabulary' (p. 139), considering them 'undisciplined', 'irresponsible' and 'grotesque' (p. 147) - 'although for a few years Luther occupied the stage of history with some of the exhibitionistic grandeur of a Renaissance man, there is no doubt that he concluded his life in an obese provinciality' (p. 194).

Young Luther, on the other hand, is considered a gifted but severely disturbed youth whose 'cause' became his cure. Indeed, Luther's case history is said to consist of marked periods of manic productivity that alternated with severe depressive breakdowns in which his inclination towards gaiety was eclipsed by his chronic *tentationes tristitiae*, or even by utter despair. Three psychopathological highlights are distinguished: (1) his fit in the choir at Erfurt when, roaring in rage, but also in

---

36 A linguistic device employed by the church as well. Cf. the first line of *Exsurge, Domine* , the famous papal bull that condemned him: 'Rise to Your feet, o Lord, for a wild boar intends to damage Your vineyard'. But quite unlike Luther's merry abuse, relentlessly directed toward the Pope and clergy, the Church's response is far from gay - rather, it is full of hatred, it is *merely* inimical.

37 'Tristitia instrumentum Sathanae' [3:2840].

laughter, he suddenly cried out *Ich bin's nit*, (2) the famous Thunderbolt Experience near Stotternheim and (3) the Tower Experience at Wittenberg, which will be considered in the next section.

Apart from his psychological ailments, Erikson studied his physical problems as well. Luther appears to have suffered from lifelong constipation and urine retention,[38] notably due to chronic melancholia and kidney problems which he, after leaving the monastery, tried to counter by consuming huge amounts of beer and eating ravenously. Erikson suggests, however, in view of his immobile circumstances, already during his stay at the Wartburg but also later in life, that his enjoyment of food and beer greatly aggravated his sadness and his constipation as well as his preoccupation with the lower parts of his body. Erikson tells us: 'He would speak of "being on labour" when his kidney stones made him swell up. When they had passed, he announced the elimination of Gargantuan quantities of fluid: eleven buckets at one time' (p. 245).[39] Indeed, he was 'bawdy' about his 'bulky body', 'obviously enjoyed hearty food and plenty of beer', as well as 'belching and farting'. His grotesque body language and his 'bawdy jokes' are explained as expressions of neurotic symptoms, as 'regressed, defiant obstinacy', and his obscenity is said to express the 'needs of his manic-depressive nature' while his repudiative and anal witticisms as well as his 'many nasty and provocative statements' (with which he set 'a lasting bad example to his people') are considered an indication of regressive, obsessive transference. Up to a certain point, Erikson claims, Luther's body language could be explained as being in accordance with contemporary aesthetics: '[P]eople in those days expressed much more openly [the emotional implications] of the primary bodily functions. We permit ourselves to understand them in a burlesque show, or in circumstances where we can laugh off our discomfort; but we are embarrassed when we are asked to acknowledge them in

---

[38] Apart from all of this, Luther also suffered from a constant buzzing and whizzing in his ears, which Erikson attributes to a chronic middle ear infection. He even suggests that Luther's spiritual weapon, his 'inner voice', might be explained by this fact (p. 244), much like Nietzsche suggested that Socrates's 'inner voice' could be attributed to ear problems - '*So ist vielleicht auch das Dämonion des Sokrates ein Ohrenleiden, das er sich gemäß seiner herrschenden moralischen Denkungsart nur anders, als es jetzt geschehen würde, ausgelegt*' (*Human, All Too Human I*, § 126).

[39] Luther was in the habit of keeping his friends well informed about his physical condition. 'The Lord has kicked me in the ass', he writes in a famous letter to Melanchton from the Wartburg, 'and my stool is so hard that it takes a lot of pressure and sweat to get rid of it' (12 May 1521). Indeed, he begs Melanchton to pray for a healthy stool. In his letter of 27 February 1537, once again to Melanchton, he reports that, as he got up one night and tried to piss in vain as usual, God suddenly opened up his ureter and bladder and enabled him to release a huge amount of the kind of liquid which is considered inferior by others but of precious value to Luther himself. Moreover, he reports that this very letter had been written while alternately pissing and writing.

earnest' (p. 205). In his later years, however, 'when Luther's freedom of speech occasionally deteriorated into vulgar license, he went far beyond the customary gay crudity of his early days' (p. 206) - and Erikson cites the following line taken from the *Prandial Conversations* as an example: 'I am like ripe shit, and the world is a gigantic ass-whole'.[40] In the closing section of this chapter, Erikson's psychological, psychoanalytical evaluation of Luther's life will be reviewed more critically. Instead of considering Luther's anal witticisms a symptom of a neurotic, obsessive concern with defecation or of psychic decline, I will point to the general features of the grotesque speech genre to which they belong, and in which excremental images, rather than conveying a negative mood, are associated with reproduction, fertility, and life, with birth, dying and being reborn, with laughter.

Luther adheres to a grotesque understanding of the body which is displayed throughout his prandial conversations, of which many examples could be cited. For example, he refers to the nose as the head's latrine, with the implication that God has to accept prayers which are said from underneath a privy.[41] Furthermore, he considered someone's capacity for defecation (which in his case had been greatly affected by monastical life) a sign of good health [3:3006]. Moreover, according to Luther, as the physical desire of eunuchs was known to increase instead of decrease with emasculation, he recommends that one should rather put on a second pair of testicles than to have his natural pair cut off [3:2865]. And during a conversation with Lukas Cranach (referred to as a person of comparable gaiety) which took place in an orchard, Luther pointed out that they in fact feeded themselves from a peasant's buttocks whose shit contained the seeds which had produced the trees, etc. [3:3210a]. Even Luther's relationship with the Devil displays all the features of grobian laughter such as can be found in the writings of Rabelais and other contemporaries. Indeed, due to grobian laughter, the terrible gothic creature is transformed into a jovial companion. In his later years, Luther had come to accept the devil's company [3:3154; 3: 3208], although at times they would still quarrel and Luther would be disturbed by his presence, taking on a dog-like disguise and afflicting him not only spiritually but also physically. Luther justified the obesity of his latter years by saying that he wanted to grow sufficiently fat in order for the devil, if by any chance he were to swallow him, would be choked by him, or at least feel forced to spit him out again. He defines sexuality mainly in terms of the physical necessity to rid oneself of bodily discharge, and discusses it in a down-to-earth, peasant-like manner. It is a cure against melancholia inflicted by a devil. Luther continued to believe in the presence of all kinds of demons and devils, hiding in forests, waters and marshes

---

40 'Ich bin der reiffe dreck, so ist die welt das weite arschloch... Ich danck dir, lieber Gott, das du mich lessest unter deinem geringen heufflein sein', 5:5537.

41 'Nasus enim est latrina capitis, *sthet einem uber dem maul*, immo ipse Deus *mus alle gebet und Gotts dienst unter dem scheishaus geschehen lassen*' [3:2807].

and also in clouds, producing all kinds of weather effects which, according to Luther, were mistakenly attributed to unknown natural causes by philosophers and physicians [3:2829]. At times, the Devil would tempt someone to enter a theological debate with him, or cause nausea or some kind of physical ailment. While residing at the Wartburg, Luther claims to have thrown walnuts at him [3:2885].

All this reveals and verifies the Renaissance mood of laughter at work in Luther's mode of speech. Yet, the most prominent of all the Luther lie-gends (one which happens to be true, and Luther himself is the source of it) concerns his basic experience of revelation, the very turning point of his spiritual life - a story which continued to embarrass his followers, while providing his enemies with the easiest of targets for ridicule: the decisive experience which came to be known as the *Turmerlebnis* - or 'tower experience'. What happened?

4. THE TOWER EXPERIENCE

Before turning to the tower experience itself, let me just briefly summarize the events to which it provides a (comic) plot. All biographers agree that Luther experienced a gloomy, gothic childhood and adolescence, full of hardship and terror. The summit of this gothic mood of terror was the so-called Stotternheim experience. While still a student and on his way from Eisleben to Erfurt, near a small village north-east of Erfurt called Stotternheim, he was caught in a tremendous thunderstorm which terrified him to such an extent that, startled by a flash of lightening, he made his famous vow to Saint Anne (the domestic saint of miners like his parents were and quite popular in rural areas at that time) to become a monk. Rather than being terrified by the storm itself, he was struck with fear and despair at the prospect of facing divine judgement. Indeed, he was overwhelmed by all the ghastly terrors of late medieval life.[42] Subsequently, while trying to become a perfect monk, his sensibility remained rather medieval and melancholic. His basic experiential mood was one of fear and despair rather than laughter. He desperately tried to subdue his sense of guilt by means of a rigid regime of fasting, freezing and isolating himself in his cell - all to no avail. At a certain point, however, at a time when he was completely absorbed by his reading of the Psalter and the Epistles of Saint Paul (notably the ones addressing the christians of Rome and those of Galatia) Luther experienced a spiritual transformation in which the thunderbolt experience near Stotternheim found its reversal. Indeed, this new experience constituted its *comic double*. Luther himself described it briefly but tellingly during one of his prandial

---

42 '...*alle Schrecken des Mittelalters fallen über ihn her*' (Preuss 1946).

conversations.[43]

In those days, while still being under the sway of papal doctrine, he tells us, those terrible words 'just' and 'justice' used to strike him like lightning and it terrified him merely to hear them uttered. For in his mind justice was inevitably associated with punishment. But once, while lingering in the tower in which the monk's privy was located, reflecting on that most obscure of lines in Saint Paul's Letter to the Christians of Rome where it is suggested that those who are justified through faith shall live (1:17), it suddenly dawned on him that justice, rather than indicating divine punishment for our sins, implies that it is God's justice by which we are justified, or rather, rectified and saved from sin.

Now for the modern reader it is a difficult task to understand the true significance of this remarkable, epoch-making revelation, this outcome of Luther's persistent *re*reading of the Psalter and the Epistles.[44] Indeed, we tend to fall silent for a while, or feel urged to read these lines over and over again, without gaining a clear understanding at first. What is Luther pointing at? What has happened? What we in fact witness here is the basic truth of the spiritual movement that came to be known as the Reformation, formulated for the very first time in its primitive, untrimmed,

---

43 The prandial conversations contain three different versions of the tower experience: 'Haec vocabula Iustus et Iustitia in papatu fulmen mihi erant in conscientia et ad solum auditum terrebant me, sed cum semel in hac turri (in qua secretus locus erat monachorum) specularer de istis vocabulis: Iustis ex fide vivit, et: Iustitia Dei etc., obiter veniebat in mentem: Si vivere debemus iusti fide per iustitiam et illa iustitia Dei est ad salutem omni credenti, ergo ex fide est iustitia et ex iustitia vita. Et erigebatur mihi conscientia mea et animus meus, et certus reddebar iustitiam Dei esse, guae nos iustificaret et salvaret. Ac statim fiebant mihi hic verba dulcia en iucunda verba. *Dieße kunst hatt mir der Heilige Geist auff diesem thurm geben*' [3232a].
'Iustus, Iustitia. Haec vocabulo Iustus et Iustitia Dei erant mihi fulmen in conscientia. Mox reddebar pavidus auditor: Iustus, ergo punit. Sed cum semel in hac turri speculabar de istis vocabulis: Iustus ex fide vivit, iustitia Dei, mox cogitaveram: Si vivere debemus iusti ex fide iustitia Dei debet esse ad salutem omni credenti, mox erigebatur mihi animus: Ergo iustitia Dei est, guae nos iustificat et salvat. Et facta sunt mihi haec verba iucundiora. *Dise khunst hat mir der Heilig Geist aiff diser cl. [cloaca] auff dem thorm gegeben*' [3232b].
'Nam haec verba: Iustus et Iustitia Dei erant mihi fulmen in conscientia, quibus audutus expavescebam: Si Deus est iustus, ergo puniet. Sed Dei gratia cum semel in hac turri et hypocausto specularer de istis vocabulis: Iustus ex fide vivit. et: Iustitia Dei, mox cogitabam: Si vivere debemus iusti ex fide et iustitia Dei debet ad salutem omni credenti, non erit meritum nostrum, sed misericordia Dei. Ita erigebatur animus meus. Nam iustitia Dei est, qua nos iustificamur et salvamur per Christum. Et illa verba facta sunt mihi iucundiora. *Die Schriefft hat mir der Heilige Geist in diesem thurn ofenbaret*' [3232c].

44 The modern reader will have similar difficulties to understand why those enigmatic and riddle-like statements known as the 95 theses could provoke such a tremendous uproar (he will find it difficult to understand them at all).

original version. The bulk of Luther's theology (a theory about to shake Europe to its very foundations) is contained in these few, remarkably comic lines, that rather read like a *parody* of revelation. They illustrate what Luther, many years later, had in mind when he stated that a fart produced in Wittenberg was audible in Rome. In these few lines it is claimed that we are completely incapable of improving ourselves by means of works or exercise and that we remain guilty before God, who nevertheless takes pity on us by saving and rectifying us - *some* of us. In short, *we are irreparably doomed, nothing can save us, ergo God will save us*. Of course, this revelation, notably the use of the word *ergo*, has nothing to do with propositional logic; it is a truth of faith, which cannot be recapitulated by reason. On the contrary, from a rational point of view such a line of reasoning seems utterly absurd. And yet, once we allow this 'truth' to enter our mind, once we really open ourselves to it, it becomes irresistible: it is not something which can be denied or rejected. We are overwhelmed, reassured, brightened by it - it makes us laugh, or cry, or defecate, or whatever. It is an experience which reminds us of Nietzsche's wonderful definition of 'gay science', cited in Chapter 2: the *saturnalia* of a mind who has patiently resisted a persistent pressure of long standing; a kind of recovery, almost like a state of drunkenness, where many a foolish and unwise thing will emerge, an experience which reveals the basic connection between truth and laughter. Luther's response to the gothic truth (we are doomed, our works fall short in comparison to our sins, we will remain guilty before God, nothing can save us) is the gay and liberating truth that God *himself* will save us, regardless of our sins. It is, moreover, a perfect example of what I referred to as *re*reading. Indeed, Luther himself refers to the 'art of reading' with which he claims to have been equipped by the Holy Spirit while he was busy attending to his daily physical needs. Those very lines which seemed to support the gothic regime of terror, suddenly announced the Dawn of Day.

At first glance, gothic terror is exaggerated to the extreme by claiming that the human soul is fundamentally corrupted by original sin and that our guilt is beyond reparation. There is no hope of correcting or improving ourselves, nor can man's basic inclination towards evil be overcome by 'works' or exercise (the medieval 'solution'). At that point, however, when we are about to be overwhelmed by utter despair, the liberating truth dawns on us that only God *can* and therefore *will* save us, that is, pardon our sins through an act of grace. In other words, we are rectified through faith, while 'works' and exercise (the hard core of spiritual existence and monastical life during the gothic Middle Ages) are rendered insignificant. Delumeau (1965) and others have explained that Luther's theology provided an answer, a solution to the general experience of fear and bewilderment that dominated the twilight of the Middle Ages by pushing gothic belief to its extreme and then turning it upside-down. That is, he relied on the 'parodical' devices of exaggeration and reversal. Like Socrates, Luther apparently had a clear, intuitive grasp of what was happening, particularly in the German regions at that time, and his case presented a solution, his theology a kind of cure. This explains the astonishing impact of views which today are bound to strike us as exaggerated, excessive and pathological. His tower experience transformed him to such an extent that the one-time melancholic suddenly changed into an astonishingly energetic maniac who, apparently undisturbed by physical suffering and the frightfully complicated political, social, and religious conflicts in which he became involved, produced a gigantic corpus of writing, encompassing, apart form his translations of and glossaries on the Bible, a great number of theological and polemical treatises which decisively influenced modern thought. Although those who claim that Luther retrospectively came to idealize his tower experience by turning what had actually been a gradual process into a sudden, mythological event are probably right, his autobiographic anecdote does point to a significant change in Luther's basic state of mind: the (sudden or gradual) expulsion of terror by laughter.

His sudden marriage in 1525 with a nun who had managed to escape from her convent marked another turning point in his life. The jesting, mocking, demonic rebel turned into a jolly *pater familias*. His body changed, and grew into the obese figure with whom he is now usually identified. As Delumeau puts it, towards the end of his life he grew fat, developed a drinking habit, and found pleasure in shocking his visitors with obscene witticisms.[45] Yet at times his merriment would still give way to severe fits of depression. Moreover, he became increasingly hostile and dogmatic towards fellow ringleaders of Protestantism - with the exception of Melanchton. He retorted the civilized irony of Erasmus by the powerful, brutal violence of his style. His prandial speeches, collected from 1529 onwards, present us with a vivid picture of his mature years. Until the end he continued his intense reading of the Bible. Luther basically remained a reader, and his writings as well as his prandial conversations basically contain a protocol of his reading.

These *Prandial Conversations*, which contain, among many other anecdotes, the comic account of Luther's decisive revelation, seem to constitute the prolonged, merry echo of the roar of laughter which overtook him *in hac turri, in qua secretus locus erat monachorum*. Notwithstanding several efforts to do away with Luther's carefree account, or even to interpret it *modo allegorico*, as an allegory of spiritual captivity - Wrampelmeyer, one of the editors for instance, claimed that the tower was a symbol of papal oppression[46] - notwithstanding all such efforts it is clear that Luther is simply being frank about the fact that he experienced his decisive moment of revelation in a lavatory, and that he, during a retrospective discussion of the

---

45 'Vers la fin de sa vie, il avait beaucoup grossi; il aimait de plus en plus le vin; il se plaisait à choquer l'auditoire par des boutades parfois grivoises', p. 97.

46 'Wrampelmeyer deutet komischerweise die Worte *in hac turri, in qua secreta locus erat monachorum* auf das Papsttum'. Tischreden 3, p. 228, n. 4; 2, p. 177, n. 3.

events which were to cause the spiritual upheaval in Germany called the Reformation, was at the same time narrating a simple, comical story to those who happened to share his table and merry temper.

A famous scene from the history of philosophy might further our understanding of Luther's grotesque autobiographical note, the one concerning the ancient Greek philosopher Herakleitos, recorded by Aristotle and commented on by Heidegger (1967, p. 185-186). Once upon a time, Herakleitos was discovered by visitors while sitting near a backing oven where he kept himself warm. He invited them in and, noting their embarrassment, encouraged them to proceed by adding: 'Here too the gods do dwell'. According to Heidegger, common opinion expects to find a famous philosopher in a more suitable position, absorbed in his thought. They want to meet a *thinker*. Instead, these visitors are confronted with an inconspicuous, everyday, commonplace scene: someone in the habit of warming himself near a backing oven, taking care of everyday, down-to-earth, physical needs. Perhaps those interested in the origins of Luther's theology would likewise expect him to have experienced his revelation in a more proper location, while engaged in a more proper and lofty exercise, reading the Bible, for instance, or writing, or contemplating, absorbed in his thoughts. But Luther laughs at them, adding, 'Here too the Holy Spirit dwells' - a scene emphasizing the remarkable proximity of the commonplace and the sublime, a truly *genealogical* scene, revealing the comic, trivial, down-to-earth origin of moral truths.

Luther's comic, auto-biographical connection of the spiritual experience of revelation with the physical experience of defecation was triggered by the fact that in both cases it had been a difficult delivery. According to Bakhtin, Socrates' self-characterization as a 'midwife' can also be considered a case of carnivalesque debasement, transforming the spiritual experience of enlightenment into a physical achievement of the body's lower half. After all, defecation and delivery are two of the principal events in the life of the grotesque body (1968, p. 319). Bergson (1940/1969) likewise points out that, as soon as the body is allowed to interfere, and infiltration of the comical is to be dreaded, and this is why in serious genres (like tragedy for example) the hero's physical needs are hardly ever mentioned. He neither eats, nor drinks, nor warms himself in public. Even to sit down and have a rest is hazardous.

Some biographers, particularly those belonging to the catholic party, have been severely criticized for having taking advantage of Luther's jolly frankness and lack of prudishness by over-emphasizing the supposedly negligible details of his decisive tower experience. They are criticized for over-emphasizing the residual *context of discovery* in their apparent effort to ridicule its serious content. One of them is H. Grisar, a Jesuit and the author of an impressive, three-volume standard biography of Luther (Grisar 1911/1912). In the first volume of this monumental work, the tower experience is considered *the* decisive turning point in Luther's spiritual development - a judgement quite in agreement with Luther's own appreciation of the event. For apart from the actual account in the *Prandial Conversations* cited above, Luther also emphasizes its importance in the introduction to his collected writings in latin. Here he claims that, due to papal doctrine and medieval custom, divine justice had come to be identified with divine punishment. While trying to become a perfect monk, however, Luther noticed that he a remained a sinner and even felt inclined to hate such a severe and punishing God. He came to develop and nourish a profound grudge against God, as well as against Saint Paul. At times he even hoped there was no God at all. The world at large seemed transformed into an enormous, dirty, diabolical 'latrine'. But then, while absorbed in his effort to understand the Psalter, an apparently unprecedented reading of the word 'justice' was revealed to him by the Holy Spirit: divine judgement is an act of grace rather than punishment. The term 'justice' should not be taken as suggesting some kind of economical relationship with God, implying that one's account will be settled and one's sins balanced against one's works. Rather, we are 'rectified' by God through faith - an explanation which is supported by the etymology of the German word for 'justice' (*Gerechtigkeit*) - we are not judged, but rectified, erected, resurrected, and this is an act of grace. We cannot 'earn' our deliverance, nor can we demand to be delivered in view of our achievements or performance during our lifetime, because God does not keep accounts. The very lines that had been impeding his understanding of the Scriptures for so long now became his 'gate to paradise' - and he felt as though he had been re-born. Thus, the tower experience was regarded as decisive by Luther himself and attributed to a revelation by the Holy Spirit.

Now it has been argued, as was already pointed out above, that the claim that such a reading of the word 'justice' was quite original and unprecedented, is in itself untenable and incorrect.[47] It had already been used by others, whose work Luther was quite familiar with (as a matter of fact, he had been using it himself before he grasped its true significance). This does not diminish the fact, however, that for Luther himself the tower experience constituted a basic change of mood, and that from now on he considered himself as being in possession of a decisive truth. One cannot deny that, although the idea as such was apparently far from new, the remarkable way *Luther* came to use and appropriate it somehow changed its significance. Something unprecedented and incommensurable had occurred.[48] And in view of the decisive significance of this event, which came to symbolize the very

---

47 Luther refers to it as the 'passive' reading of *justice*, as opposed to the 'active' reading which implies that salvation has to be earned by us.

48 Perhaps it can be compared to Marx' concept of surplus-value which, although it had already been used by others, contributed to a decisive rupture due to the specific, strategic way Marx eventually used it.

renaissance of the Gospels, indeed of Christian gaiety and freedom as such, the actual circumstances as recorded by Luther himself became the cause of substantial embarrassment to his serious, pious, or even hagiographic readership to such an extent that to refer to it was a serious tabu. In their effort to conceal these all-too-profane details, some readers went so far as to claim that the 'tower' was merely a metaphor that indicated the spiritual prison in which Luther spent his monastical years. When Grisar cautiously points out that the tower experience actually took place in a monk's cloaca, located in a tower that was apparently part of the adjacent city-wall (the sewage having egress outside the town boundaries, an arrangement quite customary at that time, p. 323), he raised a storm of indignation among his Protestant reviewers. Grisar was severely criticized for taking Luther's comic reminiscence from his monastical life literally. They even claimed that Grisar's objective was to make strategic use of the locality of Luther's revelation, similar to the way in which the Catholic Church in its struggle against Arianism had successfully exploited the fact that Arius had died in a latrine.[49] In view of this criticism, Grisar added a substantial supplement[50] in which 'the issue of locality' - *die Lokalfrage* - is given due attention. As a result, the fact that Luther really used the words 'secret', 'heated' room, as well as 'cloaca' and that he did so in a frank and straightforward manner is now considered to be beyond doubt. It could not have been his monastical cell because it was not heated, nor was he granted another private cell somewhere in a tower in order for him to quietly pursue his reading, as has also been suggested, nor is it likely for these words to have been added by impious rogues in later versions of the manuscript. Ultimately, however, both Grisar and his Lutheran critics agree that, notwithstanding the amount of work and ink spent on it, the issue of locality is quite trivial and unimportant in itself since it is only the *content* as such that really matters.

From the point of view of laughter, however, one feels obligated to side with Luther and to remain loyal to his original account rather than accepting the compartmentalization of the serious and the residual. Luther's recognition of the true significance of Paul's troublesome phrase was an experience of deliverance, an

---

[49] A few days before his death, Luther informed his wife that he himself almost died in a latrine, due to a huge stone in the ceiling that happened to come off (Letter to his wife, 10 February 1546). The comic technique of degrading someone by having him die in a latrine was a stock element in the serio-comic genres of ancient literature, cf. Seneca's *Ludus morte Claudii* where the emperor dies at the moment of defecation (Bakhtin 1968, p. 150) - another exemplification of the remarkable vitality and persistence of what Bakhtin refers to as 'genre memory'.

[50] Vol. 3, pp. 978 ff.

experience of both spiritual and physical relief.[51] And the tower- (or cloaca-)scene is a perfect Rabelais-like rendering of this decisive event. Rather than separating content from context, we ought to discern their basic connection. Luther's experience of revelation corrobates the basic truth of genealogy as a philosophical method, most notably its claim that the historical beginning of a serious discourse (such as Protestant theology) is human, all too human or even ridiculous, that it is something which has to do with nutrition, digestion and defecation, with food, drink and bodily existence, and that truth is something which is excreted by the body rather than something which descends from heaven.[52] The image of a monk contemplating on the Scriptures while lingering in a latrine reads like a scene borrowed from the popular genres of laughter. The terrible is overcome by connecting it to the body's material lower half. Fear and obstipation (both mentally and physically) are finally overcome by a roar of laughter, making life possible again, and allowing Luther's vitality to produce an enormous bulk of writing.[53] Luther finds himself delivered form his spiritual burden which had caused him to detoriate physically as well.[54] Never again is he to renounce his laughter, his merry truth. The ghastly obscurity of the gothic night finally gives way to the break of day, and his basic laughter will prevent his mind from ever being drawn into the realm of fear again. It is a scene of laughter that represents the complete transfiguration of spiritual life Luther experienced. As a youth he was 'dead drunk' with papal teachings and almost drowned by them. His desperate, persistent struggle

---

51 'A revelation, that is, a sudden inner flooding with light, is always associated with a repudiation, a cleansing, a kicking away; and it would be entirely in accord with Luther's great freedom in such matters if he were to experience and to report this repudiation in frankly physical terms... Scholars would prefer to have it happen as they achieve their own reflected revelation - sitting at a desk. Luther's statement that he was, in fact, sitting somewhere else, implies that in his creative moment the tension of nights and days of meditation found release throughout his being - and nobody who has read Luther's private remarks can doubt that his total being always included his bowels' (Erikson, 1958/1962, p. 205).

52 Marx, Nietzsche and Freud, rather than being the 'masters of suspicion', revealed the 'human, all too human', down-to-earth origins of everything lofty and serious.

53 Erikson points out that, after the tower experience, Luther changed from a highly restrained and retentive individual into an 'explosive' person. Moreover, Luther at times refers to himself as incontinent, unable to keep it up any longer, etc. when it comes to writing. Cf. 'Will er aber nicht aufhören, so las er mich mit seinen buchlein, die der Teufel aus im speiet und scheisset' (Tischreden, 5: 5659]. The comparison of writing with defecation is a popular tradition of long standing (cf. Van Buuren 1982).

54 As Nietzsche puts it, the soul needs a cloaca too in order to rid herself of her burdens and her waste - most notably the idea of God (Human, All Too Human II, The Wanderer and his Shadow, § 46).

to understand the very phrases that terrified him so much finally enabled him to understand that, rather than judged and damned (the gothic experience) we are rectified (*gerecht gemacht*), an act of grace. From now on, the Scriptures presented quite a different aspect, a gay promise, and Luther entered a new way of reading the Bible, one that made life possible again, instead of impeding it. It was his second birth, and the tower scene was a perfect rendering of this experience, quite in accordance with the basic features of the genres of popular laughter.

Someone who greatly deplored the persistent effort of Luther's readership to conceal the grotesque aspects of his achievement, is Lacan (1986, 7:2). He stressed that Luther's digestive and excremental images perfectly articulated the sense of exile and forlornness experienced by Luther and his contemporaries at the close of the gothic epoch. The gothic solution proved untenable as human impulse, the forces of the body, seemed to defy all efforts to subordinate and organize them by means of exercise and work. Luther's images pushed to its extreme an experience of despair that, according to Lacan, is still audible in contemporary forms of uneasiness and discontent because it is the very experience to which modern culture tried to provide an answer - albeit an unsuccessful one. Lacan fails to add, however, that apart from giving voice to an experience of despair by depicting the human world as the devil's privy, Luther's digestive and excremental images contained an *answer* in their own right as well, a moral solution that differed considerably from the subsequent modern one. The tower experience indicated that Luther managed to transform the gothic into the grotesque, and utter despair into a peculiar kind of optimism. While overcoming his physical constipation, that is, while transforming the very part of his body that had worked as a barrier to his physical waste into a locus of exuberance and relief, the very part of the Scriptures that had been hampering his reading and writing suddenly became what he referred to as 'the gate to paradise'. Luther's grotesque laughter revealed that the human condition is not hopeless and tragic beyond prospect and repair, as Lacan would have it, but that it is still possible to *laugh* at the tragic truth of life instead of being pounded to pieces under its weight. The gap between is and ought, one of tragedy's basic truths, is a basic truth of comedy as well. Tragedy does not constitute the only alternative to the serious but concealing discourse of the modern human sciences.

The monk's privy is indeed a symbol, not in the sense of representing something else but in the sense that, in Luther's experience, it embodied and exemplified the quintessence of gothic life.[55] He really had experienced the gothic world as constituting one huge latrine, governed by papal edicts (*Dekretalen*) which were parodically referred to by Luther as 'excrementals' (*Drecketalen*) and which were to

---

[55] It is a symbol in the sense of what Freud (1900/1942, p. 284 ff.) refers to as condensation ('Verdichtung'), not in the sense of what he refers to as displacement ('Verschiebung').

148

be answered by means of a series of farts rather than argued with, although at the end of his life Luther agrees that it is about time he refrains from continuously burrowing the Pope's filth.[56] The tower experience, as an experience of laughter, liberated Luther from the intimidating truth of gothic life, allowed the world to emerge in a different light, produced the kind of moral subjectivity presupposed by Luther's theological doctrine. But although the truth experienced by Luther was articulated in the form of a proposition, it was not propositional (or doctrinal) in itself. Rather it was an experience of revelation, one that (under certain historical circumstances) allows certain doctrines or propositions to emerge, but cannot be reduced to, or replaced by, their (theo)logical content for all eternity. On the contrary, the affinity between laughter and theological doctrine embodied by Luther, turned out to be short-lived and before long laughter began to ridicule the pretension to extra-temporal validity of this new, but increasingly serious truth it once supported.

5. WHETHER FOR THE SAKE OF THEIR CONSCIENCE OR FOR THE SAKE OF THEIR PAUNCHES

Notwithstanding the sense of rupture, of something unprecedented in his achievement, Luther was still a perfect example of the kind of author who relied on and remained responsive to the 'word of the other' rather than creating something *ex nihilo*. Luther *responded*, and his writing was closely connected with his reading. Every year, we are told, he would read the complete Bible twice, while keeping a watchful eye on the writings of his contemporaries. We cannot understand Luther's work without a persistent awareness of its responsiveness and answerability.[57] He responded both to the word of the Other and to the discourse of others. In an at times polemical, at times jocular vein he addressed the others, in order to retrieve and restore the word of the Other. His work was an effort to retrieve the word of God and

---

56 All of these anal phrases (and some more) are used in 'Wider das Papsttum zu Rom, vom Teufel gestiftet' (1545).

57 Luther's way of reading can be defined as active and dialogical. Perhaps it meets Bakhtin's idea of the 'responsible act'. As Anton Simons stresses in his reading of Bakhtin, the word longs to be understood and is desperately in need of a responsive, responsible, righteous reader, anticipated by the word form the very beginning, although he may not belong to the readership initially addressed by it. It is the task of the reader to become the one who will rescue and preserve the desperate word, so that the dreadful apprehension of remaining forever misunderstood will give way to the genre-producing joy of recognition, bound to produce an opening to the future (A. Simons, unpublished manuscript). In the case of Luther, the very word 'righteousness' ('justitia') called for a righteous reading and provided this aperture to the future!

his translation of the Scriptures into the German vernacular remains his most outstanding achievement - a *Sprachereignis* (Ebeling 1964), a discursive event of epoch-making significance. In his effort to respond to the language of the Bible, he created the German language. The bulk of his writing basically consisted of comments on the Scriptures. One might even say that his proper genre was *parody*, provided this word is not used in its modern or technical sense (referring to a particular comical genre), but taken literally (*para-oidia*), a subsequent, accompanying chant, an effort to respond to, to appropriate, retrieve or revive an already existing, but apparently obscured primal word. His word was basically responsive. Moreover, being responsive is not the same as being repetitious. Parody means responding in such a way as to establish something of significance in its own right. Luther's basic objective as a translator was not to provide his readership with a literal and accurate rendering but to restore the original to life again, to participate in its vitality, to retrieve the directness and liveliness of a text which had become too official and momentous. At times, such an endeavour is to produce the comical effect which came to be identified with parody as such, but this is not necessarily the basic feature or objective of the genre. Yet in Luther's translations of the Bible, the bold and comical aspects of parody (as well as its responsive aspects) are nonetheless present.[58] Luther succeeded in familiarizing the Bible. Likewise, the first French translation of the Bible, done by Olivétan, reflects the influence of Rabelais' language and style (Bakhtin 1969, p. 100). It is, as Bakhtin phrases it, nearer in style to Rabelais, to Calvin in thought.

According to Bergson (1940/1969), the transposition of a certain idea (or phrase, or line of thought) into a different tone of voice, a different environment, is always comical. This notably applies to the effort to translate ancient, solemn ideas into the colloquial language of contemporary life. In such a case, the solemn idea (the lamentation of an ancient Jewish prophet, for example) suddenly finds itself transferred into an environment, a generic key in which it cannot be expected to feel quite at home (sixteenth century grobian German, for example). Now the ancient idea may have been less exalted in its own original environment, but due to the historical distance it has acquired a lofty air which is bound to put up considerable resistance against being vulgarized (transformed into Luther's early modern version of the *Vulgata*). To familiarize, Bergson stresses, is always comical, and the transposition of the solemn into the familiar - which is what Luther basically tried

---

[58] According to Bakhtin (1988) the same goes for Calvin's use of the French language: 'The language of French literary prose was created by Calvin and Rabelais - but Calvin's language ... was an intentional and conscious lowering of, almost a travesty on, the sacred language of the Bible' (p. 71). The middle strata of the national languages, represented by Calvin and others, were perceived as a denigrating travesty of higher spheres. The language of Calvin (and, one might add, of Luther) were 'to a significant extent born out of parody' (p. 71).

to do - is parody. Although parody will often imply an element of degradation, this is not its basic objective. It intends to familiarize, not necessarily to degrade, and degradation is but one mode of transposition among others. Transposition becomes 'parodical' in the reduced (and often abusive) sense of the term if it is done in a mechanical and insensitive manner (if the translation is too literal, for instance).

Let me give one example of Luther's parodical technique. In *On councils and Churches* (1539) Luther points to the original and proper meaning of the word *ecclesia*. According to Luther, *ecclesia* actually means a bunch of people.[59] For instance, in chapter nineteen of *The Acts*, Paul's claim that the Greek deities were nothing but idols and human artifacts produced great commotion among the silver smiths of Ephesus. Not only was their craft in danger, but they also feared that the temple of the great goddess Diana would be despised. So one day they marched towards the theatre, shouting 'Great is Diana of the Ephesians'. When the town clerk finally managed to appease the general confusion, he referred to the crowd there gathered as *ecclesia*. Thus, although Luther's translation of *ecclesia* as 'a bunch of people' at first seems rather grobian and comical, his basic objective is to reveal that in its true and proper sense, *ecclesia* has nothing to do with the official, momentous, hierarchical institute with which it came to be identified. As a translator, Luther considered it offensive that the Pope assumed that *ecclesia* referred not to just any gathering of Christians but exclusively to *his* particular squad of fools.

In fact, Luther justified his technique quite eloquently in *Vom Dolmetschen (On Translating*, 1530). He had been severely criticized for having translated *arbitramur hominem justificari ex fide absque operibus* with *Wir halten, daß der Mensch gerecht werde ohne des Gesetzes Werke, allein durch den Glauben.*[60] Now the German translation, which contains the word *allein* ('only'), suggests that the original contains the word *sola*, which is actually absent and the literal translation would read *through faith* instead of *only through faith*. Apparently Luther added it so that the original would support his theological views. To begin with, however, Luther denies the papal asses (*Papstesel*) the right to judge his translations, for it is a profession in which he himself happens to excel.[61] Furthermore, many translations into German which seem accurate at first very often prove not be German at all but a ridiculous kind of quasi-German, bound to be misunderstood. Luther, however, had simply wanted to write proper German, and in German (like in English), the word *nicht* or *kein* is accompanied by the word *allein*. For instance, when we say *Der Bauer bringt allein Korn und kein Geld* - 'The farmer brought only corn and no

---

59 '*Die Kirche, das ist ein Haufen Leute*'.

60 'We take it that man is justified regardless of his works of Law, but *only* through faith'.

61 And he cites the Roman satirist Juvenalis to support his view.

money' - we notice that *allein* ('only') is added to *kein* ('no'). And in this respect, the German language differs from Latin or Greek. Now the translator should not consult the Latin or Greek original as to how German should be spoken or written. Rather, he should pay attention to the housewife, the children in the street, the ordinary people gathered on the market-square, watching them closely while they speak, and then he will learn how to speak or write German. And when in the Gospel of Saint Luke the angel addresses Mary in the following vein: *Ave Maria, gratia plena*, 'gratia plena' should not be translated as 'full of grace', for no German would ever talk like that and the odd phrase would make him think of a barrel full of beer. Thus, in order to become a translator, one has to acquire a profound knowledge of the vernacular German, and this is what Luther had trained himself to do, quite unlike his papal contemporaries who simply repeated (that is, obscured) rather than retrieved the Word of God. He felt compelled to write the way he did by the German language itself, and maintained that it was not his translation that offended but the Word of God itself, which was brought to light again at last. His sole objective simply was to allow the Word of God to enter the German language - to *create* the German language as a written language.

Luther's technique allowed the language and idiom of the market-square to appear in print and enter published discourse.[62] As in the case of Rabelais, many words borrowed from popular discourse were used in a written form for the first time by Luther. And, as Bakhtin observed in his book on Rabelais, it is a language whose grotesque inner logic relies very much on references to the body, notably its material lower stratum. It is this, rather than an unconscious, highly individual and idiosyncratic anal 'complex' or 'pathology'[63] that explains why Luther writes the way he does. For example, while discussing the decline of monastic life, he takes the (albeit quite reasonable) position that, should some of the monks prefer to remain in the monastery, 'whether for the sake of their paunches or for the sake of their conscience', they should not be driven out by force. It is one of the countless images put to use by Luther that express and constitute his being-in-the-world, his

---

[62] Cf. Janssen (1915): 'Er schöpfte aus den reichen Quellen der Volkstümlichen Redeweise; in volkstümlicher Beredsamkeit kamen ihm wenige gleich' (p. 252). Indeed, Janssen emphasizes that, as a writer, Luther borrowed from the rich resources of popular speech. And yet at the same time the concise, cheerful statements in which he articulates the profundity of his faith are sublime. In Luther's writings, the vulgar, the down-to-earth and the sublime somehow seem to coexist.

[63] Cf. Brown (1957/1970). Although the psychoanalytic perspective is not without considerable merits, I consider Luther's laughter as a collective and historical, rather than as a purely individual phenomenon. Moreover, I do not consider it pathological in the pejorative or clinical sense of the term, but rather in the sense of not being devoid of pathos (cf. further below).

basic way of coming to terms with the actual situation.[64]

In the case of Rabelais, Bakhtin stresses the enormous importance of extra-literary sources and I suspect the same argument is fully applicable to Luther: 'Rabelais' first and foremost source was the unofficial side of speech, with its rich store of curses ... with its various indecencies, the enormous weight carried by words and expressions connected with hard drinking. To this very day, the unofficial side of speech reflects a Rabelaisian degree of indecency in it, of words concerning drunkenness and defecation and so forth, but all this is by now clichéd and no longer creative' (1988, p. 238). Like Rabelais, Luther incorporated into his writings the 'crude frankness of folk passions', the jokes, short stories, proverbs, puns, catchwords and sayings of popular culture.

Instead of trying to separate the theological 'content' of Luther's writings for their grobian 'rhetoric', we must recognize that its grotesque images are essential to its content. At that time, in the second decade of the sixteenth century, the basic truth revealed by Luther could only be accessed by laughter. Where Ebeling (1964) talks about *Luthervergessenheit*, it is the grobian and grotesque aspect of his achievement that fell into oblivion. The official picture of Luther became one-sided and incomprehensible. Apparently, experts recognize this, as Ebeling himself does when he points to the fact that, although Luther's work is often considered the dawn of the modern age, his proximity to medieval life should not be neglected, nor should the fact that in some important respects he even severely retarded and impeded the development of modern, civic society. All such efforts to distinguish between *modern* content and *medieval* residue, however, obscure the fact that, from his spiritual transformation called the tower experience onwards, Luther belonged neither to the Middle Ages, nor to the modern age but to the sixteenth century, an epoch in its own right (although short-lived), dominated by the mood of laughter. According to Ebeling, the tendency to conceal certain aspects of Luther's achievement must no doubt be attributed to something rather 'uncanny' in his work, something of which the modern reader would rather not be reminded. I quite agree with such a claim, but not with the subsequent effort to neutralize this 'something' by considering it a medieval (that is, residual) remainder. Rather, Luther's grotesque laughter was a product of his final break with medieval life rather than a remainder of what he had already left behind. The 'uncanny' is something which intrinsically belongs to

---

64 Even Luther's account of events that were to gain considerable historical prominence (such as, for instance, his dispute with Cajetan in Augsburg) are remarkably down-to-earth and read like comical scenes from everyday life. For example, his description of how Cajetan's intermediary takes his leave with an 'Italian gestus', a contemptuous movement of his finger, or his description of how Karl von Militz, negotiating with Luther on the Pope's behalf, asked some women who stayed at their inn for their opinion on the Holy Chair. They replied that they first had to see this 'chair' before they could judge it.

Luther - something that *is* Luther rather than a residue. The tower experience, Luther's tremendous, Herculean roar of laughter, was an experience which allowed an unprecedented but responsive form of moral subjectivity to constitute itself. This and not the 'theological content' of the experience explains its astonishing impact on German spiritual and political life. It was an experience quite at odds with and welcomed in defiance of those tremendous efforts to further etatism and top-down centralism which were developed at that time, by both church and state, both the Emperor and the Pope. It was an experience that derived its energy and vitalism not from some psychological or psychoanalytical 'anal drive' (Brown, 1957/1970) but from popular laughter.[65]

Indeed, virtually every introduction to Luther's work contains a cautionary note not to pay too much attention to his 'grobian' laughter, even though it is Luther's most important literary technique, one quite current in the sixteenth century[66] and one which Luther happened to master wonderfully. Those who feel embarrassed by it are reminded of 'mitigating' circumstance such as the fact that Luther's adversaries relied on jeering as much as he did, and he was simply giving them back their own, so to speak. Yet even though one might object to grobianism as such, it cannot be denied that Luther did quite well in it. Still, it is argued that, rather than being a significant achievement, his grobianism does not affect the nucleus, the basic content of his work and that therefore any time Luther calls the Pope names, referring to him as a hog or an ass, or to his edicts as an ass's farts, we should ignore such 'medieval' residue and concentrate on Luther's theological substance. Ebeling (1964), for example, admits that at times Luther's *uncanny gift* for polemical discourse exceeds all proper limits and simply becomes unbearable. But he

---

[65] In *Life against death* Brown (1959/1968) takes the psychoanalytical point of view and pays much attention to the tower experience as well as to the 'anal' features of Luther's writing: 'Luther with his freedom from hypocrisy, his all-embracing vitality [...] records the scene of his crucial religious experience with untroubled candor' (p. 182). In Luther's work, Brown claims, the devil emerges as an 'anal' character, continuously throwing shit on everyone, showing his posterior and spreading horrible smells, while Luther himself also relied on anal devices (such as producing a fart) in order to defend himself. Rather than considering such anal gestures to be the expression of idiosyncratic personality traits, either of Luther or of Protestantism in general, I would emphasize that all these images were quite at home in the popular comical literature, the time-old 'wisdom of folly' (p. 202) which Luther (much like his contemporary Rabelais) happened to represent.

[66] Saint Grobianus was first mentioned in 1494 by Sebastian Brant in his *Narrenschiff* ('Ship of fools'), who called him a 'coarse fool'. In 1549 Friedrich Dedekind, a student at Wittenberg, produced a poem in Latin entitled *Grobianus*, which before long was translated into German by Kaspar Scheidt, father-in-law of Johann Fischart. Fischart was to produce a famous versification of the *Eulenspiegel* novel - a literary work that, according to Bakhtin (1968) and others, represented the genre *in optima forma.*

feels it is the spirit of the age that is to be blamed for this while the true impetus behind his work must be located elsewhere.[67]

This characteristic solution to the general embarrassment experienced by Luther's modern readership must be regarded as a perfect example of what has been referred to as the method of separation or compartmentalization, a method I believe is absolutely fatal with regard to understanding the discursive phenomenon called Luther. Rather, his grobianism points to a basic truth only accessible to laughter - and laughter is indispensable for recognizing it. According to Luther, it is quite pointless to *argue* with one's opponents as long as their basic mode of thinking and reading remains gothic, that is, incompatible with the one adopted by Luther. Grobianism is not an ornament that the modern reader no longer appreciates. Luther sincerely felt he could not but consider the spokesmen of the official, established truth a bunch of fools. His grobianism is the expression of a fundamental difference that cannot be solved by argument. Laughter is a basic mood or mode of thought, an *apriori* which, now that the time to remain silent has passed, allowed him to raise his voice. It is his way of being-in-the-world, confirming his break with the gothic still of the night - the basic mood of fear - that had condemned him to melancholy and silence. Luther was reformed, transfigured by laughter. The truth is that Luther did *not* give his antagonists back their own, and the effort to consider both kinds of laughter as symptoms resulting from the same deplorable but temporal atmosphere of grobianism is basically mistaken. For while his enemies still relied on a 'gothic' kind of jeer, one that did not really laugh but was instead vicious and offensive, Luther's laughter was truly gay. The truth is not that Luther was more gifted, but that he practiced a different genre of laughter and that by entering a different genre he had entered a different era, a different basic mood. It was the basic mood of laughter that allowed the Word to re-emerge and ensured that, while he was 'drinking beer in Wittemberg' (a famous centre of beer brewing at the time, which was its main industry) the Word was doing its work all by itself. Still, it is important to keep in mind that it was not his 'grobian' laughter *as such* that was unprecedented (since Luther borrowed it from the carnivalesque genres of popular culture) but the fact that the very strongholds of medieval seriousness, all the serious genres of theological discourse, were suddenly invaded and overwhelmed by it without being able to offer sufficient resistance. The long-lasting, gothic compartmentalization of life into a comic and a serious realm - expelling laughter to popular and rural quarters and genres - collapsed while in extensive parts of Germany monastic life itself drowned in a Gargantuist burst of laughter.

---

67 We are to recognize 'daß ganz anderswo als in solchen extreme Symptomen das eigentliche Movens zu suchen ist, was ihm zu schreiben treibt' (p. 51).

6. THE COURT JESTER'S PRIVILEGE

In his introduction to the first volume of his collected writings in German,[68] Luther emphasizes, while appealing to Saint Paul, that the Holy Scriptures is bound to turn all other books into utter buffoonery. The more one becomes acquainted with the Bible, the more one is likely to dislike even one's own writing and discard it as mere knavery. Luther suggests that those who do happen to take pride in what they have written grab hold of their ears, for they are bound to discover them to be of the length of an ass's.

The year 1520 was the one in which Luther published several of his most important writings, such as *To the Christian Nobility of the German Nation: On How to Improve the Christian Ranks* (*An den christlichen Adel deutscher Nation: Von des christlichen Standes Besserung*) in which the famous 'three walls' of the papal stronghold or regiment are pulled down (particularly the Pope's authority when it comes to interpreting the Scriptures). This treatise is preceded by some introductory remarks in which Luther refers to himself as a fool or court jester who still owes the world an act of foolishness - in accordance with the popular saying that, whatever the world should undertake to do, a monk ought to be present, even if one had to be painted. Furthermore, Luther points to the fact that, more than once, it has happened that a fool uttered a wise thought, and quotes the inevitable line taken from Saint Paul's first letter to the Corinthians: *Let no man deceive himselfe: if any man among you seemeth to be wise in this world, let him become a foole, that he may be wise. For the wisedome of this world is foolishness with God* (1 Corinthians 3:18). Because of his caps and bells he claims a right to frank or unrestricted speech.[69] Subsequently, Rome is compared to the Antwerp Fair, while Luther explains how the papal regime itself parodied, abused and inverted certain devices that once were of serious origin. Indeed, Luther appeals to the court jester's privilege of unrestricted speech (*[Ich] sage nach meinem Hofrecht frei heraus*) when he incites all monks, nuns and priests to violate their vows of chastity - a ridiculous vow which ought not to be demanded from any human being since it is utterly impossible to observe, and bound to produce whorishness and a tormented conscience. It is as idiotic to ban sexual intercourse as it would be to ban eating, drinking or defecation. All annual fairs and feasts are to be abolished since they only encourage alcohol abuse and idleness, and are to be made working days, for the only

---

68 *Werke*, 50, pp. 657-661.

69 On Luther's comparison of himself to a court jester see for example his letter to Elector Frederick the Wise from the Wartburg (24 February 1522) as well as the remark during one of his prandial conversations cited in chapter two: 'Wir haben einen frommen keiser... Er ist stille und frum. Ich halte, er redet in einem jar nicht so viel als ich in einem tage' [3:3245].

days that are holy are working days.[70] It is about time for the Germans to stop roaming about like wandering scholars or mendicant monks, forget about their foolish monastic vows, cease their whorish existence, and start earning a decent living. Mendicant orders and peregrine guilds are to be dismantled, they merely serve as a cover for tramps to continue their roaming existence. Universities are to be reformed, and Aristotle to be expelled. Finally, Luther announces that, notwithstanding the many efforts to make him shut up, the fool will continue to shout his truth and sing his little song about Rome. In short, this treatise is a remarkable, unstable mixture of laughter and discipline. The demand to turn all holidays into working days, for example, is an instance of comic reversal and exaggeration as much as a plea for discipline and labour. Luther's speech remains ambivalent. To a considerable extent it relies on the time-old, comic and popular device of unmasking. In opposition to the lofty and official interpretation of phenomena like pilgrimage he sees in them *nothing but* a pretext for idleness and alcohol abuse, serving bodily rather than spiritual needs - a popular wisdom of long standing.

The same goes for other 'serious' treatises as well. In *On Christian Freedom* it is claimed that, as no man remains completely devoid of evil desire, the Law forces us to despair and exposes us to terror, whereas the Word of God contains the promise that the faithful will be rectified by divine grace, an insight which produces a gay and Christian conscience.[71] And in *On Marital Life* he again claims that sexual intercourse is as natural and unavoidable as eating, drinking and defecation.[72] To make a vow to abstain from intercourse for life is utter foolishness and one cannot reasonably expect someone to keep it. We cannot *choose* to abstain from intercourse, for such a choice is beyond our capacity, and any effort to do so is bound to result in whoring, masturbation, and a bad conscience. One had better pledge to bite off one's own nose.[73]

---

[70] Luther rejected 'works', but was very much in favour of work. According to Nietzsche, Protestantism succeeded because it promised the same reward using less effort (only faith, no 'works'). Yet whereas Protestantism managed to seize the northern parts of Europe, the southern parts soon recognized that less 'works' implied more 'work'. They preferred God to do the work for them rather than working too hard themselves (*Human, All Too Human II*, Mixed Opinions and Aphorisms, § 97).

[71] 'Von der Freiheit eines Christenmenschen'. *Werke*, 7, 20-38.

[72] 'Vom ehelichen Leben'. *Werke*, 10 (2), 275-304.

[73] Moreover, Luther claims that married women do not have the right to refuse intercourse, for they have bestowed their bodies on their lawful partner. Should a married woman refuse to grant her husband the right to have intercourse with her, she should be forced to do so by the government or put to death, because women are created to carry themselves to death and their life is to be as intense as it is short. A rather cynical view

In short, even the more 'serious' parts of his writing are far from devoid of gaiety, foolishness, and laughter, much like the 'grobian' parts are far from devoid of truth. Thus, the method or strategy of compartmentalization, which aims at separating the 'serious' from the 'residual', is doomed to fail. Although perhaps some parts of Luther's work are relatively serious while others are somewhat more grobian, serious truth and grobian laughter seem to remain basically connected. But is this really the case? Virtually all Luther experts tend to agree that there is one particular text that is quite devoid of serious content while abounding in grobianism to such an extent that the very fact that Luther ever came to write it is to be greatly deplored: his disagreeable libel against Heinrich von Braunschweig-Wolfenbüttel, known as *Wider Hans Worst* (*Against Harry Sausage*).

Luther's libel *Wider Hans Worst* (1541) is generally considered the *acme* of his grobianism. In fact, Luther joined a defamatory polemics that had been going on for a while between Friedrich von Sachsen and Heinrich von Braunschweig-Wolfenbüttel. Luther took the floor because Heinrich von Braunschweig-Wolfenbüttel had accused him of calling Friedrich von Sachsen 'Hans Worst' - 'Harry Sausage', a buffoon-like figure belonging to popular grobian literature, and included, for example, in the cast of Brandt's *Narrenschiff*. To start with, Luther claims to enjoy being abused, for it makes him feel gay which is the perfect mood for writing - *Blessed are ye, when men ... shal say all manner of evill against you falsly for my sake. Reioyce, and be exceedingly glad* (Matthew 5:8). Furthermore, he admits that he often refers to the fat, coarse and clumsy oaf 'Hans Worst', particularly while preaching, but maintains he never used this name with regard to Friedrich von Sachsen.[74] Heinrich von Braunschweig-Wolffenbüttel *himself* must be considered the perfect 'Hans Worst'. After this introduction, Luther persistently refers to Heinrich as Harry Sausage, and this is one of the basic techniques of the grobian genre, of which Luther displays his mastery in a remarkably carefree way.

Now it is generally agreed upon that this deplorable libel in which Luther clearly violates all limits of decency should not be considered when it comes to discussing Luther's 'content'. In my view, however, this is unfortunate, for in addition to the fact that it informs us of the manner in which theological 'content' and grobian 'rhetoric' are intrinsically connected, it is also a remarkable treatise with regard to its content as such. Luther himself never deplored the fact that he wrote it.

In fact, grobianism seems necessary for invoking a certain mood which allows for Luther's basic insight to be appreciated. In *Wider Hans Worst*, Luther distinguishes between two worlds. The one is the dark, gothic world of terror, alcohol abuse and foolishness, a world surging between abyss-like nothingness and

---

on womanhood. Is Luther being serious here?

[74] *Hans Worst* or *Wurst* is one of those 'national clownish characters' of popular culture that are 'called by the names of national dishes' (Bakhtin 1968, p. 298).

boundless jest. The other is the world of a gay and Christian truth. And grobianism is the indispensable hinge that allows us to close the one and enter the other. By mocking terror, truth becomes possible. Grobian laughter means expanding one aspect of the gothic world (the fool's laughter) to such an extent that its somber and fearful aspect, the ghastly abyss of divine punishment, is bound to collapse. If gothic seriousness can be compared to the still of night, grobianism is the break of day, and the modern truth regime that will be constituted afterwards, broad daylight. All this is hinted at in Luther's contempted and rejected libel.

Luther himself refers to his grobianism as 'merely speaking plain German'. He simply uses it in order to make himself quite clear and to prevent any misunderstandings. Furthermore, he appeals to the Bible, some parts of which (such as *Ezekiel 23*) surpass even Luther's libel in coarseness.

According to Luther, the Word of Christ seems to have vanished from the earth without a trace and human beings are once again wallowing in the mire like hogs. And this is *not* a metaphor or figure of speech for, deprived of the Word of God, man *really* is bound to become something like a hog wallowing in the mire.[75] This is what he himself had been doing, Luther emphasizes, when suddenly he found himself rectified by the Word of God. And the Pope is the coarsest ass of all - again a phrase which must be taken literally instead of being *merely* considered a grobian figure of speech. For unlike human beings, Luther argues, animals like asses and hogs are *unable to make some basic distinctions* - for example the distinction between human (the teachings of the church) and divine (the Word of God). And as the Pope continues to suggest that the Word of God is something to negotiate about, a kind of constitution as it were, drafted by human authority, he was unable to make the most significant of all distinctions. One cannot negotiate about matters of truth, and the truth of faith is not something that can be 'settled', since this would imply that we will inevitably tumble into the abyss of uncertainty, a terrifying prospect, unless one happens to be a papal sow or ass, for they are bound to remain gross fools, basically indifferent to truth.[76] Unlike the papal one, the *true* church does not negotiate, nor would she be willing to give in or compromise. Rather, it is the unwavering foundation of truth (*Pfeiler und Grundfest der Wahrheit*) and unwavering ground of truth (*ein grundfeste und fester Grund ... ein Grund der Wahrheit*).

In the case of those who have been transformed, uncertainty has come to an end and the truth is finally revealed. But their adversaries are still referred to as asses and

---

75   Erikson (1958/1962) refers to such images as 'porcography' (p. 197).

76   In *On the Papacy at Rome* a similar claim is made. Since the papal blackguards do not belief in the existence of God, nor in a life to come, they live and die like cows, saws and other cattle. The idea of being reformed is sheer folly to them and they are bound to carry on with their life of heavy drink and idleness for ever.

hogs because *this is what they really are*. They remain indifferent towards truth, being unable to recognize the basic distinction between the human (that which can be settled) and the divine (that which cannot be settled because it is not at our disposal). They are not rectified, nor transfigured into true human beings, but continue to live like a hog - much as Luther himself did while being a monk. The Word is a light that shines in the still of night, allowing some to proceed while others remain in darkness. The true church is the ground of truth and cannot err,[77] a grounding secured by the simple phrase *Haec dixit Dominus*. This is the only voice to which a true Christian should pay attention. Luther simply *has* to shout and abuse in order to shout down the terrible noise produced by the hogs and asses, the sophists and epicurians, concealing the quiet voice of truth. Luther has recourse to grobian speech because one *truly* experiences oneself to be a bag of maggots when faced with the majestic Word of God. Those who read the Bible but do not share this experience, are not simply *like* a saw trying to play the harp, they *are* a saw, because the basic precondition required to have this experience, to play this instrument, has not been realized. The ability truly to comprehend the Bible is an act of grace. We have to become a certain kind of person, someone who no longer belongs to the gothic world of fools, blackguards, pilgrims and monks who were merely *terrified* by the Bible, not *rectified* by it - we have to become someone who 'like a bride' only pays attention to her Husband's voice.

Tetzel[78] was one of those shouting voices, a *grosser Clamant* at the market-square of gothic life, turning the Bible into a fool's cap, not someone to negotiate with but to abuse, for this was the only language he understood.[79] And this goes for Harry Sausage too. The subsequent passage, the *acme* of Luther's grobianism, runs something like this: Now you infamous Harry, refrain from writing books on matters like church, faith, obedience and revolt, because you know yourself to be an infamous fool who should only write a book when he happens to hear the fart of an old sow, on that occasion you should open your mouth and say, Thank you,

---

[77] *Ecclesia non potest errare*.

[78] The unfortunate Dominican who happened to be selling indulgences in Wittenberg on behalf of Saint Peter's Dome when Luther took the floor.

[79] Experts inform us that Tetzel, really a dedicated intellectual, was badly mistreated by Luther. Many of the burlesque scenes attributed to him by the Protestant tradition were in fact borrowed from late medieval popular literature such as *Pfaffe Amis* and *Fahrende Schuler*. Well known examples are the story that Tetzel once used his rhetorical talents to present the Roman satirist Juvenalis as a Saint, or the story, mentioned by Luther in *Wider Hans Worst*, that he only just managed to escape from being drowned in the Inn as a punishment for his sexual licentiousness.

Nightingale, for now I hear a piece which is mine.[80] Luther's objective, however, was not simply abuse. His aim was to expose a certain world, a certain basic mood (the late medieval gothic mood), the way it perceived, was terrified by, and laughed at reality, and he did so by exaggerating its laughter, at the expense of its terror. When *we* read the 'indulgence' distributed by Pope Leo X to raise money for Saint Peter's Dome - 'Confession, fasting, a visit to seven churches, saying five Paternosters and five Hail Mary's ... and a small alms for Saint Peter's Dome' - it raises a smile that still relies on Luther's original, violent roar of laughter. It is like a faint echo of *his* original laugh, one that made modern sensibility possible.

Bakhtin's view on the carnivalistic tradition of laughter, notably his observations regarding the phenomenon of praise/abuse, can be of considerable assistance when it comes to furthering our philosophical appraisal of Luther's grobianism. Carnivalistic abuse, Bakhtin tells us, does not *merely* degrade its target, for it becomes *familiarized* as well. The terrifying powers of church and state are humanized as the intimidating distance between power and subject is reduced. Terms of abuse are nicknames, conveying the basic insight that we humans are all basically equal because the daily life of our bodies (notably of the body's lower half) remains basically similar, regardless of official (that is, artificial) separations of class, profession and political (or ecclesiastical) influence.[81] Reality is familiarized and the object is brought up close, although the old truth still pretends to be extra-temporal and absolute, and its representatives still strut majestically, threatening their foes with eternal punishment, unable to perceive their own origin, limitations and end, unable to recognize the comic nature of all pretensions to eternity and immutability (Bakhtin 1968, p. 212/213). Due to jolly abuse, these frightening silhouettes, the representatives of eternal truth, turn out to be human beings just like us. Or, as Marx phrased it, they turn out to be the comedians of a world order whose real heroes have already died. Jolly abuse implies perceiving the world fearlessly and impiously. The gay and triumphant tone at work in it ought not escape us. Human beings are reconciled by the physical proximity that is suggested by grotesque, degrading images and Luther's jolly abuse echoes the experience of the collapse of gothic intimidation. The jolly abuse with which he addresses church and state officials is in sharp contrast, however, with his verbal treatment of the revolting peasants. In the latter case, his rhetoric is *merely* abusive and, by implication, terrifying. His language becomes violent and grim, intimidating and frightening. Quite unlike abusive terms like 'papal asses', by means of which the terrifying is

---

80 'Du solltest nicht ehe ein Buch schreiben , du hettest denn ein Forz von einer alten Saw gehöret, da soltestu dein Maul gegen aufsperren und sagen, Dank habe du schöne Nachtigal, da höre ich einen text, der ist fur mich' (p. 373).

81 According to Bakhtin, the modern euphemism 'mudslinging' refers to an ancient gesture of besmirching, not with mud but with excrement.

transformed into the familiar, the familiar is now transformed into the terrifying and the peasants are depicted as hordes of gothic devils, to be exterminated without consideration or delay - in short, Luther's speech suddenly suffers a significant and disastrous generic shift.

Another perfect specimen of the parodical/grobian genre is Luther's treatise *On the Papacy at Rome, Against the Celebrated Romanist at Leipzig* - a title which is ironical since the Romanist at Leipzig who had attacked him was not that famous.[82] To begin with, Luther claims that although he had already been suffered quite a bit of slander, now suddenly a giantesque and well-equipped figure enters the ring. Fortunately, however, on further consideration, he proves to be ridiculous rather than of frightening: an idiot on stilts. Furthermore, Luther justifies his recourse to jest by indicating that his adversaries had been treating the Scriptures disrespectfully, almost as if they were mere fairy tales produced by a professional jester on Shrove Tuesday. Since the Word of God evokes no more respect than a fool's prandial speech, Luther feels compelled to suspend seriousness and resort to jest: gross fools have to be addressed in a gross manner. Moreover, the Papal blackguards had been mocking pious German simpletons long enough, pulling their legs for quite some time, convinced that they could get away with it, but the German drunkards had finally come to recognize that they had let themselves be taken in too many times.

Luther's argument focusses on his adversary's claim that, just as a body cannot do without a corporeal head, neither can the church. According to Luther, this is Shrove Tuesday dialectics. His line of argument, aimed at ruthlessly demonstrating its ridiculous nature, is tedious at times, but he basically argues that since the church is a spiritual community, it is in need of a *spiritual* head (i.e. Christ) but can perfectly do without a corporeal one. In fact, a corporeal head would fit a spiritual body like a painted, Shrove Tuesday mask would fit a corporeal one. Moreover, if Luther were to use the Scriptures as arbitrarily as his adversaries did, he would easily succeed in proving that *Rastrum* (a cheap beer consumed in considerable amounts by students at Leipzig, who compared it to a *rastrum*, a pick-axe, because of the disastrous effect it had on their bowels) surpasses *Malvasier*, an excellent brand of white wine quite famous at the time, in quality. Only a Shrove Tuesday fool would see the Pope as a head. Luther no longer allows his legs to be pulled by such sophisms. And because God endowed him with a gay and fearless mind, he considered it his vocation to show ruthlessly that the claims of his 'Romanist' opponents were the braying of a donkey.

Once again, a great number of elements of the popular culture of laughter are present in this treatise. For example, the giant on stilts represents the famous grotesque strategy of transforming the terrible into the ridiculous - a strategy

---

[82] 'Von dem Papsttum zu Rom, wider den hochberühmten Romanisten zu Leipzig'. *Werke* 6, pp. 285-324.

162

employed by Luther throughout his life time by continuously mocking the once dreaded spokesmen of official truth. Furthermore, he jocularly refers to several instances of comic prandial discourse, such as the fool's speech on Shroves Tuesday, as well as to student drinking habits and mock debates. His final jest entails showing that this spokesman of official truth is himself mocking the Pope by comparing him to a head - again an image borrowed from grotesque popular culture and used brilliantly by Luther, provided that his performance is judged by the standards of the genre involved. Yet Luther's speech is far from being unequivocal. Although devoted to the principle of laughter himself, he at the same time distances himself from it, announcing the possibility of new forms of official speech taking the place of outdated forms which had been sufficiently ridiculed and were about to collapse.

7. A FINAL JUDGEMENT

In the previous sections it was claimed that in the early sixteenth century, laughter had become indispensable to allow for the collapse of gothic seriousness as well as the emergence of unprecedented forms of moral subjectivity - forms that transgressed the medieval compartmentalization of moral life into the serious and the grotesque. If one agrees with such a claim, it is still be possible to maintain that, although laughter *as such* had indeed become indispensable, the excessive and idiosyncratic coarseness and crudity of *Luther's* laughter, notably during his later years, must still be considered deplorable, even pathological. The laughter of some of his contemporaries (notably Erasmus), although displaying a fair amount of gaiety as well, did so in a more humane and civilized manner. In this final section, therefore, I will ask whether it is still possible to side with Luther here, whether his laughter really was gay, or 'grobian' rather than 'gay'. In order to arrive at an answer, I will briefly point out the difference between Luther's laughter and Erasmus' laughter, and subsequently go into the seemingly 'pathological' features of Luther's laughter as analyzed by Erikson, before turning to the question of what form of moral subjectivity it supported.

In order to compare Luther's laughter with Erasmus', one must be aware of the fact that both antagonists had already made this comparison themselves. Erasmus reproached Luther for being excessively violent and crude, and Luther reproached Erasmus for being too consistent in his ambivalence. According to Luther, Erasmus laughed at everything and everyone, persisting in his ambivalence even in the face of Christ. Let us have a closer look.

I already pointed out that Luther's works, notably his *Tischreden*, contain many comic scenes which can be considered perfect examples of the popular comic genres of the sixteenth Century (in which both he and Erasmus proved themselves true masters). One could easily compose a comic novel out of them and in my opinion, Luther's talents as a comic novelist still do not receive the attention they deserve. Take, for example, the story about the lazy priest who, instead of saying his obligatory prayers, was in the habit of reciting the alphabet, adding, 'Lord, please receive these letters and be so kind as to compose from them the canonical chants Yourself [3: 2973]. Or the story about the butcher's dog who mistook his master's testicles for the bowels he was cleaning and swallowed them - a story which arose during a discussion on the etymology of the word 'monk' which, according to Luther, was derived from *Mönch* ('castrated horse', 3:2981). Or the story about the priest who, as he witnessed a dog urinating in his censer, asked whether the animal had turned Lutheran. Such gay-hearted stories, narrated by Luther over his hospitable table, contributed considerably to the merry atmosphere of his prandial conversations. Indeed, the world seemed full of gaiety, with everyone mocking everyone else, and Luther joined in with Renaissance laughter, with one exception: only God was not to be trifled with.[83] Whenever that happened, his gay laughter immediately gave way to furious rage. And on this point Luther distinguished himself from Erasmus, whom he reproached for laughing at everything and everyone, including (the Word of) God, whereas he himself, although given to gross mockery when dealing with his fellow human beings, remained pious to God. Erasmus stopped at nothing and finally seemed to include even Christ in his ridicule, or at least in his ambivalence, but Luther maintained that one can laugh at everything except for the Scriptures [3: 2834, 2866, 3010]. In short, Luther reproached Erasmus for being indifferent towards this one basic constraint. But he eventually reproaches Erasmus' laughter for being *too restricted*. Although at first Erasmus' relentless laughter seems more consistent, he still leaves something, or rather, *someone* out, namely himself. While exposing everyone to ridicule, he himself claims to be wise. According to Luther, this is his basic flaw, for whoever wishes to remain faithful to God must become a fool in the eyes of the world, which is what Erasmus refuses to do.[84] By means of his ambiguous, 'amphibolic'

---

[83] Diabolus ridet omnes, sed eo excepto, de quo Paulus dicit: Non irridetur, 3: 2993; cf. 3327: 'Ich kann auch scherzen, trinken, lachen, frölich sein, possen reissen etc, sed quidquid de verbo tractatur aut tractandum est, da verzir mich keiner und lasse viel lachen'.

[84] I focus on Luther's judgement of Erasmus without passing a judgement on the latter myself and without verifying whether his laughter is really ironical and self-assertive, for such an endeavour would be beyond the scope of this chapter. I will not conceal, however, that my personal judgement is much more sympathetic than Luther's and that I consider Erasmus' laughter less restricted and, above all, less 'ironical' than is suggested here. Huizinga (1950a, 1950b) stresses his wittiness and jest. *Praise of Folly* is considered the paragon of Renaissance laughter. Even the Scriptures become the target of his playful wit. According to Huizinga, modern man is unable to appreciate Erasmus' gaiety and jest

language [3: 3010, 3284, 3302], which threatens to ridicule even Christ, he is protecting *himself*. Although on the surface it seems as though he will not stop at anything, eventually he is *unable to laugh at himself*. In the case of Luther's laughter, however, his own Self is clearly included. By making a fool of himself, proclaiming himself a buffoon and a simpleton, he is showing his regard for Christ.[85] Ultimately, it is Luther who stops at nothing - nothing in this world. While Erasmus' laughter comes to a halt before his own genius, Luther includes himself in his universal derision. He laughs at lazy priests, at unfortunate butchers, and also at himself. He stops at *no-thing*, but does stop at God. Idols can be ridiculed, God cannot; we can laugh at ourselves, but not at God. The *stultitia mundi* does include *us*, but not *Him*. Erasmus's laughter is an experience of Self-assertion rather than of de-subjectivation: the laughing Self remains unchallenged. According to Luther, however, the only Self who had a right to exclude Himself from ridicule was Christ.[86]

An unsurpassed and gifted reader of the Bible, however, Luther clearly recognized the ambivalence of many of its phrases, its vulnerable spots, its susceptibility to a parodical or even grotesque reading. He considered this the work of the devil, to whom he referred as a rogue who, finding himself unable to challenge the Word of God directly, ridiculed it from within by coining phrases which allow or even suggest grotesque associations with bodily functions, thus contributing significantly to the merriment of idle readers. Luther mentions as an example a line taken from the *Psalter - Flabit spiritus, et fluent aquae* - which could be interpreted as suggesting that God produced a fart so that the waters would be stirred. Indeed, Luther adds, many a good line was sullied in this way.

---

because Luther's earnestness and resoluteness has alienated us from it. We tend to consider his devotion superficial or even deficient. In this chapter I pointed out that the tension between Luther and Erasmus cannot be identified with the one between earnestness and folly. Luther's laughter prevents him from becoming serious and dogmatic - he is a Renaissance figure in his own right.

85 In his prandial conversations he often refers to himself as a fool, and prays that God may act as guardian of simpletons like himself - 'Unser Herrgott muß der narren furmundt sein' (3: 2835), cf. 'Wir sint hanswurste' (3: 2849).

86 This appraisal of Erasmus of Rotterdam, as well as the opposition between irony and piety, is supported by Kierkegaard. Apart from the fact that he considers Erasmus an outstanding example of irony (p. 261) he stresses the extent to which Erasmus' laughter differs from what he refers to as the 'devout mind': '[Much like the ironic subject] the devout mind [or pious mentality] also declares that all is vanity but ... it makes no exception of its own person ... on the contrary, it also must be set aside. In Irony, however, since everything is shown to be vanity, the subject becomes free. The more vain everything becomes, all the lighter, emptier, and volatilized the subject becomes. And while everything is in the process of becoming vanity, the ironic subject does not become vain in his own eyes but rescues his own vanity' (p. 258).

Nor did it escape Luther's attention that at times Christ himself had recourse to mockery. The grains of mockery contained in some of His speech acts did not escape him. In *Tischreden 3:2842*, for example, he points to several instances of mockery and ridicule where Christ *hat spottisch geredt*.[87] In fact, he regarded his own prandial conversation - his discourses *über Tische*, his *colloquii convivali*, in which he emerges as an amiable fellow, referring to himself as a simpleton and to his mates as rogues[88] - as similar to the ones conducted daily by Christ and his disciples, referred to by Luther as *iundissima et familiarissima* [3: 3286]. But ultimately, the connection between faith and gaiety goes much deeper yet and pertains to the basic truth of faith itself. Everything we believe in, everything that is revealed by the Scriptures, Luther claims, is a ridiculous lie from the point of view of reason and experience.[89] And yet we cannot resist this truth, however ridiculous it may seem. Erasmus, however, refuses to become a fool and simpleton, that is, a true Christian.[90]

Now provided we grant this, provided we agree with Luther that Erasmus' laughter - quite unlike 'Christian' laughter - suffered from this one basic flaw, then what about the next charge, the one concerning the excessive *coarseness* of his laughter? Why did he find it necessary to call the Pope, the rebellious peasants, etc. all these awful names, considering them to be the devil in person - although at times he was so generous as to allow for the possibility that perhaps the Pope acted out of stupidity instead of maliciousness, and therefore was to be regarded an ass rather than a devil.[91] As was mentioned in a previous section, Erikson takes a psychogenetic, psychoanalytical perspective of the problem of Luther's grobian excess. What does it amount to?

---

[87] According to Nietzsche, however, Christ is outmatched by Socrates in this respect - 'Vor dem Stifter des Christentums hat Sokrates die fröhliche Art des Ernstes und jene *Weisheit* voller Schelmenstreiche voraus' (*Human, All Too Human II*, The Wanderer and his Shadow, § 86).

[88] Ex animo laetus erat et iocabatur cum amicis et mecum et extenuabat suam eruditionem: Ich bin alber, saget er, und ir seitt ein schalck... 5: 5284. One is reminded of Nietzsche's remark: *Freie Geiste: Gesellen mit denen man lacht* (*Human, All Too Human I*, § 2).

[89] 3: 2843, 3022b, etc.; but notably 3:2970b where, after citing a line pronounced by Christ Himself, he laughs and claims that, form the point of view of reason, it is a gross lie: 'Deinde ridens dixit: Ratio dicit: *Das ist ein grosse lugen*'.

[90] Nietzsche would no doubt have sided with Erasmus, for he accuses Christianity of having discredited reason (cf. chapter 2)

[91] 'Aut asinus fuit papa aut diabolus; asinus quod stupidissimus suos errores non intelligit, Diabolus, quod eos fovit et confirmavit' (3: 3027).

In the first chapter of Erikson's case study it is announced that the author 'will interpret in psychological terms whatever phenomena clinical experience and psychoanalytic thought have made [him] recognize are dependent on man's demonstrable psychic structure' (p. 21), implying that Luther's achievements as well as his ailings and idiosyncracies are to be explained in terms of his neurotic or manic-depressive state of mind and character traits or else regarded as expressions of his 'partially unsuccessful solution of the identity crisis of youth' (p. 242).[92] Some clues to such a psychoanalytic explanation are provided by Kierkegaard, who already referred to Luther as a 'patient' - not in the clinical sense though, but in the sense of being someone with a passion for expressing and describing his physical and spiritual suffering.[93] Moreover, Kierkegaard unequivocally supports the view that, in his later years, Luther's personality as well as his achievements suffered a severe decline. He complains about the mediocrity and staleness of his table-talks as well as his folksy witticisms (such as the claim that a fart produced in Wittenberg is audible in Rome). As we have already seen, Erikson basically concurred to this view. Whereas young Luther's *cause* became his *cure*, in Luther's later years his rage as well as his laughter turned histrionic and grotesque.

Contrary to Erikson's position, however, I will contend that *laughter* was the thing that cured him, and that the laughter of his later years was still truly gay and quite in tune with the roar of laughter known as the tower experience. The 'grotesque' story about the monk who experienced a sudden revelation while taking care of his bodily discharge in a latrine, told by Luther in his later years, should not be separated from the (perhaps more gradual) spiritual transformation that actually took place in Luther's youth. Both episodes (the tower and the dish) represented (albeit in their own way) the principle of laughter as it resounded during the early sixteenth Century. Whereas in the case of the tower experience Luther's laughter was still rather isolated and a perfect example of the experience of laughter as explored by Bataille, the convivial laughter of his later years was perhaps even more gay in the Bakhtinean sense of being carefree, comical and hospitable. Let me therefore further elaborate my position by means of a pair of decent arguments, one of them being of a 'historical' nature and the other of a 'moral' nature. The parentheses are added

---

92   An approach which exemplifies Bakhtin's observation that in the modern image of the body 'sexual life, eating, drinking, and defecation have radically changed their meaning: they have been transferred to the private and psychological level' (1968, p. 321).

93   Freud refers to Luther only once and apologizes for doing so. In his book on Moses, he quotes from Luther's translation of the Bible: 'ich bitte um Verzeihung, daß ich mich in anachronistischer Weise der Übersetzung Luthers bediene' (1946, p. 195). However, as he uses the Luther quotation in a discussion on Michelangelo's statue of Moses and the Renaissance attitude toward Biblical sources (p. 197) his apology seems somewhat out of place.

because, basically, both arguments are intimately connected. In fact, they have already been briefly mentioned in the course of this chapter.

Beginning with the historical argument, often too much emphasis is laid on one particular aspect of the gothic frame of mind which, in the nineteenth century, came to be identified with the gothic *per se*: the aspect of gloomy terror. In reality, the gothic world had *two* aspects. Besides terror, atonement and chill, reinforced by the somber chorus of the mendicant orders, there was the popular cult of carnival, of license and leisure, relief and release. These aspects existed side-by-side, and the early sixteenth century did not witness the resurgence of extinguished laughter so much as the sudden expansion of one aspect of gothic life - its laughing aspect - at the expense of its counter-aspect - the somber backdrop of terror which had accompanied it for centuries. For a gloomy, nineteenth century picture of the 14th and 15th Century, Huizinga's *The Waning of the Middle Ages* is often cited, but then in a biased and one-sided way, for besides terror and decline, Huizinga's account also includes gay poetry and popular farce, companies of fools and bursts of laughter, jolly festivals and comic processions. Therefore, instead of emphasizing a basic rupture between the gloomy, terrible Middle Ages on the one hand and the gay and merry Renaissance on the other, one has to point to this basic continuity, to Luther's indebtedness to medieval popular culture, and to the grotesque, pre-modern nature of his laughter. Young 'gothic' Luther had been a gloomy and depressed but also gay fellow (*ein guter Geselle*) blessed with a musical gift, a remarkable fondness for lute-playing and singing, which he was to keep up for the rest of his life. He was someone who appreciated the parodical, comical features of traditional student rituals and, many years later when it was his turn to hold a 'deposition' (a kind of initiation speech, addressing a crowd of 'burse' or hostel residents who accompanied some novices, comically dressed up with pig's teeth, long ears and horns) he played on the word 'deposition' (which in Latin, apart from 'swearing an oath', also means 'humiliation') and urged them to honour at all times the magistrates and the female sex, provided they 'did not piss in public' [*Tischreden* 4:5024].

The monastery constituted an environment that, by means of its rigid regime of fasting, silence, isolation, and other forms of deprivation, aimed at conditioning depression and abolishing laughter. But, as Erikson noted, Luther developed his own, albeit 'folksy', way of resistance: a highly ambivalent *overobedience*, an effort to make monkshood absurd from the very start and from within by obeying its rules too scrupulously - a *parodical* strategy of rebellious mocking in the form of exaggerated obedience. Although initially one might feel inclined to consider excessive fasting as an expression of the total dominance of monastic power over the vital body, on further reflection it might turn out to be a phenomenon of resistance. After having confessed for hours Luther would ask for special appointments in order to correct previous statements or add fresh exaggerations concerning his 'sins', thereby upsetting monastic efficiency. In fact, those 'sins' consisted, apart from spontaneous ejaculations, mainly of a chronic inclination towards mockery, profanation and blasphemous abuse while celebrating Mass.[94] His mentor Staupitz, however, replied to his pupil's rebellious mockery adequately - with humorous replies.

Luther's final outburst of laughter in the tower was far from ironic or otherwise subdued. It was a roar of irresistible laughter that before long turned into a collective experience, the impact of which was simply astonishing. Its outcome was one of renewal and liberation rather than destruction. And it was, of course, grotesque. This meant, in the first place, that it was closely connected with the body, with bodily resistance. It started as an experience of release associated with defecation, and before long became associated with abundant digestion, that is, Luther's comic reversal of medieval asceticism, his body growing voracious and grandiose, consuming and discharging gigantic portions, while his conversation abounded in references to the body's lower half, to eating, drinking and sweating. Asceticism, as it was introduced by early Christianity, gave way to the recurrence of grotesque laughter, a change further encouraged by Luther's Gargantuan production of published speech. This was his primal achievement and act of renewal: the transposition of the gay, unpublished spheres of speech into printed discourse, which resulted in the official being overwhelmed by the vernacular and the colloquial. Those three former monks (Rabelais, Erasmus and Luther) were true contemporaries indeed.

The extent to which Luther distanced himself from official ecclesiastical and theological views on laughter is truly astonishing. Medieval theology had been marked by a tension between two incompatible views on laughter, the Aristotelian and the ascetic one.[95] The Aristotelian view, which has already been discussed in chapter three, aimed at a middle ground between boorishness and buffoonery, between annihilation and excess. According to Clemens of Alexandria, for example, human nature must not be smothered and repressed but managed and organized according to some ethical standards. Likewise, laughter may well be balanced and used in an appropriate manner - an ideal commonly referred to as 'urbanity' (as opposed to primitive provincial village laughter).[96] Before long, however, the

---

94 Perhaps these abuses are remainders of the ancient pagan habit of mocking and insulting the deity by means of comic pledges and oaths, already referred to in chapter three as ancient cultic forms of abuse and derision.

95 Cf. for example Posthumus Meyjes (1992).

96 In his *Poetics* Aristotle (1927/1960) tells us that, according to some, comedy was derived from *komai*, a Dorian dialect noun referring to 'outlying villages'. The comic poets used to wander from village to village, being excluded contemptuously from the city.

ascetic view gained dominance. Laughter was no longer tolerated but denied all civil rights. It was stressed that, unlike the pagan deities, the Jewish-Christian God did not laugh.[97] Christian devotion was considered to be incompatible with any kind of laughter and John Chrysostom declared that jest and laughter are not from God but from the devil (Bakhtin 1968, p. 73). Yet the idea of *urbanitas* as well as the idea of an *opportuna iocatio* (the appropriate joke) was never abolished altogether. In fact, the Aristotelian view was rehabilitated by Thomas Aquinas: laughter is natural and admissible provided it is civilized rather than excessive. Protestantism was usually opposed to laughter and countless Protestant moralists explicitly rejected popular carnivalesque cheerfulness, while Calvin himself rebuked Rabelais in a rather stern manner (1984, pp. 138-140).[98] Yet according to Luther, gaiety (even if 'excessive' at times) should count as an appropriate Christian mood, while a bold prank (even if considered less-appropriate by some) should count as an argument. In short, he rejected both the Aristotelian and the ascetic view, in favour of unrestricted laughter.

Lutheran orthodoxy, however, made every effort to turn theology into a serious genre once again. The distinction between nucleus and residue, still present in virtually all of the introductions to Luther's work, at times even producing allegorical interpretations of straightforward and candid jest, was one of the basic devices of what Toulmin referred to as the Counter-Renaissance, granting only a thoroughly revised Luther access to the *Temple du Goût* of modern discourse, even if it meant stripping him of something basic, presenting him as someone who merely *prepared the way for a new seriousness*, a herald of Counter-Renaissance, of a new, etatistic alliance between church and state. Still, one cannot deny that some aspects of Luther's performance do seem to support such a reading. His libel *Hans Worst*, for example, or more generally his preoccupation with firm foundations and certainty, seem to justify such an approach. Indeed, Luther's writing constitutes a strategic field in which several discursive forces compete with one another. One of them is Counter-Renaissance etatism, which announces itself at times, but without being able to silence laughter, not even in the case of the elderly Luther, for he also had his share of laughter. But in order to consider this issue more thoroughly, a second and 'moral' line of argument has to be included.

In *Human, All Too Human*, Nietzsche explains what he considers to be the truly pagan as opposed to the truly Christian.[99] It is a tolerance for the comic, the vulgar, the excessive: in short, the 'other' side of human life. In ancient Greece all natural

---

[97] With some exceptions, for example Psalm 2:4.

[98] As to Calvin - 'the agelast Calvin' (Bakhtin 1968, p. 350) - his view on laughter differs considerably form Luther's. Unfortunately, however, a comparison of the latter's views with those of other protagonists of Protestantism is far beyond the scope of this book.

[99] *Human, All Too Human II*, 'Mixed Opinions and Aphorisms', § 220.

instincts and inclinations were granted certain festivities or appointed days during which it was allowed to exhibit and satisfy them, or even to grant them full rein. Instead of being jeered at, they were tolerated and acknowledged, albeit within certain fixed, temporal boundaries. Every natural force, provided it displayed a certain impact on human behaviour, was considered divine. All natural inclinations were included in public life instead of being rejected or denied. There were certain occasions on which they could be discharged. This arrangement was a precaution against the risk of being suddenly overwhelmed by the fury of the elements that one would no longer be able contain. Morality was attuned to human existence as a whole rather than being the restricted, ascetic regimen of some sacerdotal caste or other. Paganism displayed a sense of realism, moderating the passions instead of trying to abolish them. This no doubt explained the pagan sense of connectedness of the comical (or even the obscene) with the religious, of the burlesque and the ridiculous with the sublime, displayed for instance during the festivities of Dionysos and Demeter (§ 112). Christianity, on the other hand, has always displayed a tendency towards asceticism as well as excess: although it aimed at abolishing, repressing, or gradually extinguishing certain comic or carnal aspects of human life, other serious or spiritual aspects were pushed to their extreme (§ 114). In fact, Nietzsche discerns a historical development of progressive repression of laughter. As culture became more civilized, he claims, more and more realms of human existence were cleansed of mockery and jest. In the sixteenth century, marriage and the church had almost been *laughed* into oblivion, but now the epoch of seriousness has finally dawned on us (§ 240).

In terms of Nietzsche's historical tale of continuously increasing seriousness, Luther no doubt occupies a turning-point, and above all a temporary relapse. It becomes increasingly clear that the details of the tower experience are far from residual. First of all, they indicate that, after a long period of asceticism, the 'other', comic, carnal side of human existence finally asserted itself. Furthermore, the details of this breakthrough emphasize a deeply felt connectedness of the comical and the obscene with the religious and the sublime as experienced by Luther throughout his life. The violent recurrence of the repressed culminated in an irresistible experience of laughter. Yet there is another side to laughter, recognized by Nietzsche, Bataille and Foucault, which must be included in our account: its connection with fear.

In the first volume of *Human, All Too Human* a remarkable section is included on the origin (*Herkunft*) of the comical (§ 169) in which human history reaches far beyond the dawn of ancient Greece, leading us into the very twilight of prehistory. For hundreds of thousands of years, Nietzsche claims, man had been a frightened animal, living in a permanent state of anxiety. Anything sudden or unexpected posed an immediate threat to survival. In view of this, it is not at all astonishing that a sudden or unexpected event, although frightening at first, will give rise to laughter as soon as it proved to be harmless. Now according to Nietzsche, this transition from short-lived fear to short-lived recklessness, conditioned long ago but still discernable in man, is called the comical.

Apparently there are two sides to laughter. In the sections mentioned above, laughter was the sudden manifestation of a vital force, bound to assert itself in a violent manner should its basic rights be neglected. As such, it was an experience of release, of being overwhelmed by laughter. In the section just mentioned, however, laughter is triggered by the sudden collapse of fear, that is, by the awareness that the apparently fearful object or event is in fact quite harmless. As such, laughter is a triumphant experience, one of recklessness and sovereignty, connected with a sudden awareness or insight: a gay truth which is suddenly revealed. Indeed, the tower experience provides us with a perfect example of laughter in which both aspects manifest themselves. Retention gives way to release while fear gives way to recklessness. Indeed, the terrifying object ('God') turns out to be well-disposed. Luther's experience of laughter is truly triumphant and truly gay. Both Pope and Emperor are taken aback by the reckless laughter of a mere monk. From now on the 'other' side of human life becomes more and more recognized: celibacy gives way to marriage, Latin to the vernacular, and the official ecclesiastical idiom to colloquial speech genres.

It is interesting to note that the 'Etna experience' recorded by Bataille is similar in some respects to the tower experience narrated by Luther. Note, for instance, that young Bataille left his shelter 'in order to satisfy a certain physical need'. Perhaps the volcano itself symbolizes something like the earth's latrine, producing nothing but dung and wind. Exposed to this horrible sight, he suddenly laughs, an experience of revelation and triumph.

Nietzsche recognized that, apart from being an experience (the aspect of laughter emphasized by Bataille), laughter is also a practice (the aspect of laughter emphasized by Bakhtin). The comic festivities of Dionysos and Demeter, for instance, are to be interpreted as efforts to 'dramatize' laughter and turn it into a practice or, rather, a genre: a comic cult with its peculiar chants or modes of speech. In the case of Luther, several efforts to turn laughter into a genre can be discerned. As a youth, he developed his parodical game of concealed mockery, his parodical practice of overobedience, his foolish, rebellious parody of asceticism which in the end was *justified* by the tower experience. Finally, the one-time gloomy, silent monk of the Erfurt monastery was transformed into the jovial chatterer of the table-talks, who initiated a merry genre, the dramatization of hospitable sympathy and merriment.

The tower experience marked the conclusion of Luther's ascetic phase, his life of isolation and deprivation. Its details clearly show that, all of a sudden, a comic foolish monk had become the herald of a new gay truth, for it is in the fool's discourse that new truths first make their appearance. He is granted the privilege of articulating them for the first time. After having descended from the tower where he experienced his revelation, he once again seeks the company of men. He reaches the market-square and runs into Tetzel, *der grosser Clamant*, a loud, advertising voice selling his ecclesiastical merchandise - until he finds himself exposed and ridiculed by Luther's relentless laughter, which before long will bring about the irrevocable collapse of the gothic demarcation of the serious and the popular, the ascetic and the grotesque.

In his introduction to the first volume of *Human, All Too Human* Nietzsche relates the origin of freethinking in such a way that Luther's biography inadvertently crosses one's mind. It starts with the experience of suddenly breaking free from former ties, from the dark corner (the 'monastic cell', for instance) into which one had withdrawn oneself, as well as from one's sense of duty and reverence for everything holy. It is a sudden startling experience of awakening, of eruption, of being torn away from one's 'home'. It is an experience of freedom, evoking a frank and carefree mood. From now on, a state of excessive health becomes one's goal. Life had become a problem, but now it is made possible again. Before living life to the full, however, the free-thinker will cast a final glance on his former life, gratefully enjoying his 'panoramic, bird's-eye view' - his *Wartburg* so to speak.[100] The world he left behind has completely lost its significance to him. Finally, the history of free-thinking implies the discovery of one's basic task, one's 'inner tyrant'.[101] From a literary point of view, Luther's outstanding achievement after descending from his dwelling in the 'realm of the birds' was to allow the popular, comic and burlesque genres entrance to published speech, to admit popular diction and dialect to a discourse which until then had exclusively been devoted to spiritual issues, and to make use of a great number of the free-floating popular speech genres (all those forms of *franc-parler* that are present in his work). In doing so he created the German language. In his later years he became the founding father of Christian gaiety professing to be able to write only when in a merry mood. Although he did not actually claim to be writing *while* eating and drinking, both activities became intimately associated with each other. He became one of those remarkable authors who applied comical devices to spiritual issues. His unprecedented practice of writing became his 'remedy' (although not necessarily a psychotherapeutic one), his effort to regain his health, which had been corrupted by medieval asceticism. As

---

100 As Nietzsche talks about 'Vogel-Freiheit', 'Vogel-Umblick', 'Fernblicken und Vogelflügen in kalte Höhen' it is interesting to note that in his letters Luther uses similar expressions to refer to his stay at the Wartburg as well as at the fortress at Coburg: 'Im Reich der Vögel', 'Aus dem Reich der Vögel', etc.

101 *Human, All Too Human II*, § 4.

Nietzsche pointed out, [102] writing can become a cure, a way to organize free-floating energy suddenly set loose. What does this mean?

In the early sixteenth century, due to the decline of late medieval forms of moral subjectivity, the human subject was in danger of being overwhelmed by the tyranny of unorganized instincts and forces that could no longer be contained by means of the moral and political devices which had been developed to this end. They had been applied successfully for quite some time, thereby securing a moral regime of long standing. Suddenly, however, it was on the verge of collapse. There were basically two possible remedies. One was etatism: containment by expanding state and/or ecclesiastical power, allowing it to penetrate human life to an unprecedented extent - the etatistic, top-down option that was used, for instance, in the violent repression of the peasant revolt. It was the emperor's option as well, although his imperial version of it was eventually frustrated by the emergence of a new political phenomenon called the nation-state. Finally, it was this same remedy that inspired the Counter-Reformation, a tremendous effort to centralize, codify and restrain spiritual life on an unprecedented scale.

The other remedy hailed the breakdown of established morality, for it would allow unprecedented forms of moral subjectivity to become established. This was Luther's initial, bottom-up solution to a problem he himself experienced so vehemently - the sudden awareness of the insignificance of that which had been terrifying him, while at the same time finding himself overwhelmed by certain aspects of spiritual and bodily existence which had been neglected by the established regime and which, due to the collapse of gothic seriousness, were suddenly released. This experience of collapse, breakthrough and laughter initiated a writing practice which allowed the serious and the comic to be reconnected - and in the course of this writing practice, a new form of moral subjectivity, one quite in tune with the Renaissance state of mind, was established. In short, Luther allowed himself and others to become a different kind of person.

The collective instead of merely individual, the 'moral' instead of merely 'psychological' nature of this transition is an indication of the deficiency of a psychopathological or psychoanalytic understanding (of which Erikson provides us with an outstanding example). 'Humor', he claims, 'marks the moment when our ego regains territory from oppressive conscience' (p. 169). Now this could be considered merely a redescription or adaption, in a somewhat different vocabulary, of an insight already articulated above, namely that laughter is effected by a sudden decline of oppressive fear. Basically, however, Erikson's remark relies on what he refers to elsewhere as 'man's demonstrable psychic structure' (p. 21) - that is, on the claim that the basic structures of human subjectivity are universal and permanent, and captured once and for all in terms of the ongoing struggle between Ego, Id and

---

[102] *Human, All Too Human I*, Introduction, § 1.

Super-ego (or conscience) as recorded by Freud. This basic assumption is to be challenged. Apart from the fact that one might challenge the validity of Freud's account as far as the present is concerned, it seems inadmissible simply to transpose it to incomparable historical circumstances. Conscience as we know it, for instance, is not at all an enduring and universal phenomenon, but rather the temporary outcome of a particular historical development. Hegel in his *Philosophy of Law*, for instance, points to the fact that the Greek did not yet have a conscience, whereas Nietzscheans like Foucault have pointed to the fact that the Ego presented to us by Freud is a 'recent invention' and of modern ('Cartesian') origin - an outcome of what Toulmin refers to as the Counter-Renaissance. By taking current, modern (or even 'postmodern') forms of moral subjectivity for granted and by imposing them without further reflection on experiences like the one recorded by Luther, we are likely to produce a distorted picture of those (likewise temporary) forms of moral subjectivity that were allowed to become established in the early sixteenth Century. Notwithstanding the significance of the psychoanalytic view as a genealogical and 'bottom-up' perspective, the Freudian claims regarding the basic structures of moral subjectivity must not be taken for granted as extra-temporal because the transformation of moral experience that occurred during the early sixteenth century affected the very structures of subjectivity as well. As has been stressed by Nietzsche and Foucault, the moral subject has a history, it is historical rather than permanent. Luther's laughter indicated the collapse of a particular historical kind of 'ego-formation', some aspects of which were included in the new formation, while others were laughed into oblivion. Although it initiated a profound reorganization of vital forces, its outcome - Luther - was not yet a modern subject. The tower experience was a positive, affirmative experience in its own right and the form of moral subjectivity it produced was not merely a transition but the Renaissance state of mind. It did not *merely* tear down some obsolete forms of seriousness so that new forms of seriousness could take their place.

But what about Luther's subsequent etatistic turn? Did he not side with etatism against the peasants and become more and more infected by it as he grew older, transforming gay Christianity into a state-church?[103] Luther should not be considered one of those 'political maniacs' to which Nietzsche refers, heading for revolt but unable to establish something new[104] (a judgement which, according to Luther, applied to the rebellious peasants), but perhaps what he eventually established turned out to be something serious and modern? As we have seen, Nietzsche maintained that Luther still represented a medieval, backward state of

---

103 Whose basic maxim was captured in the famous line *Cuius regio, eius religio.*

104 *Human, All Too Human I,* § 463.

mind,[105] notably his stubborn 'peasant' assumption that there is something like an undisputable truth which we must 'posses' or everything is lost - a state of mind which, according to Nietzsche, greatly impeded unbiased enquiry and science, that is, the dawning of the *modern* state of mind, which entails *searching* for truth rather than claiming to posses it.[106] After *re*reading Luther as thoroughly as we have done, one senses that such a judgement is one-sided, to say the least. Nietzsche's remarks seem to suggest that he actually adhered to the opposition between, on the one hand, a primitive, pre-scientific state of mind and, on the other, a modern, scientific one. In chapter two, however, we have already drawn the conclusion that such a scheme, although at times apparently adopted by Nietzsche, eventually found itself disrupted by the truth of laughter. Therefore, rather than accepting that Luther can be disposed of in such an unsatisfactory manner, we must recognize that he embodied a philosophical principle in its own right.

In my view, Nietzsche's remarkable analysis of Socrates's remedy, discussed in the final section of chapter three, applies to Luther as well. Reference was made to Plato's efforts to contain the gay and carefree laughter of the 'true' Socrates, which had managed to retain its regenerative power and joyful tone in several of the dialogues. Nietzsche claimed that, at that time, established morality as well as the established modes of exercising power suffered a severe decay. Human subjectivity was in danger of being overwhelmed by the tyranny of unorganized instincts that apparently could no longer be contained, neither in a moral nor in a political manner. Laughter not only confirmed the breakdown of established, serious morality but also gave voice to the omnipresence of free-floating energy that allowed unprecedented forms of moral subjectivity to become established. Such a situation temporarily demanded a Socratic bottom-up solution, but is was short-lived and eventually overcome by rationality and etatism (that is, incorporated in the Platonic top-down policy of establishing a new, stable, centripetal and rationalistic moral regime). Luther's performance could be judged along the same lines and in much the same vein. His remarkable writing practice constituted a temporary effort to allow the free-floating energies to be organized in a gay and non-etatistic way before being absorbed by a new set of moral, religious, scientific and political disciplines referred to by Toulmin as the Counter-Renaissance. Indeed, as Foucault indicated, there was something unstable and unendurable in Renaissance laughter which hinted at its collapse from the very start. But this does not allow us to regard it merely as a transitional phenomenon, an aftermath of medievalism, or a precursor of modernism. Rather, it constituted a state of mind in its own right. Indeed, to laugh, to mock, to deplore, to curse - those were Luther's basic modes of speech and Spinoza's rejection

---

[105] *Human, All Too Human I*, § 26, § 237.

[106] *Human, All Too Human II*, 'Mixed Opinions and Aphorisms', § 631, § 632, § 633.

clearly conveyed the awareness that the modern state of mind entailed a rupture with the gay science of the Renaissance, most notably its basic mood of laughter.

It is not my contention, of course, that modern laughter should become completely identical with Luther's gay-hearted laugh, nor do I deny that the basic conditions of moral criticism have significantly changed. We will have to produce our own responsive laugh. Public discourse is no longer dominated by the theological and ideological constraints of late medieval Christianity. Compared to public discourse in Luther's days, our language has become remarkably free and democratic (cf. Bakhtin 1988, p. 71). On the other hand, however, it must be stressed that at the close of the nineteenth century a new set of official speech genres has been established, known as the social and human sciences, overshadowing even late medieval theology's ability to penetrate and dominate public (as well as 'private') discourse, contributing significantly to the establishment of moral subjectivity. Instead of being peaceable and neutral these genres successfully deflated, disqualified and diminished their generic rivals (such as, for example, ecclesiastic theology) and became an important stronghold of contemporary etatism. Perhaps the particular branch of moral philosophy that aims at solving some of the policy problems of contemporary liberalism in a more or less scientific manner, discussed in chapter one, is one of them. Perhaps moral philosophy will even try to take their place.

Be that as it may, our situation is comparable to Luther's in certain respects. Or perhaps we should say that both epochs mirror one another. The sixteenth century witnessed the rise of the nation-state on the political level, the formation of national languages on the cultural level, and the launching of Reformation and Counter-Reformation on the ideological level. At present, however, we witness the sudden but apparently irreversible decline of these challenged, or even staggering forms of national, linguistic and religious unity. No doubt this will allow for unprecedented forms of moral subjectivity to emerge. Whereas in the sixteenth century imperial efforts to bring about the political unity of Europe were thwarted by the rise of the nation state, we now witness the nation-states rapidly losing their political significance and being incorporated into a unified Europe. Whereas in the sixteenth century the short-lived revival of Latin as a *lingua franca* for science was thwarted by the formation of national languages and the translation of Latin sources into the vernacular (a development to which Rabelais and Luther contributed significantly), we now witness the rise of a new *lingua franca* of science (a certain standard version of the English language) at the expense of the national vernacular. Moreover, all of a sudden we witness the disappearance of all those adversive ideological camps (Reformation and Counter-Reformation, Communism and Democracy, etcetera) whose mutual struggles and tensions dominated the political history of modernity. It is under such circumstances that society increasingly tends to rely on 'ethical expertise' to find support for her policies of containment (much like in the sixteenth century, centripetal imperial forces enlisted the support of ecclesiastical theology), although moral philosophy's effort to comply with this demand will be considerably hampered by the fact that basically, moral philosophy is a centrifugal rather than a centripetal mode of speech.

In view of the fact that what we experience today may be considered as the very reversal of the moral transformation that took place in the sixteenth century, a philosophical reconsideration of Luther's basic experiences and principles undoubtedly gains significance. Once again, laughter may serve as an epistemological prerequisite for exposing the limitations, delusions and complacence of official genres that mistakenly consider their basic insights to be indisputable. The frank and gay vocabulary of parody might still serve to challenge the stabilizing tendencies of the sufficiently neutralized and generalized nomenclature of (either social or moral) science. If seeming neutral is just another word for being dominant, we are left with no alternative. Gay laughter does not call for political revolt, or things like that, and its objectives are not of a political nature in the top-down sense of the term. As has been stressed in my reading of Luther, he also exemplified a bottom-up solution, established a new form of moral subjectivity, a new form of Christian piety. [107] Whether, in view of contemporary moral circumstances, laughter once again will provide such a remedy, is the subject of the final chapter.

---

[107] 'Ich will from Leute haben, nicht eine neue politiam anfangen - *Christum nullam relationem habet ad politiam*' [*Tischreden* 3:3126].

Chapter 5

The Transfiguration of the
Moral Subject: a *Re*reading of
When We Dead Awaken

1. DID IBSEN LAUGH?

In chapter two several philosophers of laughter were introduced, and in chapters three and four, two *heroes* of laughter made their appearance, one ancient and one early modern. And now I have to come up with a third, a modern 'hero of laughter', someone who made *our* laughter possible and whose laughter would render the strategies of avoidance and compartmentalization described in chapter one untenable.

I suspect that it will come as a surprise that Ibsen is supposed to meet this description and that he of all people is regarded as someone who makes us laugh. From pictures and portraits of him, one gets the impression that the silent, tight-lipped poet hardly ever smiled, and when the writer Jonas Lie tells about convivial evenings with Ibsen - 'The more his good humour grew, the more he beamed and laughed and shone' until at last he became good, kind, and talkative (Beyer 1978, p. 168) - these remarks are interesting *because* they are so much at odds with the great majority of observations of those who met him, usually bearing witness to his gloomy character and cheerless, even cynical mood. The great majority of his plays are not generally considered comical, seeming rather to convey a gloomy, sinister and tragic view of life. Furthermore, apart from the fact that Ibsen does not seem to excel in any comic genre whatsoever, he neither is generally considered a severe critic of a progressive, liberal ethic. On the contrary, he is often considered an advocate of liberalism and someone who was in support of a rather liberal approach to issues like suicide, euthanasia and the emancipation of women.

But perhaps the reader will allow me to remind him of the fact that, in the case of Socrates and Luther, the basic mood of laughter also had to be *recovered* at the expense of a well-established, *serious* reading of long standing. True laughter, instead of being self-evident, seems to escape us at first. Therefore it is not inconceivable from the very outset that a more or less similar result could be the outcome of my effort to *re*read Ibsen - implying that the Norwegian playwright would meet the aesthetic demand formulated by Socrates in *The Symposium* that a writer of tragedy ought to excel in comedy as well.[1] Thus the question is whether Ibsen was indeed an 'agelast' (something which seems to be generally agreed upon) or whether he did laugh. If he did laugh (and it goes without saying that I will contend that he did) what was the nature of his laughter? Finally, the implications of his laughter with regard to the liberal strategies of compartmentalization will have to be taken into consideration. The claim that he supported a liberal ethic, although it is considered a firmly established fact by some, will be challenged.

In the case of Socrates and Luther, Nietzsche's judgement (or rather his *judgements*) of them served as a starting-point for my own evaluation, but in the case of Ibsen such a procedure seems out of the question since Nietzsche hardly knew the work of his contemporary. The only Ibsen play he appears to have read was *Pillars of Society*, a transitional work and not one of Ibsen's major achievements as a creative writer. Moreover, although he *does* incidentally refer to him, he seems to focus on his political 'convictions', his progressive 'cause', rather than on his creative work. In *Ecce homo*, Nietzsche calls him a 'typical old spinster' and 'accuses' him of supporting the emancipation of women.[2] According to Nietzsche, emancipation is a phenomenon of resentment, a symptom of being unable to procreate, and the only way to 'cure' a woman is to make her pregnant - in short, he accuses Ibsen of not endorsing the negative-ascetic view on women, discussed in chapter two. In the *Nachlass*, Ibsen is mentioned as someone who represents moral liberalism, and as someone who, notwithstanding his robust will to truth, did not succeed in freeing himself from the illusions of morality, someone who is unable to grasp that 'freedom' is merely another manifestation of the will to power and that those who demand 'freedom' and 'justice' are the powerless and the weak.

These incidental remarks, which we will consider more carefully at a later point, seem rather disappointing at first. To begin with, no mention is made of the fact that Ibsen has provided the modern theatre with what could be considered a solution to 'the problem Wagner' as it was formulated by Nietzsche himself. For although Ibsen started his career as a playwright of historical pieces (such as *The Vikings at Helgeland*) that were similar to Wagner's historical operas in certain respects, he finally rejected the romantic-historical genre, preferring modern life as a dramatic setting, although he never neglected the profoundly historical, even genealogical origins of modern life's dramatic plots and problems. Furthermore, it has been stressed by many that some of Ibsen's dramatic heroes (most notably Sollness and Borkmann) should be regarded as personifications of a Nietzsche-like ideal, transcending the moral boundaries of duty, guilt, and other aspects of what Nietzsche

---

[1] Although all of his plays constitute a mixture of comic and tragic elements, his 'epilogue' could perhaps be considered his 'satyr-play', comical above average and added to the somewhat more tragic series of plays preceding it.

[2] 'Warum ich so gute Bücher schreibe', § 6.

180

referred to as slave morality.[3] Nietzsche's remarks do not even hint at this. Still, I will point out that Nietzsche's judgement, although apparently incorrect as such, will further our understanding of him - in a *negative* manner.

I will start reading Ibsen without my usual intermediary. Moreover, instead of judging all of his work, I intend to focus my attention on just one play. My preference for *When we Dead Awaken* is perhaps arbitrary, and some other play might have served just as well. Yet there is something final in this play, which is Ibsen's final work and presented to the audience as an 'epilogue'. Moreover, I consider it Ibsen's greatest achievement, but perhaps this is merely my personal opinion. Ibsen is generally considered the founding father of modern theatre, and rightly so. In his mature plays, he came to reject the aesthetic criteria of Romanticism. They are written in prose and deal with modern individuals rather than historical persons. Moreover, instead of focusing on the lofty and the sublime, they deal with less exalted human experiences and moods such as uneasiness or discontent, nausea, disappointment and boredom. Now where does laughter come in? To begin with, I will claim that Ibsen continuously mocks his characters, or rather, that they mutually mock each other. They reveal each other's true and basic objectives by mocking the feigned, 'official' ones. And eventually I will suggest that an even more basic *mood* of laughter seems to pervade his creative work, although it is often unnoticed.

But first allow me to summarize the play.[4] Its setting is a mountain area and its main characters are professor Arnold Rubek, a sculptor, Maia, his wife, and Irene, who, several years ago, served as model for his master piece, the statue that made him famous, entitled 'Resurrection Day'. After spending many years abroad, Rubek and Maia have returned to Norway. They are bound for a journey to the Arctic. In the first act, outside a hotel at a spa, they are having breakfast with champagne. The professor is described as a distinguished-looking elderly man, and Maia is described as being quite young, with gay, mocking eyes. They experience the uncomfortable, overpowering quietness of their native country. Furthermore, according to Maia, professor Rubek has come to dislike his fellow-men. Ever since he finished his great masterpiece, he seems to have lost all pleasure in his work. Life bores him. At first 'Resurrection Day' really *was* a masterpiece, but later adaptions affected its sublimity. Yet it brought him fame as well as many commissions for portrait busts. Whereas (due to the superficial nature of their judgement) his clients usually discern a 'striking likeness' of their bust to the human original, they all fail to notice the

---

3 Cf. for example: 'He [Sollness] could also be, as has been suggested, a Nietzschean superman, but one tragicomically undone by the fascinating young woman he could not keep in her (according to Nietzsche) properly servile place' (Chamberlain 1982, p. 201)

4 All references to Ibsen (1964/1982) with one exception: I prefer the usual translation of the title to the one used in this version ('When we dead wake').

mocking grin beneath. They all fail to understand that Rubek has in fact been mocking them, actually modelling their busts after the head of a horse, a mule, a dog, a hog, or some other farm animal.

Rubek and Maia are provided with all the conveniences required to feel comfortable, but Rubek appears to have noticed something strange and disquieting: a mysterious white lady who walks about the ground at night, accompanied by a dark figure. The hotel manager informs him that it must have been one of the guests, a certain Madame de Satoff, who is in fact accompanied by a nun. And when Rubek subsequently meets her, he recognizes her: it is Irene. In the course of their conversation it becomes clear that, after their separation, Irene began to reproach him for having used her as his model, consuming her living body to produce a work of art, persuading her to obliterate herself and to dedicate four years of her life to their joint effort - their 'child' as Irene calls it - the statue. She gave up her human vocation (to get married, to have children, etc.) in order to become his servant. But when Rubek finally finished his masterpiece, he thanked her for what he referred to as an 'episode' - a phrase immediately grasped by Irene as an allusion that he no longer needed her. After that word, she left him. Her fury was caused by the fact that, during the course of their collaboration, he remained a self-collected artist, approaching her and perceiving her *merely* as an artist's model, and never as a person. He *transfigured* a living body into a marble statue that was eventually stowed away in what Irene refers to as a sepulchre: a museum. He did not love her as a woman, but simply used her for his masterpiece. Rubek confesses that he has a troubled conscience with regard to their 'episode'. Furthermore, he indicates that later on he made some alterations and adaptions that affected the statue's sublime beauty. He allowed reality to intrude upon its purity by broadening the pedestal, moving the central figure back a little, and adding a host of human figures with secret animal faces. And his new conception demanded also that her face, which was at first transfigured with joy at seeing the light, was subdued a little, expressing life as Rubek came to see it later on.

According to Irene, Rubek 'killed' her by transforming her into a statue - and from the day of her departure onwards she considered herself dead. Now, finally meeting Rubek once again, she awaits her second and final transfiguration, her 'resurrection', and counts on being brought back to life again. For Rubek, their second meeting is first of all a chance to rid himself of his feeling of guilt about Irene. Moreover, from the day of his model's departure, his creativity was diminished, and now he hopes that he too, as an artist, will be restored to life.

Rubek and Irene, the 'tragic' couple, find themselves accompanied by what could be referred to as a comic double: Maia and Ulfheim, the latter a professed bearhunter whom she meets during their stay at the spa. Ulfheim represents the intrusion of laughable, folksy and burlesque reality, someone with unkempt hair and beard and a loud voice who speaks a sturdy hunter's dialect, continuously making up wonderful stories and persuading Maia to join him on a bear hunt, with the intention of making advances toward her. Although he does in fact know his way about the mountains, he is a rather clownish figure, referred to by Maia as the living image of a satyr. Maia is very eager to join Ulfheim on his trip. She has noticed that Rubek is bored by her presence. Furthermore, she very much longs to see the overwhelming mountain landscape and to experience the dangerous beauty of the area. Maia is prepared to leave Rubek should this be his wish, but he seems to prefer a *ménage à trois*. Apparently he still considers her presence useful. When Maia sees Irene striding along 'like a marble statue', she takes her leave, granting Rubek and Irene a chance to reconsider their 'episode'.

Because of her encounter with Rubek, Irene seems to have awoken from a deep, deathlike slumber and risen from her grave now that she has finally returned 'home to her lord and master'. When Rubek confesses how he wasted their 'child', she draws a knife but hesitates to kill him. Rubek professes his sense of remorse after a wasted life. Never in all eternity will he be free to live the 'resurrected life'. Irene indicates, however, that mere feelings of guilt and remorse will not settle the account. She reminds him of a sunrise they once witnessed when Rubek had enticed her to climb a mountain with him, promising her she would see 'all the glory of the world' (one of Rubek's lofty figures of speech) if she followed him to the heights, adding however that there is no resurrection for a partnership such as theirs. All that is left for them to do is to continue playing. Then Maia and Ulfheim pass them on their way to the mountains, and Maia proclaims that she feels like she has been awakened and that she is finally going to live. Irene and Rubek promise each other to meet again that very night on the mountainside. Finally, Irene contends that we only see the irreparable when we understand that we have never lived.

In the third and last act, we encounter Maia and Ulfheim on a wild mountainside surrounded by precipices. Suddenly Rubek and Irene appear, having managed to climb a precipitous track. All four of them spent the night on the mountain. Ulfheim draws attention to the storm that is approaching. Rubek observes that the gusts of wind sound 'like the prelude to Resurrection Day'. Ulfheim urges him and Irene to take shelter in a mountain hut, promising to send a party of men to rescue them, while he starts to rush down the track with Maia. Rubek and Irene, however, fearlessly approach the demonic upheaval of nature in order to hold their marriage feast. When Rubek invites her to follow him to the promised heights, she consents and obeys her master and lord 'as if transfigured'. They intend to pass through the mist up to the topmost peak gleaming in the sunrise, but disappear from view and are buried under an avalanche sliding down at a terrific pace. The nun, Irene's gloomy companion, arrives on the scene just in time to witness their destruction and utter a *pax vobiscum*.

2. ARTISTIC CALLING

When we encounter Rubek and Maia in the first act, they are engaged in a debate on whether they consider themselves happy. Rubek hesitates: 'No... to tell you the truth, I don't think I am - not entirely happy' (p. 224), but later on he claims: 'I *am* happy, Maia - really happy. In a way...' (p. 229). Somehow their apparent freedom and happiness is subdued by a chronic sense of discomfort or even boredom. Rubek, once a zealous artist, seems to have lost all pleasure in his work. It has become a daily routine for him. Like a modern Faust, although he excels in his art, he feels sickened by it. Instead of creating works of art, he has settled for producing commissioned portrait busts. Yet he distances himself from this routine - in a parodical manner. He does not simply produce portrait busts, but busts that seem to parody the conventions of the genre, and although his clients do not seem to notice it, the artist takes considerable delight in it. Something is staring at them, mocking them, from behind the surface of those busts:

> RUBEK: Only I can see it - and how it makes me laugh! On the surface, there's the 'striking likeness', as they call it, that they all stand and gape with wonder at. [*Lowering his voice*] But deep down underneath, there's the pompous self-righteous face of a horse, the obstinate muzzle of a mule, the lop-eared shallow-pated head of a dog, a greasy hog's snout... and sometimes the gross, brutal mask of a bull! (p. 229)

It goes without saying that the portrait bust is a serious, official genre. Since it portrays the acknowledged representatives of official life rather than selecting its models or subjects for aesthetic reasons, it is bound to convey, or even reinforce a more or less official view on life. Yet, being exposed in such a manner, those who happen to have commissioned a portrait bust become highly vulnerable from the point of view of artistic laughter. The parody involved is not *merely* comical. The animal figures that support the human surface seem to reveal what these individuals really look like, what human beings truly and basically are. At the hands of Rubek, the portrait bust as a genre becomes the very reverse of those ancient, grotesque little statues, the *Sileni* mentioned in *The Symposium*. For that which seems rather serious on the outside, is actually hiding something ridiculous: a grotesque grin. The serious exterior is mocked and ridiculed by that which is buried inside. Basically, what is conveyed by this parody, the portrait genre as it came to be reshaped by Rubek, is that the official human world is really a comedy. Its true aspect is temporarily concealed but by no means silenced by the official, boring countenance of earnestness.

184

Perhaps Rubek's parodical and degrading device can be considered as a subdued version of Luther's more impudent and straightforward ('grobian') comparison of high church officials to mules, hogs and other animals. In fact, Bakhtin also refers to 'the grotesque character of the transformation of the human element into an animal one' and adds: 'the combination of human and animal traits is, as we know, one of the most ancient grotesque forms' (1968, p. 316). Apparently Rubek is carrying on a comic tradition of long standing.

At the same time, however, Rubek himself is mercilessly exposed as a rather comical figure by Maia. He certainly appears to be a rather serious or even tragic character at first. But once we notice how she continually (and rather successfully) mocks him, the comic aspect cannot escape us any more. Ibsen's play suddenly reads like a comedy rather than a tragedy, which is how it is usually interpreted. Rubek's pretence to seriousness, to the lofty and the sublime as well as his rhetoric of the artist's vocation, is exposed time and again by Maia's degrading mockery. For example, she is in the habit of mockingly quoting Rubek's favorite figures of speech, which tend to be rather exalted indeed. Moreover, she ruthlessly exposes Rubek's inflated rhetoric about the artist's vocation, revealing it as a veil that conceals his calculating, utilitarian way with other people, counting on their loyalty and servitude, relying unconditionally on their availability, but ridding himself of them when they are no longer needed.

PROFESSOR RUBEK [*tapping himself on the chest*]: Inside here, you see, I have a little casket with a secret lock, and in that casket lies all my vision as an artist, but when she [Irene] disappeared without a trace, the lock snapped shut. She had the key, and she took that with her. You, my dear Maia, had no key... and so all that is in the casket is lost to me. And time is passing - And there's no way for me to reach the treasure.

MAIA [*struggling with a subtle smile*]: Then get her to unlock it for you again ... After all, she's here. And it's clearly because of the casket that she's come ... My dear Rubek! Is it really worth making all this fuss and commotion over such a simple thing? ... Just attach yourself to whomever you need most (p. 261/262).

When subsequently Irene arrives on the scene, Maia addresses her in the following vein:

MAIA: Professor Rubek is up there waiting for you, madam.
IRENE: What does he want?
MAIA: He wants you to help him open up a casket that has snapped shut (p. 263).

Or consider the following quotation, taken from the second act, in which he confesses that he has come to experience his relationship with Maia as a hindrance to his creative aspirations, his creative revival.

> PROFESSOR RUBEK: [...] Do you know what's the most appalling thing of all? Can you guess?
> MAIA [quietly defying him]: Yes, it must be that you have got yourself tied to me - for life!
> PROFESSOR RUBEK: I shouldn't have put it quite as heartlessly.
> MAIA: That wouldn't make your meaning any less heartless.
> PROFESSOR RUBEK: You haven't the least idea how an artist's mind works.
> MAIA: Good heavens, I haven't any idea how my own mind works.
> PROFESSOR RUBEK [continuing imperturbably]: I live at such a pace Maia, we artists do [...] I've come to realize that it isn't in me to find happiness in idle pleasure. Life doesn't go like that for me and my kind. I must keep on working - creating work after work - till the day I die. [Managing to say it] *That* is why I can't go on with you any longer, Maia; not with just you.
> MAIA [calmly]: Does that mean, in plain words, that you've got tired of me?
> PROFESSOR RUBEK [violently]: Yes, that's what it means. I've grown tired of this life with you - unbearably tired and slack and irritable. Now you know (p. 260/261).

Notwithstanding the rhetoric of artistic calling, Rubek's objectives are rather obvious. He has been using Maia, and now he has finally grown tired of her companionship. He seems about to experience a new artistic upheaval, to which he expects her to be unable to contribute. Indeed, Rubek's official countenance, his 'portrait bust' so to speak, finds itself mocked and challenged by Maia's degrading, down-to-earth interpretation of his rhetoric. A hidden, calculating grin is thereby exposed. An exalted genre (the lofty pretence to artistic vocation) is interpreted as the outcome of something mean and trivial and commonplace - the common human tendency to exploit one another as soon as the opportunity to do so presents itself.

Irene was Rubek's first victim. He demanded her subservience for four years, without paying her any money of course, and without eventually settling the account the way she seems to have been expecting - by marrying and subsequently impregnating her. She had wanted to serve him 'in all things' (p. 245), but he simply wanted her to serve him as a model for his work. She happened to be exactly what he needed and willingly consented to serve him although they had different expectations with regard to their bargain from the outset. She generously gave him four years of her youth - 'What a spendthrift I was in those days!' (p. 249) - but all he did was express his gratitude for what he referred to as an 'episode'. After this word, and because of it, she left.

Once again the rhetoric of artistic calling proves to be merely a veil that conceals *real* objectives: the will to power, our continuous efforts to exploit one another. Rubek managed to subdue and master her, much as he succeeded in mastering the material he worked with, while remaining a self-possessed artist, successfully refraining from exposing his human vulnerability, most notably his sexual desire. Ulfheim explains somewhere that a block of marble has something to fight for too, and will resist 'with might and main' rather than let itself be hammered into life - the very reversal of the fate which befell Irene. She was a living, warm-blooded human being that was hammered into stone.When she found herself defeated, she *really* wanted to became a statue, a piece of marble, and refused to continue to live, ruining her own life as well as that of others and aborting her pregnancies. Yet she gained a victory as well. After her disappearance, Rubek's dependence suddenly became manifest. She was to remain his only true model and the statue that resulted of their joint effort was his only masterpiece. After that, he was to settle for trivial and routine modellings.

In short, Nietzsche's judgement of Ibsen seems to suggest the very reversal of what his plays are really like. As pointed out above, he blamed Ibsen for his apparent failure to grasp the fact that moral demands like 'freedom' and 'justice' are to be interpreted in terms of the general struggle for power. They are tactical devices used by the powerless and the weak to defend themselves against an excessive display of power by the strong. But now we must recognize that Nietzsche's judgement was mistaken, for this omnipresent strive for power in terms of which human relationships are to be interpreted is the very truth that Ibsen discerned. Or, to put it differently, Nietzsche's judgement furthers our understanding of Ibsen in a 'negative' manner. Although he says that the very features which actually prove vital to Ibsen's work are missing, he describes them, thereby helping us to recognize them. We find a male artist and his female model, engaged in a struggle for power. And now, having tasted defeat and finding herself exploited without sufficient reimbursement, the former model demands 'justice', a fair settlement: he is to restore her to life again, 'to bring the pulsing blood of her youth back to life again', or else she is determined to take his. Her basic motives are. resentment and revenge.[5] Moreover, Ibsen even agrees with Nietzsche that her basic objective was to subdue her male opponent by getting pregnant and giving birth to a child. Yet Rubek, after having used her body merely as an instrument to produce a 'child', a work of art, rejected her 'justified' claims with regard to a partnership for life, and now she has returned to take revenge. Getting pregnant was her primary desire, and her

---

5 Although Irene's predominant tone of voice is one of accusation, there is a share of mockery in it as well, cf. 'At the same time she accuses him and mocks him' (Beyer 1978, p. 188).

willingness to help Rubek create his work of art was actually part of a tacit but violated agreement. She had been a living, warm-blooded human being and he had drained the life out of her, transforming her into a piece of marble. She subsequently refused to continue her life, refusing to become pregnant until the account was settled, in the meantime taking revenge on substitutes - two unhappy husbands who we are informed she drove to despair.

Yet, Rubek's victory proves to be illusory, for by leaving him Irene deprived him of his creative powers. His efforts to manipulate others did not produce the happiness he desired. In the general struggle for power every victory can only be partial, relative and temporary, accompanied by significant drawbacks - we are faced with a strategic situation. And now Rubek has lost all interest in his wife Maia, even giving her the impression of hatching some hidden plot against her. He seems about to terminate another 'episode', for he has discovered that he is once again in need of someone 'truly near to him', who is willing and able to be one with him in all his aspirations. His attachments to others is instrumental, strategic and temporary, rather than solid or 'moral', and he is able to forget very easily (p. 255). We may conclude that, in Ibsen's perspective, all 'official' (that is, *super*ficial) goals and objectives of individuals are to be interpreted as mere disguises for the basic impetus that is at work: the will to power. And rather than being 'a typical old spinster', Ibsen as a playwright succeeded in exploring those very aspects of human existence which came to be recognized by Nietzsche in a philosophical manner.[6]

One may doubt, however, whether the will to power does constitute the final truth of Ibsen's play. Although Rubek's way with others is clearly manipulative, the will to power as such cannot in itself be considered a convincing ultimate motive. A more basic attachment seems to incite him to manipulate, a basic readiness to respond, a basic sense of vocation, and (later in life) a sense of failure - all of which seems to amount to something more than *mere* rhetoric. His power game as such is not an end it itself, but is a means to achieve a certain goal: living up to one's vocation. Rubek's effort to remain self-possessed in the presence of his former model's fascinating beauty was not merely a decisive masterstroke in their mutual combat. His judgement, his considering asceticism a basic condition for artistic creativity, might have been adequate, and his words convey something more than mere pretence when he claims that he was:

---

[6] When Irene left him, Rubek did not merely loose a model, but the very thing a true artist needs most, someone who is able to offer resistance. In order to be creative, Nietzsche claims in *Twilight of the Idols*, one needs enemies rather than friends, and preferably strong enemies, for serious opposition allows one to excel oneself. According to Desirée Verweij (1993, p. 139), this notably applies to Nietzsche's views on the 'eternal struggle' between the sexes.

An artist first and foremost. And I was sick with longing to create the great work of my life... You were so exactly what I needed... I could use you - you and no one else. To me, you became something holy - not to be touched except in reverent thought... I was filled with the conviction that if I touched you, or desired you sensually, my vision would be so desecrated that I should never be able to achieve what I was striving after. And I still think there was some truth in that... Condemn me if you like, but in those days my great task dominated me completely - filled me with exultant joy (p. 246).

In his *Poetics* Aristotle points out that comedy aims at representing men as worse than they are, tragedy as better than they are (II, 4). Notably the genre of parody is mentioned by him as representing men as worse than they really are. In Ibsen's play, Rubek aims at representing himself as a tragic figure, compelled by a lofty sense of duty, a design successfully countered by Maia (and Irene) who mockingly reveal that his basic motives are simple, common and even comical. Whereas Rubek tries to exalt himself, Maia aims at degrading him. Both efforts seem rather one-sided as compared to the complicated person Rubek 'really' is. For although successful in dominating and manipulating others, he himself still feels *dominated* in a very fundamental way - not by some human individual or other, but by his calling, his artistic sense of duty, his *demon* so to speak. His readiness to manipulate seems to have been motivated by a basic drive beyond his control, forcing itself upon him. And now he finds himself overcome by a basic sense of failure. Time is running out for him, and he seems unable to settle the account. Indeed, he has been an over-generous 'spendthrift' himself, wasting his talents on portrait busts that do not put in much weight, since they do not count as truly artistic. His relationship with Irene had been a violent struggle, rather than a partnership, a violent encounter, a struggle for power the outcome of which proved to be rather ambiguous. She took revenge by leaving him - *her* master stroke, one that deprived him of his creativity. She killed him as an artist. They both died and they both long for what they refer to as Resurrection Day, they both desire to be transfigured. This is represented by the basic symbol[7] of the play, the statue of a woman of sublime beauty, filled with a holy joy at finding herself unchanged at Resurrection Day, that is, at finding herself transfigured into a warm-blooded, living being once more.

---

7 The statue is a symbol in the sense of being a condensation of the basic desire at work rather than a displacement (Freud 1900/1942). It is the perfect symbol of Rubek's and Irene's artistic episode in much the same way as the Erfurt cloaca was a symbol of Luther's monastic episode (cf. chapter four).

3. TRANSFIGURATION

Now the play enters its final phase. As Rubek and Maia separate, they are replaced by a tragic couple (Rubek and Irene) and its comic double (Maia and Ulfheim). Each couple is heading for its own plot - Rubek and Irene ascending to tragic heights, Maia and Ulfheim descending into the comical and the absurd - and yet they cross each other's track.[8] Still one wonders whether Rubek's and Irene's self-destruction is truly tragic. The sudden ending bends towards exaggeration, towards the absurd,[9] and the sudden appearance of the nun emphasizes this. It is as if Ibsen had somehow forgotten her and is suddenly reminded of her existence, needing her to ridicule the apparently tragic. She speaks as a jester who is granted the final word, allowed to utter a parody (not coincidentally in latin) of what is supposed to be a tragic line. The whole scene is a parodical reversal of Resurrection Day. Freezing to death, they become like marble. And the very last sound that is heard is Maia ridiculous song in the distance, floating up from further down the mountain.

In my view, this quasi-tragic ending symbolizes perfectly the inevitable collapse of what Strawson refers to as the demarcation between the sphere or morality and the region of the ethical (as well as Rorty's separation of the private and the public realm, of private irony and public solidarity). All individuals, Strawson claims, are fascinated by some personal ideal, seizing them, holding them captive, being true in a very fundamental way. A perfect example of such an ideal is Rubek's ideal of living a truly artistic life - the very thing he failed to do. In the so-called sphere of morality, however, we are constrained by certain non-controversial rules and principles that regulate social discourse (for instance, do not harm others). The moral experience articulated by Ibsen in his play is one of transgression rather than of consolidation of this basic platitude of liberalism. It is a work of art which refuses to be rendered harmless by transferring it to some kind of separate realm. Rather, it reveals the intimate way in which the 'ethical' and the 'moral' remain connected. In order to live up to our ideal, we need the support and, at times, even the resistance of others. According to Ibsen, human individuals constantly support one another, harm one another, combat one another, driven by a basic will. Nietzsche claimed that notions such as justice, solidarity, etc. - in short, the whole vocabulary of liberal

---

[8] 'Maia and Ulfheim return to what they think is life but what Rubek and Irene regard as death, while Rubek and Irene climb upwards to what the others regard as death but they regard as life' (Meyer 1967/1985, p. 826).

[9] Cf. Meyer's comment: 'The shortness of the last act is a mystery; not merely its shortness but its (to my mind) inadequacy. [It is possible that] he [Ibsen] felt some strange compulsion to leave it as a fragment. It is an unfinished, imperfect fragment' (Meyer 1967/1985, p. 826). In my view, however, it is inadequate *from the point of view of tragedy*, that is, according to the aesthetics of the sublime, but it is, in fact, parodical, and adequate as such.

morality - must be interpreted as a set of devices put to use in a strategic setting. To what extent is this picture of human life shared by Ibsen?

I already pointed out that Ibsen's way of revealing the strive for power as a basic impetus at work underneath the official motives of individuals was through laughter. I mentioned several instances of mockery in Ibsen's play (and many could be added) by means of which Rubek's manipulative strategies, for example, were ruthlessly exposed. But I did not yet sufficiently point to the basic mood of laughter conveyed by the play *as such*. In Ibsen's play laughter is an experience of intrusion, causing the demarcation between the private and the public to collapse. As an artist, Rubek represents the intrusion of laughter into the serious genre of the portrait bust. By abusing others, he manages to remain self-collected. By *harming* his clients, he partially or temporarily manages to live up to his basic sense of obligation, or to subdue his sense of failure. But there is an intrusion of laughter in the final scene as well. Initially, Irene is overwhelmed by fear. She speaks 'in terror', 'in mounting horror', and so on. But as Rubek and Irene are about to ascend the mountain, they boldly raise their voices, for once in their lives they intend to live it to the full - and call it a 'feast'. Fear is finally overcome by a burst of laughter. They have been harming each other ruthlessly, allowing each other to become the person they have been, and now the account is about to be settled. Their laughter, Ibsen's laughter, is not, of course, of an ironical, *harmless* kind. Rather, it is a burst of laughter, making life possible 'to the full', risking self-destruction. Moreover, it is a grotesque, parodical laughter, exaggerating tragic conventions.

It is an experience of laughter that perhaps resembles the one described by Bataille when he himself climbed a mountain slope and was faced with the violent, non-human aspect of nature. The physical exhaustion, the experience of suddenly perceiving reality in a different light, the sense of horror suddenly overcome by a burst of laughter, all these ingredients are present here.

Ibsen's play urges a redescription of the basic features of moral life. In the liberal view, the public and the private realm, as well as public and private morality, are to remain separated. Liberal laughter does not laugh, is of a harmless, ironical kind, a laughter that meets liberalism's basic demand: not to cause harm to others. In Ibsen's view, however, both realms remain intrinsically connected, and they continuously intrude upon each other. The intrusion of laughter is an experience of transgression. The 'non-controversial' demands of the public sphere are rendered superficial by a compelling (rather than 'private') sense of duty. Rubek's sense of guilt, for example, although at first seeming to pertain to the harm he has inflicted upon Irene, eventually proves to be identical to his artistic sense of failure. What is contested by Ibsen's play is not the awareness *as such* that moral life is enacted on different levels or in different realms, but rather the way this basic experience is interpreted by liberalism. What is rejected is the claim that these basic levels or realms or aspects of moral life can be compartmentalized and separated from each other. Rather, the very tension between these basic aspects of moral life is the principal object not of some separate branch of ethics, but of ethics *as such*. This tension is our basic moral problem, although under different historical circumstances and conditions, different solutions will present themselves.

By 'solution' I mean the way moral subjectivity is allowed to establish itself in response to this basic tension. In Ibsen's later plays, a certain form of moral subjectivity appeared for the first time, a form which, notwithstanding liberalism's continuous effort to abolish it, was to maintain itself up to the present - a form of subjectivity which continues to resist compartmentalization into a personal and an institutional Self. It was articulated by psychologists and philosophers like Freud ('discontent'), Heidegger ('inauthenticity'), Sartre ('bad faith') and others. In all cases, however, although often quite different terms were used, compartmentalization as a form of moral subjectivity is presented as something inadequate, in need of a solution. For although apparently it is a comfortable position, it nevertheless conceals rather than articulates the basic tension of contemporary life and therefore is bound to produce a chronic sense of uneasiness or bad faith. Yet, at the same time it is emphasized that such a solution seems to be denied to us. Most notably, a 'political', 'etatistic', 'top-down' solution seems out of the question, and those political movements which presented themselves as providing a way out, soon headed for terror and despotism. Some bottom-up strategy has to be employed, a strategy which would enable the modern individual to renounce his desire for 'final solutions' (such as the prospect of 'transfiguration') but without urging him to resignate, that is, to settle for what seems to be our inevitable present condition (the prospect of compartmentalization). What we need is a form of laughter that laughs at everything 'inevitable' or 'final' and that would allow for a rival understanding of moral subjectivity to become viable, one that remains incompatible with the liberal understanding of moral life, mistakenly considering itself the inevitable 'solution' to the basic tension of moral existence.

According to Lacan, this rival understanding, offering obstinate resistance to the platitudes of liberalism, is to be found in the tragic (rather than the comic) view of life. He claims that the impossible object of our desire - for example, Rubek's artistic vocation - is far beyond our grasp and in his review of Lacan's seminar on the ethics of psychoanalysis, Van Haute (1996) explains Lacan's insights in such a way that they actually seem to provide us with an astonishing clarification of the final scene of Ibsen's play. He points out that the beautiful, the work of art, is not something (some 'thing') within our reach but an echo from outside, a point of transition, a last defence, where human existence becomes frightfully vulnerable. Van Haute refers to a violent illumination, a glow of beauty, which coincides with the moment of transgression when beauty lights up and desire becomes manifest -

phrases that indeed remind us of Ibsen's dramatic plot. The desire for the perfect (for example, the perfect work of art or the phantasy of resurrection) entails a risk of destruction. As for ethics, it is neither about human happiness or well-being nor about avoiding harm and suffering. Rather, it is about finding a possible way of relating to the ultimate object of desire without being overwhelmed by it. This is indeed the basic insight conveyed by *When We Dead Awaken*. Yet in Ibsen's play the comical and the tragic remain intimately connected. Moreover, the tragic view of life is finally overcome by ridicule. Because of the intrusion of laughter, a basic truth of human existence is revealed. The basic truth of tragedy (i.e. the recognition that the ultimate object of our desire remains forever beyond our grasp and that excessive desire for final solutions entails the risk of self-destruction) is the truth of comedy as well, revealed for instance by Aristophanes in the *Symposium* when he tells the comic story about biped human beings, forever separated form their counterpart, forever deprived of the prospect of resurrection, even intimidated by Zeus who threatens to bisect them once again should they refuse to settle for their present condition. Or, as Bataille phrased it, laughter is a non-tragical way of discerning the fearful truth of tragedy. Laughter is a viable way of relating to the ultimate object of desire, it allows for a viable form of moral subjectivity to become established. *When We Dead Awaken* reveals the intimate connectedness of the truth of tragedy and the truth of laughter. Eventually the modern individual, trying to find his way out of an 'impossible' situation, will have to rely on the strategies of laughter.

4. BEYOND CYNICISM

If the modern individual is to rely on a comical rather than a tragic view of life, what *form* of laughter do we have in mind? In the previous chapters irony ('reduced' laughter) was already rejected in favour of parody ('true' laughter). There are some reasons, however, for considering Ibsen's play as cynical rather than parodical. Apart from the fact that Ibsen himself was often described as cynical, some obvious ingredients of cynicism can be found in *When We Dead Awaken* as well. The mocking grin, for instance, secretly smuggled in by Rubek and added to his portrait busts, seems full of scorn and contempt and therefore could be regarded cynical rather than parodical (for cynic laughter is contemptuous rather than gay). Moreover, as to Diogenes the Cynic, the founding father of cynicism, Diogenes Laertius (1925/1979) narrates a famous anecdote about how he lit a lamp in broad daylight and said, as he went about, 'I am looking for a man' (6:41), apparently implying that he considered actual human beings to be far below his moral standard. This seems to be the kind of attitude that is conveyed by Rubek's grin as well. In addition, I already indicated in chapter two that both Foucault and Sloterdijk pointed to the significance of cynicism. Therefore, I will have to explain why I prefer parody to cynicism. But first allow me to introduce the basic features of cynicism as a form of laughter in its own right.

In the 'standard account' of the history of serious mainstream philosophy, Socrates is represented as its founding father. Yet he also inaugurated the philosophical tradition that constituted its 'comic double', namely cynicism. Cynics like Antisthenes and Diogenes are presented by Diogenes Laertius as Plato's mocking contemporaries - his 'bad conscience' so to speak, for they reminded him in an obtrusive and pushy manner of those aspects of his highly esteemed teacher he increasingly tried to obscure in his own dialogues: the comic, plebeian, scandalous, mocking ones. Many Cynics were of humble or even questionable descent. Their philosophy constituted a way of life rather than a doctrine - one of poverty, abstinence, hardship and jest. To the Cynics, philosophy primarily meant physical and mental exercise, and they excelled in adapting themselves to all possible circumstances. Instead of arguing with Platonic or Academic philosophy or other branches of scientific discourse, they aimed at refuting it by means of practical jokes and 'dramatized' ridicule, using food, bodily members and bodily fluids as visual aids. For example, since Plato had defined man as an animal, biped and featherless, Diogenes plucked a fowl one day and brought him into the lecture room with the words, 'Here is Plato's man'. As a result of this, 'having broad nails' was added to the definition (Diogenes Laertius 1925/1979, 6:40).

Apart from Platonic philosophy and other philosophical rivals, public life was also ridiculed by them and in much the same manner. We are informed, for example, that Diogenes was in the habit of behaving indecently in public places, doing 'everything in public, the works of Demeter and of Aphrodite alike'[10] and using any place for any purpose (6:69). At a feast certain people kept throwing bones to him as they would have done to a dog (the word 'cynic' was apparently derived from the Greek noun for 'dog' and Diogenes was nicknamed thus) whereupon he played a dog's trick and drenched them (6:46). In short, the ancient Cynic was a solitary, eccentric, unsociable chap (generally of plebeian descent) who refuted established morality in a bold and provocative manner. His basic objective was to challenge the platitudes of established culture by means of wit rather than argument, an attitude for which Socrates had apparently set the example. Instead of preaching moral criticism, the Cynic embodied it, albeit in a provocative, exaggerated, even grotesque manner.

One remarkable feature of the Cynic mode of speech is the extent to which its content remains dependent on its context. Their speech acts are performative rather than argumentative, and always belong to (and comment on) the specific situation. In order to grasp the meaning of a particular line or phrase, the situation must

---

[10] A phrase indicating that he used to eat and masturbate in public.

194

always be taken into account. It is a performative and dramatic mode of speech.

Cynicism created its own genre: the satirical, 'counter-Platonic' dialogue. Duddly (1937) claims that in the writings of Menippus the Cynic (unfortunately no longer existent) the spirit of mockery was all-pervading (p. 70). No serious treatises were produced by him, Diogenes Laertius claims, and his books overflow with ridicule.[11] Duddley considers the adaption of the philosophical dialogue for comic and satirical purposes to have been his chief contribution to literature, although such a development had already been foreshadowed by Plato, some of whose dialogues (the 'Socratic' ones) abounded in comic wit as well (cf. chapter three).

Notwithstanding the abundance of comic wit among some of its representatives, however, Cynic laughter was scornful rather than gay and conveyed an attitude of chronic contempt - 'He [Diogenes] was great at pouring scorn on his contemporaries' (Diogenes Laertius, 6:24). I already referred to the famous anecdote that tells us how he lit a lamp and cried 'I am looking for a man'.[12] Antisthenes was criticized by his followers because, at the time of his death, although suffering great pains, he hesitated before willingly departing from life. Let this suffice as an account of ancient cynicism as it was described by Diogenes Laertius and ruthlessly ridiculed by Lucian. A few years ago, Sloterdijk and Foucault seemed to aim at something like a Cynic revival. Let us take a closer look.

In his *Critique of Cynical Reason* Sloterdijk (1983) aims at rehabilitating cynicism proper as a tradition of comic and popular resistance of long standing by referring to it as 'kynicism' and distinguishing it from cynicism in its usual, pejorative sense. According to Sloterdijk, Kynicism (rather than irony or parody) was Nietzsche's basic form of laughter. He exemplified the recurrence of kynicism as it had flourished during the first three centuries A.D. as well as during the Renaissance. Kynicism basic feature was *Frechheit* (impudence or insolence) and its style of argumentation was coarse, vulgar and 'grotesque' (p. 204). Diogenes was the founding-father of grobian, satirical resistance, of kynicism as a plebeian bottom-up philosophy, a 'street philosophy', dwelling in public spaces, boldly and impudently challenging established morality in a comic manner and with irresistible energy, using a crude, grotesque and impudent mode of argumentation (p. 203). During the Middle Ages, kynicism continued to manifest itself in the carnivalesque, the frivolous and the obscene, most notably in Germany (Harlequin, Hans Wurst,

---

[11] 'There is no seriousness in him; but his books overflow with laughter, much the same as those of his contemporary Meleager' (Diogenes Laertius, 6:99). Some, he tells us, attributed these dialogues to Diogenes himself who, writing them as a joke, made them over to Menippus as a person able to dispose of them advantageously (6:100) - an anecdote apparently meant to exemplify Diogenes' contempt for literary fame as well as for literature as such.

[12] Perhaps 'human being' would have been a better translation.

etc.).[13] Tijl Eulenspiegel ('the fool who went into the offensive') and Luther[14] are mentioned as paragons of German impudence (p. 231). Moreover, kynical wit aimed at rehabilitating bodily life and bodily functions (notably its lower parts) and argued by means of crude gestures and indecent behaviour.

Yet true kynicism suffered a dramatic decline and today the bold, impudent rogue seems to have disappeared. Already during the Protestant era laughter was transformed into mere satire, and although its critical aspect has survived, modern criticism has become a serious matter and distanced itself from the traditions of laughter to which it historically belonged. Although modern criticism is of comic descent, and critical philosophy is heir to a popular tradition of comic resistance, we hardly seem to be aware of the fact that since time immemorial moral criticism was connected with laughter.

According to Sloterdijk, the laughter of Diogenes was uninhibited, unembarrassed and unrestrained, relying on quick-wittedness and presence of mind (p. 275). Yet at the same time Sloterdijk points to kynicism's basic ambivalence. Diogenes was obviously a misanthrope and Sloterdijk agrees that his laughter conveyed a considerable amount of bitterness, resentment, discontent, scorn and contempt (p. 308-309, p. 314).[15]

Sloterdijk's effort to rehabilitate kynicism (or cynicism proper) coincided with a similar effort by Foucault. In the fall of 1983, he presented a lecture at Berkeley on *parresia* - frank or unrestricted speech. The Greek noun *parresia* (*franc-parler*) corresponds to the verb *parresiazesthai*. It appears for the first time in the plays of Euripides, although the word *parresiastes*, the *unrestricted speaker*, is of a much later date and can be found, for example, in the writings of Lucian. The literal meaning of *parresia* is to say everything without recourse to any rhetorical forms of indirect speech and without any restrictions of prudence or politeness, implying that *parresia* contains an element of impudence and risk. In the writings of Plato as well as those of the church fathers it has a negative connotation for it refers to vulgar public discourse and is opposed to the virtue of knowing when to remain silent. In most classical Greek texts, however, *parresia* usually means saying what is really true.

In ancient Greece, Foucault claims, truth is not constituted by decisive experiences as is the case with, for instance, Descartes, but by *parresia* as a verbal

---

13 Sloterdijk refers to Bakhtin and Rabelais (p. 232).

14 One of his lines is cited: 'Ein zaghafter Arsch läßt selten einen fröhlicher Furz' ('A timid behind seldom produces a cheerful fart', p. 203).

15 Sloterdijk refers to his laughter as 'unfröhliches Gelächter' (p. 329).

practice.[16] It is straightforward and sincere, as well as dangerous. It rejects and criticizes those forms of speech which protect us from an inconvenient or even dangerous truth. It is a form of speech that is devoid of rhetorical devices, or, as Foucault phrases it, it is the zero degree of rhetoric. The most prominent *parresiastes* of all was, of course, Socrates. His performance conveyed the freedom and frankness of market-square speech.

But speech forms are bound to become more restricted and rhetorical when they enter a power relationship, for instance, between a king and one of his subjects. In that case *parresia* takes the form of a contract or agreement. The king orders his subject, for example a messenger, to speak the truth on the condition that the usual restrictions and inhibitions are suspended. *Parresia* is a mode of verbal intercourse that allows the truth to become apparent. This is the way it emerges in the plays of Euripides, who was a contemporary of Socrates and, like the latter, committed to criticism and truth. Foucault emphasizes three forms of *parresia*: *parresia* between friends, *parresia* in the context of spiritual exercise, and *parresia* as criticism.

As to the critical function, special attention is paid to the role of *parresia* in public discourse in democratic Athens. *Parresia* as a problem is intrinsically connected with democratic institutions, since they tend to remove traditional restrictions on public speech and grant all citizens equal rights with respect to participation in public discourse. And this is where laughter comes in, but its connection with frankness is rather ambivalent. In fact, Foucault argues that *parresia* somehow becomes divided in itself. In this respect he refers to an anti-democratic pamphlet, dating from the end of the fifth century B.C. and written in the form of a parodical (Foucault uses the word 'paradoxical', p. 36) eulogy on democracy. Foucault emphasizes, however, that the piece is devoid of literary value because it is aggressive rather than witty. It cannot be regarded as representative of the 'zero degree of rhetoric' because it is an indirect form of speech, instrumentalizing current literary genres such as parody and irony. Its 'irony' (p. 37) is in opposition with *parresia*, and laughter seems to take sides with conservatism. Its basic contention, however, is that democracy does not foster true *parresia*, but encourages flattery, a concealing mode of speech.

A similar line of argument occurs in a more moderate and serious treatise by Isocrates. Democracy pretends to foster *parresia*, but is basically at odds with it. And the only remaining true *parresiastes* can be found in the theatre among the comedians! The indirect genres of laughter surpass the established supposedly

---

16 I thoroughly disagree with Foucault when it comes to Descartes. In his case, truth was not merely an experience but also intimately connected with a practice of unrestricted speech. - cf. his impudent claim (1949, § 1) that he would write about the passions as if no one ever discussed the topic and as if the huge body of philosophical discourse available at that time was simply nonexistent.

'unrestricted' discourse in frankness. Instead of encouraging frankness, democracy has impeded it and 'true' *parresia* joins forces with the (indirect) genres of public laughter.

In connection with the decline and fall of the Greek city state and of the democratic institutions of Athens, public life and discourse in ancient Greece were fundamentally transformed - a transformation which entailed considerable changes regarding the role and form of *parresia*. And in this respect, Foucault focuses attention on certain unrestricted forms of life and speech, in particular the movement which came to be known as cynicism. Foucault emphasizes that cynicism was a way of life rather than a philosophical doctrine.[17] Again, the relationship between cynic *parresia* and the genres of laughter is highly ambivalent. Laughter laughs at cynicism (cf. Lucian), but cynicism is also a form of laughter in its own right. At first glance cynicism appears to be a form of seriousness, of criticism and preaching mocked by poets like Lucian. The public performance of Cynics, however, was remarkably provocative and outrageous, purposely violating public and civil conventions. The lives of the leading Cynics entail a series of remarkable anecdotes and scandals which address the masses rather than the elite. These public, outrageous performances were often connected with bodily functions, such as eating, sleeping and masturbating in public. It is clear that their vileness and impudence (*anaideia*), apart from serving the purpose of contesting established customs and moral ideals, produced a comical effect as well. They criticized moral *doxa* by means of a bottom-up approach, rather than an elite, top-down approach pursued by, for example, Plato. Like Plato, however, the Cynics considered Socrates to be the founder of their school, the pioneer of their outrageous, provocative and irritating, as well as comical bottom-up approach. Although they were laughed at by the conservative elite, they were the celebrated champions of the lower classes, who greatly appreciated their practice of purposely being uncivilized and their Socrates-like, pretended ignorance (although the ignorance of the Cynics was of a practical rather than a verbal nature). Much like their jest, laughter was *dramatized* by them, and cynicism was primarily a practice, a way of life. Cynic offensiveness had both a serious and a gay aspect, although unlike the comical genres of the elite its laughter was rather lumpish and unrefined. Moreover, as a form of laughter, it was scornful rather than gay.

According to Foucault, cynicism constitutes a remarkable stage in a development in which criticism was finally bereft of its gay, hilarious aspect and reduced to rational criticism *as such*. Of course, this has not been simply a linear development. There were several eruptions of gay laughter, most notably during the sixteenth century. According to Foucault, *parresia* is part of a genealogy, it is the beginning (*Herkunft*) of the critical tradition of the West. The transformation of *parresia* into

---

17 Diogenes Laertius is hesitant about this claim: 'If we decide that Cynicism is really a philosophy, and not, as some maintain, just a way of life' (6:103).

modern criticism implied the separation of criticism and laughter, the separation of the lofty and timeless 'idea' of rational criticism from its comic origin. The fact that moral criticism evolved out of local, peculiar, non-philosophical forms of speech before it finally gained its present shape and status, is obscured by presenting rational criticism as an extra-temporal ideal. This is not the end of the story, however, and the separation of truth and laughter is far from self-evident or incontestable. It is a temporary outcome and one day the basic affinity between truth and laughter might be rediscovered.

Relying on the accounts of Sloterdijk and Foucault the following basic features of laughter in general and cynicism (or Kynicism) in particular must be emphasized. To begin with, it is important to note that, whereas in the introduction I still felt obliged to justify my 'remarkable' claim that there is moral truth in laughter, the history of cynicism and other forms of laughter reveals that, for many centuries, moral criticism and laughter were intimately connected - they were natural allies, so to speak. Moral philosophy started as a comical genre. Gradually, however, the critical aspect came to be regarded as 'content', the comical aspect as 'residue'. Although their original connectedness was obscured by a series of efforts to turn moral philosophy into a serious genre (such as Platonic as well as Neo-Platonic philosophy, early Christian theology, seventeenth Century Counter-Renaissance philosophy and theology and contemporary liberalism), the natural alliance between moral criticism and laughter tends to re-emerge in times of moral transition, such as in the first half of the sixteenth Century and the second half of the nineteenth Century.

Furthermore, since time immemorial the strategies of laughter are intimately connected with popular resistance. As Sloterdijk points out, the 'silent majorities' have always been laughing majorities, defying official views and policies by mocking them. The experience of laughter indicates that the vital forces of the human body, exploited by the established regime for decades or even centuries, can no longer be contained and are suddenly set free by laughter. It is the expression of free-floating energy, which is to be organized again (in view of the risk of pointless excess and self-destruction), but in quite a different manner than before. Laughter means breaking away from those forms of life that are acknowledged and encouraged by top-down policies and strategies of the established regime.[18] History informs us, however, that forms of moral subjectivity established by laughter are short-lived. They are (in a narrow political sense) unstable and before long tend to be appropriated, exploited and transformed by a new regime of etatism.

Moreover, like other forms of laughter, cynicism is unlikely to produce a theoretical discourse of its own accord. It is responsive rather than constructive. Its basic strategy consists of mocking established theories, exposing their questionable

---

[18] Cf. Nietzsche, *Human, All Too Human II*, Mixed Opinions and Aphorisms, § 320.

aspects to ridicule. Nietzsche's dialogue between the wanderer and his shadow is a dialogue between a philosopher and his jester.[19] What he (the philosopher) learns from his jester is not the ability to develop some grand theory or other. What he learns is to appreciate the significance, not of the lofty, the extra-temporal and the sublime, but of common things, of 'things nearby', such as food, the body, etc. - *Naturalia non sunt turpia* was one of Diogenes' famous sayings. From the point of view of laughter, the philosophical attitude is one of experimentation, of relentlessly putting established convictions to the test: the 'crucible of laughter'.

Another important aspect cynicism shares with other forms of laughter (most notably parody) is its disrespect for demarcations and compartmentalizations. Diogenes' impudence consisted of doing everything everywhere. The experience of laughter is an experience of intrusion, of displaying certain behaviours (although perhaps perfectly acceptable in themselves) in a manner which is unexpected or even indecent. Much like parody, cynicism implies, among other things, the application of accepted rules and conventions to 'inappropriate' circumstances. Moreover, it relies on exaggeration as well as on the well-known comic device of taking something which is said quite literally (cf. the anecdote about the biped fowl) - a strategy Diogenes shared with medieval comic heroes like Tijl Uilenspiegel (and one of the reasons why laughter often defies translation).

Finally, both Sloterdijk and Foucault point out that cynicism is basically ambivalent. On the one hand it is unrestricted, impudent and comical, but on the other it is never *really* gay. There is always an element of scorn and contempt in it. In short, it is a negative form of laughter, one that is at times even sarcastic. Even Mephistopheles, in Sloterdijk's eyes the summit of kynical laughter, displays a negative attitude toward life, and living life 'to the full' primarily means to corrupt and be corrupted, to destroy and become self-destructive - a fate exemplified by Faust himself. Compared to other forms of laughter, cynicism clearly excels in depicting human beings as worse than they really are. Sloterdijk tries to subdue cynicism's nasty, unappealing aspect by distinguishing true cynicism (kynicism) from more or less 'degenerated' varieties, but all the same cynicism's chronic contempt is present already in its 'pure', original form. Quite unlike Socrates' laughter, that of Diogenes was already considerably scornful and jeering. Like Sloterdijk, I appreciate the impudent, popular and comical aspects of laughter, but I prefer to refer to it as parody. In other words, I prefer Socrates to Diogenes, affirmation to contempt.

Socrates, Luther, Ibsen and others exemplify the extent to which moral criticism is basically and originally a comical genre. In the case of Socrates, the comic tradition was still very much alive, but even Luther and Ibsen somehow seem to remember this, although moral discourse had turned serious many centuries ago.

---

[19] 'Sei ernsthaft, lieber Narr!', *Human, All Too Human II*, The Wanderer and his Shadow, Introduction.

They intuitively grasp and put to use some of the hidden and forgotten possibilities of their genre. I guess the concept of 'genre memory' coined by Bakhtin will allow us to clarify this phenomenon. Genres, Bakhtin tells us, constitute fundamental ways by which we visualize and conceptualize the world. Notwithstanding the diversity of comical forms, 'one logic pervades all these elements' (1968, p. 61). He even goes so far as to invest genres with a life and memory of their own. A genre lives in the present, but always remembers its past, its beginning. While discussing the prehistory of the Dostoevski novel Bakhtin writes that it was not the author's 'subjective memory', but the 'objective memory' of the genre in which he was working which preserved the characteristics of ancient literary forms (1973, p. 100). Likewise, all the basic elements of comedy retain 'a certain memory of that mighty whole to which they belonged in the distant past' (Bakhtin 1968, p. 47). As to modern forms of abuse, for instance, a vague memory of past carnival liberties and carnival truth still seems to slumber in them, although the problem of their irrepressible linguistic vitality has not yet been seriously posed (1986, p. 28). Notwithstanding the many adaptions to refined sensibilities and proprieties of aesthetic decorum suffered in the course of its generic 'life', notwithstanding the many efforts to delete the inappropriate and to eliminate the vulgar, a certain awareness of the basic features of the generic tradition somehow maintains itself and forces itself upon those who enter it (cf. Le Blanc 1995). Like any other genre, moral criticism remembers its past. It has a 'genre memory', an 'objective memory' of its indestructible comic potential, still sensed by some. We still intuitively grasp some of moral criticism's hidden possibilities, we have some vague memory of what is absent, lobotomized, adapted in serious ethical discourse, we somehow still discern the possibilities suggested by the genre itself, ignoring or seeing-through artificial constraints. The modern effort to transform moral criticism into a serious genre and to erase all traces of its comic past, is bound to fail. Modern time is but 'a tiny island .. it has only existed for the last four hundred years' (Bakhtin 1968, p. 319).

5. LAUGHTER AS A REMEDY

I pointed out that, originally, ethics was a comic genre, transformed into a serious one later on (most notably during the Middle Ages). Ironically, one of the questions addressed by this now serious discourse affected laughter itself: could certain forms of laughter still be considered admissible or should laughter be abolished altogether? In chapter two I pointed out that, in contemporary liberal ethics, this question is dealt with by stating that laughter must be considered permissible as long as it remains ironic, that is, a private matter. No responsible politics can be extracted out of laughter. Laughter ridicules, but at the same time is said to sustain oppressive political orders.

How, then, could laughter constitute a remedy? In the course of my book a relied on Bakhtin to a considerable extent, but his work contains primarily a *history* of laughter, he nowhere systematically explains how laughter could function in the world of today. At times he seems to suggest that laughter could still be of some significance but in *The Dialogic Imagination* he explicitly points out that in modern times the functions of parody have become narrow and unproductive (1988, p. 71). Parody has become sickly, he claims, and its place in modern literature is insignificant. Moreover, he adds that we 'live, write and speak today in a world of free and democratized language; the complex and multi-leveled hierarchy of discourses, forms, images, styles that used to permeate the entire system of official language and linguistic consciousness was swept away by the linguistic revolutions of the Renaissance'. The middle strata of national languages that were successfully transformed into the official language, provide only modest space for travesty. In short, when it come to the actual ideological equilibrium, laughter is either insignificant or dangerous. A liberal democracy does not seem to be the kind of society where public laughter still applies.

The pertinence of Bakhtin's view on laughter in the context of contemporary society has also been addressed by Hirschkop (1986, 1989). Are Bakhtin's views populistic or firmly democratic? are they in favour of, or basically opposed to a scientific world-view? Such questions are difficult to answer since the clues in Bakhtin's own work seem rather inconsistent or at least fragmentary. He is consistent, however, in viewing language as the material for competing socio-ideological forces. The basic instrument of political domination by the official stratum (a 'unified' language, unfairly generalizing the experience of a limited section of the population) is mocked and contested by a popular-subversive tradition of farce and plebeian laughter and Hirschkop rightly emphasizes that Bakhtin's view on the popular strata of society is 'far removed from reactionary images of a pious and backward "folk"' (1986, p. 93). Moreover, as far as the basic opposition between higher and lower social strata is concerned, Bakhtin unambiguously sides with the latter. To a neo-marxist like Hirschkop, however, this does not automatically imply that Bakhtin must be considered as democratic and progressive. What is missing in his account, Hirschkop claims, is 'the socializing function of the official stratum ... the institutional forms within which socialization must take place' (p. 101). Bakhtin's political critique is 'unable to distinguish between the repressive and socializing functions of class rule'. What is neglected is 'the process of socialization' as well as the fact that a particular language dominates by becoming the language of crucial political and cultural institutions: 'Because he [Bakhtin] does not theorize the fact that the ideological dominance is secured by institutions like schools and dictionaries, he assumes that a spontaneously produced popular discourse will subvert it' (p. 111). In terms of political denomination, Bakhtin seems at best an anarchist and I have the impression that, in a way, Hirschkop's criticism of Bakhtin's populism copies Marx's criticism of Heinzen's grobianism, referred to in chapter two. Bakhtin is criticized for being politically unreliable and ambivalent, for advocating anarchism and populism instead of an organized and scientific view on social change. In order to further human well-being we need a state, a scientific understanding of reality as well as a democratic language.

Hirschkop's point of departure is the statement of Bakhtin just cited: 'We live, write and speak today in a world of free and democratized language' (1988, p. 71). Bakhtin described how differences in form, genre and style within a shared national language can enforce or challenge political domination and how supposedly unified modern languages must be rethought as political battlefields. According to Hirschkop (1989), Bakhtin's basic objective apparently was to provide the tools for transforming a popular language into a democratic one. Still there are some inconsistencies and ambiguities that must be dealt with. In what way do Bakhtin's concepts really further the objective of establishing a democratic language and culture in modern societies? Hirschkop emphasizes that many of Bakhtin's concepts are both descriptive and normative. Centripetal tendencies are both analyzed and criticized as repressing a language's 'natural' tendency towards stratification and differentiation (p. 5). Bakhtin's description of culture seems to be motivated by certain political and normative objectives and language is something that can be improved. But what are his ultimate political and normative objectives? According to Hirschkop there is a strong populist inclination at work in Bakhtin's writings. The plebeian masses are endowed with a spontaneous skepticism, they never fully share the ruling truth, never take completely serious the slogans of the state. Linguistic conflicts reflect the everlasting socio-ideological struggles of society. At first glance, Hirschkop claims, this might seem 'more or less the vision of society on offer from liberalism' (p. 20) - differences in language reflect differences in interest, which must be balanced, accommodated, tolerated, etc. - and 'through this line of argument Bakhtin becomes liberalism's, or, if you prefer, liberal pluralism's, best friend' (p. 20). Yet on further consideration certain aspects of Bakhtin's writings seem basically at odds both with a liberal and with a socialist view on democracy and social change. What is missing, Hirschkop argues, is any effort to connect the local, semi-public languages of the market-square to 'the larger structures of society and history', to connect 'the texture of every day life' to 'the scientific aspirations of social theory'. In Bakhtin's work, he claims, there is 'a dangerous temptation to reject the scientific aspirations altogether in favour of an unqualified celebration of the "everyday life" seemingly conjured up by heteroglossia - a gesture often made in the name of democracy. Such celebrations have only a tangential relation to

Bakhtin's theory of the novel, and arguably none at all to democracy' (p. 30). Hirschkop feels that, by renouncing cognition and social science altogether, democracy would be reduced to 'expression', disconnecting it from the need for accurate knowledge of social forms (p. 31). In opposition to such a view, Hirschkop advocates 'a conception of democracy as a collective learning process'. If the social analysis necessary to that process appears in the guise of an authoritative language, this is actually a political problem, not an excuse for dismissing social analysis as such. Rather it would entail 'the creation of new political institutions, programs for popular education, democratic forms of mass media, and so on'. According to Hirschkop, the comprehension of complex modern societies requires knowledge of a sophisticated. scientific kind rather than an uncritical celebration of everyday life. Certain aspects of Bakhtin's work (most notably his anarchist and populist inclinations) 'disregard the need for the stability and security which many think is part of the good and desirable life' (p. 32). Instead of trying to change the world in a democratic, organized and scientific way, Bakhtin's conception of a people repressed by official institutions 'leaves us with an unending struggle between a "serious" ... ruling stratum .. and an ever skeptical populace' (p. 33). After citing a statement by Lukacs implying that irony is 'the emblem of the frustration of human impulses in a world which is alien to them', Hirschkop finally concludes that Bakhtin's vision has little in common with the formal democracy on offer from the liberal state while the "democracy of carnival" is a vision which 'draws a remarkable contrast with the public life we have come to accept as norm' (p. 35).

I both agree and disagree with Hirschkop's view. Of course, in a society in which we increasingly allow a scientific world-view as well as an etatistic, top-down understanding of political change to shape our lives, laughter is bound to become a problem. I do not agree with Bakhtin's suggestion, however, that we live, write and speak today in a world of free and democratized language, nor do I share Hirschkop's belief in the primacy of science. Although historical conditions have been significantly transformed ever since the sixteenth century, some of the basic tools elaborated by Bakhtin (such as his agonal view on the relationship between official or regional languages as well as between centripetal and centrifugal forces) must still be considered significant, perhaps in defiance of his own statement, not in the least *because* of the extent to which official scientific languages have penetrated social discourse, not in the least *because* it has become the aspiration of a growing number of social genres to have themselves transformed into a science (for example, moral criticism). Laughter has preserved its ability to expose the limitations, delusions and complacence of serious genres (such as the ones referred to as 'social science', some branches of moral philosophy included). Laughter does not call for anarchy or things like that, but it does recognize the extent to which political domination is a phenomenon of language as well as the extent to which the world is transformed through language. It recognizes (not necessarily deplores) the fact that our moral subjectivity, our being-in-the-world finds itself fundamentally transformed as everyday life is increasingly explained in scientific terms. In this sense, parody remains 'corrective' laughter. Its normative ideal is neither the conservative phantasy of a folk language that managed to preserve its age-old integrity, nor the progressive phantasy of an ideal communication devoid of power and domination, nor is it the tragic desire for resurrection, the desire for a language that preserved the purity and innocence of a marble statue or some other exalted work of art - for such a desire is 'corrected' rather than supported by laughter. Basically, laughter entails an awareness of the linguistic struggles of past and present. It is a way of remaining responsive and alert, rather than responsible, an effort to recognize and expose those forms of moral violence and moral domination that try to become ideologically immunized by presenting themselves as scientific. Laughter does not involve a plea for the abolishment of liberal democracy or things like that - any other regime would be considerably more violent. The fact that liberal democracy has to be accepted or even applauded as a political system does not imply that we should allow ourselves to ignore those forms of moral violence connected with what Hirschkop refers to as 'a collective learning process', a top-down process in the course of which certain forms of moral subjectivity will be established or enhanced at the expense of others. I do not advocate a relapse into a state of nature but merely a recognition of the political nature of moral discourse. Laughter still offers resistance to the basic inclination of all official ideologies to separate social genres (such as morality) from 'the fundamental realities of life' (Bakhtin 1988, p. 237) by transforming them into a science.

It is important to emphasize, moreover, that, in the case of Hirschkop and others, 'free and fearless investigation' as well as the 'experimental attitude' made possible by laughter is mistakenly identified with science. Although Bakhtin, like Nietzsche, initially seems to support science in its struggle against the idols of superstition and religion (in short, against all forms of 'ideology') he eventually reveals that there are other forms of truth than those of science, and that the free and fearless forms of investigation and experiment made possible by laughter are not necessarily those of science. Ultimately, both Bakhtin and Nietzsche side with 'gay' rather than with 'social' science, with the moral individual rather than with the ethical expert, and with the Renaissance state of mind rather than those forms of discourse that were established by the Counter-Renaissance. 'Free and fearless' investigation should not be identified with science, but rather with gay science: its bold, comic and unofficial double.

Moreover, Bakhtin and Nietzsche may greet Freud as an ally in this respect. After desperately trying to come up with a scientific account regarding the origin of sexual desire, he finally turns to another source: 'Apart from this, science has so little to tell us about the origin of sexuality that we can liken the problem to a darkness into which not so much as a ray of a hypothesis has penetrated. In quite a different region, it is true, we *do* meet with such a hypothesis; but it is of so fantastic a kind - a myth rather than a scientific explanation - that I should not venture to produce it here, were it not that it fulfills precisely the one condition whose fulfillment we desire ... What I have in mind is, of course, the theory which Plato puts in the mouth of Aristophanes in the *Symposium*' (1959/1967, p. 100). Rather than recapitulating the truth of laughter in scientific terms, Freud acknowledges that 'here ... the moment has come for breaking off' (p. 102). Indeed, it takes a great deal of intellectual freedom and fearlessness to admit the truth of laughter into a discourse that desperately tried to present itself as scientific, and even to acknowledge that the truth of laughter, being both positive and profound, eventually surpasses the truth of science.[20]

Allow me to draw a conclusion. In chapter one, politics was initially defined as the art of government, the art of exercising power over individuals. I argued, however, that such a definition entails a restricted, top-down understanding of politics, one which tends to obscure the bottom-up aspect of political life. What is neglected in a top-down perspective is the question of what kind of moral subjectivity, what form of moral life is constituted, fostered and established by a particular moral regime.

Liberalism is both a political and a moral phenomenon. Its moral aspect is the compartmentalization of moral life into a public and a private realm. Moreover, in a liberal perspective the public realm is identified with top-down politics (with procedures, fairness, rights, etc.) whereas moral subjectivity is considered the outcome of private, individual choices. This implies that on the theoretical level, liberalism obscures what it perfectly seems to be aware of on the practical level, namely that, in order for her policies of containment to be accepted, certain forms of moral subjectivity have to be produced. Liberalism pretends to be neutral towards moral subjectivity and forms of life, for these are considered private issues. But on this level, seeming neutral is just another word for being dominant. Liberalism tends to neglect or obscure a vital part of the public, political realm, one that cannot be identified with politics in the 'strict' sense of top-down government. Its is the

---

[20] I consider this passage of far greater importance when it comes to developing a philosophy of laughter than his book on jokes (1905/1973). In this book, he contends from the very beginning that he considers the joke to differ from the comical as such, and although eventually he tries to outline the relationship between the two, he admits that he does so with considerable reluctance - 'An das Problem des Komischen selbst wagen wir uns nur mit Bangen heran' (p. 207). In his discussion of parody, however, he points out that parody aims at depriving the highly placed of their dignity and sovereignty by overemphasizing certain bodily features or by stressing that they are troubled by the same bodily (notably excremental) needs as everybody else (cf. chapter four).

agonistic realm, the public *agon* or *agora* where incompatible interpretations of the present moral condition mockingly confront each other in an everlasting competitive struggle. Such an understanding of the public realm was already endorsed by Nietzsche and other admirers of ancient and hellenistic Greece who were enticed by the Greek love for verbal competition and dispute, by the fact that Greek public life was marked by an atmosphere of verbal and physical competition where human drives could freely express themselves without being considered as endangering the political establishment.[21]

This vital but neglected part of the public realm is the working area of laughter. Although true laughter is the very opposite of government and responsibility, it certainly is public, and even political - but in a bottom-up sense of the term. True laughter, Bakhtin claims, concerns the entire order of life, including the prevailing truth (1968, p. 307). True laughter is a moral experience of intrusion which causes the compartmentalization of moral life to collapse. Socrates, for instance, was not a politician. He did not argue for political change in the top-down sense of the term. He was a midwife, someone who, in defiance of those forms of life acknowledged and fostered by the state, allowed unprecedented forms of moral subjectivity to become established, forms which no longer derived their moral standards from substantial morality (that is, from the established life forms of the Greek City State) but from philosophical discourse. And in the case of Socrates, philosophical discourse represented an intrusion of popular laughter into the public realm. Philosophical critique was once again connected with age-old popular genres of laughter. In the eyes of the 'historical' Socrates, philosophy was hilarity and fun. Rather than challenging certain political arrangements, his laughter initiated a certain form of moral subjectivity. Although not 'political' in a restricted, top-down sense, his comic performance greatly affected public and political life. It did not merely reject but also affirmed. Indeed, the forms of life initiated by Socratic laughter were to gain political significance in the years and centuries to come. Thus, his performance turned out to be 'world-historically justified'. It was a remarkable achievement. For centuries moral criticism remained intimately connected with laughter - and in my view things still could be like that. Laughter does not urge us to violate the constitution or human rights, but allows us to perceive the present in a different light and to transcend those established forms of moral subjectivity that we came to experience as restricting.

---

21 *Human, All Too Human II*, 'The Wanderer and his Shadow', § 167, § 226. Huizinga (1938) in his study on the playful ('het ludieke') points out that, whereas in the ancient Greek experience of the playful the competitive aspect had been emphasized, a shift towards the comical occurred during the Roman period, while during the Middle Ages as well as during the Renaissance the playful and the foolish remained intimately connected.

We must always keep in mind, however, that different forms of laughter can be distinguished. What kind of laughter would allow us to challenge the basic platitudes of liberalism, to expose the moral restrictions of the present? What kind of laughter would provide a timely 'remedy'? In the previous chapters and sections, we have already dismissed irony and, up to a certain point, the same goes for cynicism as well. Whereas irony is basically a means of defence against mediocrity, cynicism is basically the expression of contempt. A much more viable form of laughter has been advocated, one that, under certain historical circumstances, is allowed access to official life, a form of laughter which encroaches upon official genres whenever, due to certain historical conditions, representatives of the lower strata, the plebeian sections of society (such as Socrates and Luther) are suddenly granted access to written discourse; a form of laughter which affirms rather than rejects, and which is full of life rather than defensive. Therefore, should my judgement of contemporary liberalism be considered excessive at times, one must keep in mind that exaggeration belongs to parody as a mode of argument. Still, we should not aim at a revival of Socrates' or Luther's laughter *as such*, we should not try to laugh *like them*, for such a laugh would merely be a costume or a mask. Certain basic features of their laughter, however, might enable us or encourage us to start laughing our own genuine laugh - one that laughs at yet another moral regime that questions the admissibility of laughter; one that laughs at yet another temporary outcome of human history that considers itself to be permanent and final, peaceable and lasting.

Literature

H. Achterhuis (1984) *Arbeid, een eigenaardig medicijn.* Baarn: Ambo.

D.B. Allison (1990) A Diet of Worms. *Nietzsche Studien, 19,* 43-57.

Aristotle (1926/1959) *The 'art' of rhetoric* [Loeb ed.]. London: Heinemann / Cambridge: Harvard University Press.

Aristotle (1926/1982) *The Nicomachean ethics* [Loeb ed.]. London: Heinemann / Cambridge: Harvard University Press.

Aristotle (1927/1960) *The poetics* [Loeb ed.]. London: Heinemann / Cambridge: Harvard Univerity Press.

Aristotle (1937/1961) *The parts of animals* [Loeb ed.]. London: Heinemann / Cambridge: Harvard University Press.

H. van Bakel (1946) *Lutherlegenden.* Haarlem: Tjeenk Willink.

M. Bakhtin (1988) *The dialogic imagination. Four essays* (6th ed.). Austin: University of Texas Press.

M. Bakhtin (1968) *Rabelais and his world.* Cambridge, Massechusetts: M.I.T. Press.

M. Bakhtin (1973) *Problems of Dostoevsky's poetics.* Ardis.

G. Bataille (1931/1970) 'L'anus solaire'. In: *Œuvres complètes 1: Premiers Écrits 1922-1940.* Paris: Gallimard, 79-86.

G. Bataille (1943/1973) 'L'expérience intérieure'. In: *Œuvres complètes 5: La Somme Athéologique, Tome 1.* Paris: Gallimard, 9-234.

G. Bataille (1944/1973) 'Le coupable'. In: *Œuvres complètes 5: La Somme Athéologique, Tome 1.* Paris: Gallimard, 235-366.

G. Bataille (1942/1973) 'Le rire de Nietzsche'. In: *Œuvres complètes 6: La Somme Athéologique 2.* Paris: Gallimard, 307-314.

B. Bauch (1904) Luther und Kant. Berlin: Reuter.

E. Behler (1989) Sockrates und die Griechische Tragödie. *Nietzsche Studien, 18*, 141-157.

E. Behler (1975) Nietzsches Auffassung der Ironie. *Nietzsche Studien, 4*, 1-35.

H. Bergson (1940/1969) *Le rire. Essai sur la signification du comique.* Paris: PUF.

E. Beyer (1978) *Ibsen: the man and his work.* New York: Taplinger.

B. Bräutigam (1977) Verwegene Kunststücke. *Nietzsche Studien, 6*, 45-63.

W. Bröcker (1972) Nietzsches Narrentum. *Nietzsche Studien, 1*, 138-146.

N.O. Brown (1959/1968) *Life against death: the psychoanalytical meaning of history.* London: Sphere Books.

M. van Buuren (1982) *De boekenpoeper: over het groteske in de literatuur.* Assen: Van Gorcum.

D. Callahan (1981) 'Minimalist ethics: on the pacification of morality'. In: A. Caplan, D. Callahan (eds.) *Ethics in hard times.* New York and London: Plenum Press.

J. Calvin (1984) *Des scandales.* Genève: Droz.

A. del Caro (1983) Anti-Romantic irony in the poetry of Nietzsche. *Nietzsche Studien, 12*, 372-378.

M. de Certeau (1991) 'Das Lachen Michel Foucaults'. In: W. Schmidt (Hrsg.) *Denken und Existenz bei Michel Foucault.* Frankfurt am Main: Suhrkamp.

J.S. Chamberlain (1982) *Ibsen: the open vision.* London: Athlone.

W.J. Dannhauser (1974) *Nietzsche's view on Socrates.* Ithaca and London: Cornell University Press.

J. Delumeau (1965/1991) *Naissance et affirmation de la Réforme.* Paris: Presses Universitaires de France.

R. Descartes (1649) 'Les passions de l'âme'. In: *Oeuvres de Descartes*. Paris: Gilbert.

M. De Unamuno (1954) *The tragic sense of life*. New York: Dover.

Diogenes Laertius (1925/1979) *Lives of eminent philosophers*, Vol. 2 (Book 6 - 10) [Loeb ed.]. Cambridge: Harvard University Press, London: Heinemann.

D. Dudley (1937) *A history of Cynicism from Diogenes to the 6th Century A.D.* London: Methuen.

G. Ebeling (1964) *Luther: Einführung in sein Denken*. Tübingen: Mohr.

E. Erikson (1958/1962) *Young man Luther: a study in psychoanalysis and history*. New York: Norton.

M. Foucault (1961/1972) *Folie et déraison. Histoire de la folie à l'âge classique*. Paris: Gallimard.

- (1966) *Les mots et les choses. Une archéologie des sciences humaines*. Paris: Gallimard.

- (1971) 'Nietzsche, la généalogie, l'histoire'. In: *Hommage à Jean Hyppolite*. Paris: PUF, 145-172.

- (1975) *Surveiller et punir. Naissance de la prison*. Paris: Gallimard.

- (1983/1989) *Parrèsia: vrijmoedig spreken en waarheid* [Discourse and truth: the problematisation of parrhèsia]. Amsterdam: Krisis.

- (1989) *Résumé des cours 1970-1982*. Paris: Julliard.

S. Freud (1900/1942/1973) 'Die Traumdeutung'. *Gesammelte Werke*, Vol. 2/3. Frankfurt am Main: Fischer / London: Imago.

S. Freud (1905/1940/1973) Der Witz und seine Beziehung zum Unbewußten. *Gesammelte Werke*, Vol. 6. Frankfurt am Main: Fischer / London: Imago.

S. Freud (1946/1973) 'Werke aus den Jahren 1913 - 1917'. *Gesammelte Werke*, Vol. 10. Frankfurt am Main: Fischer / London: Imago.

S. Freud (1920/1959/1967) *Beyond the pleasure principle*. New York: Bantom Books.

H.-G. Gadamer (1960/1990) *Gesammelte Werke 1. Wahrheit und Methode. Grundzüge einer philosophischen Hermeneutik*. Tübingen: Mohr (Siebeck).

S.L. Gilman (1975) Incipit parodia: the function of parody in the lyrical poetry of Friedrich Nietzsche. *Nietzsche Studien, 4,* 52-74.

H. Grisar (1911/1912) *Luther*. 1: Luthers werden: Grundlegung der Spaltung bis 1530; 2: Auf der Höhe des Lebens; 3: Am Ende der Bahn, Rückblicke. Freiburg im Breisgau: Herder.

K.C. Guthry (1961) 'Protagoras: Introduction'. In: E. Hamilton, H. Cairns (eds.) *The Collected Dialogues of Plato*. New York: Bollingen Foundation, 308.

J. Habermas (1987) *Theorie des kommunikativen Handelns* (4th ed.). I: Handlungsrationalität und gesellschaftliche Rationalisierung. II: Zur Kritik der funktionalistischen Vernunft. Frankfurt am Main: Suhrkamp.

D. Hamilton (1951) 'Introduction'. In: Plato (1951).

A.M. Harmon (1960) 'Introduction to *The dead come to life, or the fisherman'*. In: *The works of Lucian 3* [Loeb ed.]. London: Heinemann / Cambridge: Harvard University Press, 1.

Ph. van Haute (1996) 'Death and sublimation in Lacan's reading of Antigone'. In: S. Harasym (ed.) *The missed encounter: Lacan and Levinas* (in print).

G.W.F. Hegel (1971) *Werke in zwanzig Bänden 18: Vorlesungen über die Geschichte der Philosophie 1*. Frankfurt am Main: Suhrkamp.

M. Heidegger (1927/1986) *Sein und Zeit*. Tübingen: Niemeyer.

M. Heidegger (1967) *Wegmarken*. Frankfurt am Main: Klostermann.

E. Hirsch (1986) Nietzsche und Luther. *Nietzsche Studien, 15,* 398-431.

K. Hirschkop (1986) Bakhtin, discourse and democracy. *New Left Review, 160,* 92-113.

K. Hirschkop (1989) 'Introduction: Bakhtin and cultural theory'. In: K. Hirschkop, D. Sheperd (eds.) *Bakhtin and cultural theory*. Manchester and New York: Manchester University Press.

J. Huizinga (1938) *Homo ludens. Proeve eener bepaling van het spel-element der cultuur*. Haarlem: Willink.

J. Huizinga (1950a) 'Erasmus'. In: *Verzamelde Werken 6: biografie*. Haarlem: Willink.

J. Huizinga (1950b) 'Erasmus' maatstaf der dwaasheid'. In: *Verzamelde werken 6: biografie*. Haarlem: Willink.

H. Ibsen (1964/1982) 'When we dead wake: a dramatic epilogue'. In: *Ghosts, A Public Enemy, When we Dead Wake*. Harmondsworth: Penguin.

H.W. Janson (1962/1986) *History of art*. New York: Abrams, Englewood Cliffs: Prentice-Hall.

J. Janssen (1915) *Geschichte des Deutschen Volkes 2: Vom Beginn der politisch-kirchlichen Revolution bis zum Ausgang der sozialen Revolution von 1525*. Freiburg: Herder.

K. Jaspers (1964/1975) *Die maßgebenden Menschen*. München/ Zürich: Piper.

L. ten Kate (1994) *De lege plaats. Revoltes tegen het instrumentele leven in Bataille's atheologie*. Kampen: Kok Agora.

S. Kierkegaard (1989) The concept of irony with continual reference to Socrates. *Kierkegaard's Writings Vol. 2*. Princeton N.J.: Princeton University Pess.

P. Klossowski (1963) 'Nietzsche, le polythéisme et la parodie'. In: *Un si funeste désir*. Paris: Gallimard, pp. 185-228.

T. Kunnas (1982) *Nietzsches Lachen. Eine Studie über das Komische bei Nietzsche*. München: Flade.

J. Lacan (1986) *Le séminaire VII: L'éthique de la psychanalyse*. Paris: Éditions du Seuil.

R. Le Blanc (1995) 'A la recherche du genre perdu: Fielding, Gogol and Bakhtin's genre memory'. *The Seventh International Bakhtin Conference, Vol. II*. Moscow: Moscow State Pedagogical University, 422-428.

P. Lehmann (1922) *Die Parodie im Mittelalter*. München.

Lucianus (1960a) 'Philosophies for sale'. In: *The works of Lucian*, Vol. 2 [Loeb ed.]. London: Heinemann / Cambridge: Harvard University Press, 449-511.

Lucianus (1960b) 'The dead come to life, or the fisherman'. In: *The works of Lucian*, Vol. 3 [Loeb ed.]. London: Heinemann / Cambridge: Harvard University Press, 1-81.

M. Luther (1913) 'Werke' (60 Bände). In: *D. Martin Luthers Werke: kritische Gesamtausgabe*. Weimar: Böhlhaus.

M. Luther (1913) 'Tischreden 1531-1564' (6 Bände). In: *D. Martin Luthers Werke: kritische Gesamtausgabe*. Weimar: Böhlhaus.

M. Luther (1541/1959) 'Wider Hans Worst'. *Luthers Werke in Auswahl 4*, Berlin: De Gruyter, 1959.

K. Marx, F. Engels (1845/1975) 'The holy family'. In: *Collected works 4*. London: Lawrence & Wishart, 5-211.

K. Marx, F. Engels (1846/1976) 'The German Ideology, Vol. I'. In: *Collected works 5*. London: Lawrence & Wishart, 19-451.

K. Marx (1847/1972) 'Die moralisierende Kritik und die kritisierende Moral: Beitrag zur Deutschen Kulturgeschichte, gegen Karl Heinzen'. In: K. Marx, F. Engels, *Werke 4*. Berlin: Dietz.

K. Marx (1847/1976) 'The poverty of philosophy. Answer to the *Philosophy of Poverty* by M. Proudhon'. In: *Collected works 6*. London: Lawrence & Wishart, 105-212.

K. Marx (1852/1979) 'The eighteenth Brumaire of Louis Bonaparte'. In: *Collected works 11*. London: Lawrence & Wishart, 99-198.

M. Meyer (1967/1985) *Ibsen*. Harmondsworth: Penguin.

J.S. Mill (1859/1974) *On liberty*. Harmondsworth: Penguin.

F. Nietzsche (1969/1983) *Werke* [Schlechta ed.]. Frankfurt am Main: Ullstein.

F. Nietzsche (1974) *The gay science (with a prelude in rhymes and an appendix of songs)* [Translation: W. Kaufmann]. New York: Vintage Books.

Plato (1961) *The Collected Dialogues of Plato* [E. Hamilton, H. Cairns, eds.]. New York: Bollingen Foundation.

Plato (1951) *The Symposium*. Harmondsworth: Penguin.

Plato (1955/1974) *The Republic*. Harmondsworth: Penguin.

Plutarch (1958) 'Pericles'. In: *Plutarch's lives 3* [Loeb Edition]. London: Heinemann / Cambridge: Harvard University Press, 3-115.

G. Posthumus Meyjes (1992) *Geloven en lachen in de historie. Enkele opmerkingen over de waardering van de lach in de geschiedenis der kerk.* Leiden: RUL.

H. Preuss (1947) *Martin Luther: Seele und Sendung*. Gütersloh: Bertelsmann.

F. Rabelais (1919) *La vie treshorrificque du grand Gargantua pere de Pantagruel iadis composée par Alcofribas abstracteur de quinte essence. Livre plein de pantagruelisme.* Paris: Les Éditions de la Sirène.

J. Rawls (1972) *A theory of justice*. Oxford: Oxford University Press.

J. Rawls (1987) The idea of an overlapping consensus. *Oxford Journal of Legal Studies, 7* (1), 1-25.

J. Rawls (1993) *Political liberalism* (The John Dewey essays in philosophy 4). New York: Columbia.

P. Ricoeur (1975) 'Phaenomenologie und Hermeneutiek'. In: H. Rombach et al, *Phaenomenologie heute: Grundlagen und Methodenprobleme*. Freiburg: Alber.

Ch. Robinson (1979) *Lucian and his influence in Europe*. London: Duckworth.

R. Rorty (1980) *Philosophy and the mirror of nature*. London: Blackwell.

R. Rorty (1989) *Contingency, irony, and solidarity*. Cambridge (Mass.): Cambridge University Press.

J. Salaquarda (1986) Nachwort zu E. Hirsch, 'Nietzsche und Luther'. *Nietzsche Studien*, *15*, 431-438.

A. Simons (1990) *Het groteske van de taal. Over het werk van Mikhail Bachtin*. Amsterdam: SUA.

P. Sloterdijk (1983) *Kritik der zynischen Vernunft*. Frankfurt am Main: Suhrkamp.

J. Stout (1981) *The flight from authority. Religion, morality, and the quest for autonomy*. Notre Dame: Notre Dame University Press.

P.F. Strawson (1970) Social morality and individual ideal. In: G. Wallace, A.D.M. Walker (eds.) *The definition of morality*. London.

P. van Tongeren (1989) *Die Moral von Nietzsches Moralkritik: Studie zu Jenseits von Gut und Böse*. Bonn: Bouvier.

S. Toulmin (1990) *Cosmopolis: the hidden agenda of modernity*. New York: The Free Press.

H. Treddenick (1961) 'Socrates' Defence (Apology): Introduction'. E. Hamilton, H. Cairns (eds.) *The Collected Dialogues of Plato*. New York: Bollingen Foundation, 3.

D. Verweij (1993) *Ariadne en Dionysos. Vrouw-metaforen en verlangen in het werk van Nietzsche*. Amsterdam: Thesis Publishers.

L. Wittgenstein (1984) 'Zettel'. In: *Werkausgabe 8*. Frankfurt am Main: Suhrkamp.

H. Zwart (1993) *Ethische consensus in een pluralistische samenleving: de gezondheidsethiek als casus*. Amsterdam: Thesis Publishers.

H. Zwart (1995a) *Weg met de ethiek? Filosofische beschouwingen over geneeskunde en ethiek*. Amsterdam: Thesis Publishers.

H. Zwart (1995b) *Technocratie en onbehagen: de plaats van de ethiek in het werk van Michel Foucault*. Nijmegen: Sun.